ADVANCING THE POWER OF
Economic Evidence
to Inform Investments in Children, Youth, and Families

Committee on the Use of Economic Evidence to
Inform Investments in Children, Youth, and Families

Eugene Steuerle and Leigh Miles Jackson, *Editors*

Board on Children, Youth, and Families

Division of Behavioral and Social Sciences and Education

The National Academies of
SCIENCES · ENGINEERING · MEDICINE

THE NATIONAL ACADEMIES PRESS
Washington, DC
www.nap.edu

THE NATIONAL ACADEMIES PRESS   500 Fifth Street, NW   Washington, DC 20001

This activity was supported by Contract No. 10002411 from the Jacobs Foundation, Contract No. 10002006 from the MacArthur Foundation, and Contract No. 10002289 from the Robert Wood Johnson Foundation. Any opinions, findings, conclusions, or recommendations expressed in this publication do not necessarily reflect the views of any organization or agency that provided support for the project.

International Standard Book Number-13: 978-0-309-44059-2
International Standard Book Number-10: 0-309-44059-9
Digital Object Identifier: 10.17226/23481

Additional copies of this report are available for sale from the National Academies Press, 500 Fifth Street, NW, Keck 360, Washington, DC 20001; (800) 624-6242 or (202) 334-3313; http://www.nap.edu.

Cover credit: Jay Christian Design, LLC.

Suggested citation: National Academies of Sciences, Engineering, and Medicine. (2016). *Advancing the Power of Economic Evidence to Inform Investments in Children, Youth, and Families.* Washington, DC: The National Academies Press. doi: 10.17226/23481.

The National Academies of
SCIENCES · ENGINEERING · MEDICINE

The **National Academy of Sciences** was established in 1863 by an Act of Congress, signed by President Lincoln, as a private, nongovernmental institution to advise the nation on issues related to science and technology. Members are elected by their peers for outstanding contributions to research. Dr. Ralph J. Cicerone is president.

The **National Academy of Engineering** was established in 1964 under the charter of the National Academy of Sciences to bring the practices of engineering to advising the nation. Members are elected by their peers for extraordinary contributions to engineering. Dr. C. D. Mote, Jr., is president.

The **National Academy of Medicine** (formerly the Institute of Medicine) was established in 1970 under the charter of the National Academy of Sciences to advise the nation on medical and health issues. Members are elected by their peers for distinguished contributions to medicine and health. Dr. Victor J. Dzau is president.

The three Academies work together as the **National Academies of Sciences, Engineering, and Medicine** to provide independent, objective analysis and advice to the nation and conduct other activities to solve complex problems and inform public policy decisions. The Academies also encourage education and research, recognize outstanding contributions to knowledge, and increase public understanding in matters of science, engineering, and medicine.

Learn more about the National Academies of Sciences, Engineering, and Medicine at **www.national-academies.org**.

Preface

Almost nothing drives the development of society more than investments in the nation's children. Accordingly, public and private policy makers, funders, and others have in recent years called for and sponsored the production and use of economic evidence to inform decision making on how to make such investments. The rationale for these efforts appears straightforward: better evidence should enable higher returns from such investments. Yet to date, the use of such evidence has been limited. Why? Many reasons might be ventured: politics, special interests, power of the status quo, the limits on which evidence can be quantified, and the relative adolescence of the field. Some of these reasons can be interesting from an historical viewpoint, but the more compelling question for future investments is how to improve the development of economic evidence so it can better inform those investments.

Two answers to this latter question stand out and serve as the two principles around which this report is organized: *quality counts* and *context matters*. The better the *quality* of the research, the better it is received, and the more likely it is to generate demand for future economic evidence even on unrelated investments. At the same time, if high-quality evidence is to be used well, it must be suited to the *context* in which decisions are made. It must be timely and relevant to the decisions at hand and account for many other needs of the consumer. It was in teasing out the many ramifications of these two principles that the committee convened to conduct this study responded to a 2014 charge from its sponsors—the Jacobs Foundation, the MacArthur Foundation, and the Robert Wood Johnson Foundation—to study how to improve the use of economic evidence to inform investments in children, youth, and families.

The committee focused its attention on economic evaluation, a type of economic analysis that is commonly performed to provide economic information related to investments in children, youth, and families. Economic evaluation encompasses cost analysis, cost-effectiveness analysis, benefit-cost analysis, and related methods used in an effort to quantify program costs and outcomes and potentially to make comparisons among programs. These methods are commonly employed in randomized controlled trials, but by no means does the committee discount the value of other approaches—ranging from theory to qualitative analysis to other forms of statistical analysis—and indeed, it encourages researchers reporting on economic evaluation to acknowledge what might be learned through such other means.

Perhaps not surprising, the committee identified many instances in which the quality of economic evidence was low, such as failure to account for many types of costs, or was reported in ways that could mislead by failing to acknowledge limitations of the analysis, often forced by restricted budgets. Accordingly, a major goal of this study was to recommend a number of ways in which current practices in the production of economic evidence could be improved. Likewise, this report suggests that producers and consumers of economic evidence can gain by giving considerable attention before, during, and after economic evaluations are performed to the context or broader system within which investment decisions are made. Setting and organizational capacity matter—as do politics and values, culture and management practices, and budget. This report includes a roadmap outlining a multipronged strategy for fostering multi-stakeholder partnerships to address these issues and for improving incentives for the use of economic evidence for various stakeholders, ranging from publishers of economic research results to program evaluators.

Needless to say, the topic of this study is of such breadth that the committee makes no pretense of having covered every angle. In some cases, moreover, it was necessary to apply lessons from related literatures because the literature on the actual use of economic evaluations was scant.

The committee members brought to this study a wide range of experience and expertise, as well as common sense. Their energy was unbounded; their enthusiasm strong; and their dedication to the public good through solid, professional, and unbiased research paramount. This report was truly a collaborative effort, with multiple authors and mutual editors and wide acceptance of critiques. It was my pleasure to serve with this esteemed group.

The committee's talents would have been sorely tried without the superlative efforts of the study staff, led by Leigh Miles Jackson, study director;

Tara Mainero, associate program officer; Noam Keren, research associate; and Stacey Smit, senior program assistant. Wonderful guidance and encouragement also were provided by Natacha Blain, current director of the Board on Children, Youth, and Families; Bridget Kelly, former acting director; and earlier, Kimber Bogard, then serving as director. The report also benefited greatly from the efforts of our editor, Rona Briere. They kept us on track, organized our disparate thoughts, and made extraordinary organizational and other tasks look ordinary. The committee extends its profound thanks and indebtedness to them.

Of course, this study is not about us; it is about the children, youth, and families whose lives are touched, often in crucial and profound ways, by the investment decisions that were this study's focus. It is our hope that we have advanced their well-being by describing ways to inform these decisions through better use of economic evidence. If producers and consumers of this evidence devote greater attention to its quality and the context in which it is used, we believe we will have succeeded in that task.

Eugene Steuerle, *Chair*
Committee on the Use of Economic
Evidence to Inform Investments in
Children, Youth, and Families

Acknowledgments

This report reflects contributions from numerous individuals and groups. The committee takes this opportunity to recognize those who so generously gave their time and expertise to inform its deliberations. To begin, the committee would like to thank the sponsors of this study. Support for the committee's work was provided by the Jacobs Foundation, the MacArthur Foundation, and the Robert Wood Johnson Foundation. We wish to thank Valerie Chang, Kerry Anne McGeary, and Simon Sommer for their guidance and support.

The committee greatly benefited from the opportunity for discussion with individuals who made presentations at and attended its workshops and meetings (see Appendix A). The committee is thankful for the many contributions of these individuals.

The committee could not have done its work without the support and guidance provided by the National Academies of Sciences, Engineering, and Medicine project staff: Leigh Miles Jackson, Tara Mainero, Noam Keren, and Stacey Smit. The committee is also grateful to Lisa Alston, Pamella Atayi, and Faye Hillman for their administrative and financial assistance on this project, and gratefully acknowledges Kimber Bogard, Bridget Kelly, and Natacha Blain of the Board on Children, Youth, and Families for the guidance they provided throughout this important study.

Many other staff within the Academies provided support to this project in various ways. The committee would like to thank the executive office reports staff of the Division of Behavioral and Social Sciences and Education (DBASSE), especially Kirsten Sampson-Snyder, who managed the report review process. Thanks are due as well to the staff in the DBASSE Office of Communication and Reports (Patricia L. Morison, Douglas Sprunger, Eugenia Grohman, Viola Horek, and Yvonne Wise), Janice Mehler of the Report Review Committee, the Academies Research Center staff (Victoria Harriston, Daniel Bearss, Rebecca Morgan, and Ellen Kimmel), and the National Academies Press staff.

We thank Richard Cookson, Donald P. Moynihan, Spyros Konstantopoulos, and Jeffrey Valentine for their valuable commissioned work. We are grateful to Lauren Tobias and Steve Olson for their work as communications consultants for this study, as well as to Jay Christian, Francesca Moghari, and Michael Dudzik for their creative efforts in our graphic design projects. We also wish to thank Justin Ingels, Nathaniel Taylor, Rebecca Walcott, Laura Wiese, and the project's intern, Alia Sani, for the superb research assistance they provided. Finally, Rona Briere and Alisa Decatur are to be credited for their superb editorial assistance in preparing this report.

This report has been reviewed in draft form by individuals chosen for their diverse perspectives and technical expertise, in accordance with procedures approved by the Report Review Committee of the Academies. The purpose of this independent review is to provide candid and critical comments that will assist the institution in making its published report as sound as possible and to ensure that the report meets institutional standards for objectivity, evidence, and responsiveness to the study charge. The review comments and draft manuscript remain confidential to protect the integrity of the deliberative process. We wish to thank the following individuals for their review of this report: Richard P. Barke, School of Public Policy, Georgia Institute of Technology; Jere R. Behrman, Department of Economics, University of Pennsylvania; Janet Currie, Department of Economics and Center for Health and Wellbeing, Princeton University; Paula M. Lantz, Research and Policy Engagement, Gerald R. Ford School of Public Policy, University of Michigan; Henry M. Levin, Economics and Education, Teachers College, Columbia University and Education and Economics, (emeritus), Stanford University; Rebecca A. Maynard, Education and Social Policy, University of Pennsylvania; Lawrence A. Palinkas, Department of Child, Youth and Families and Behavior, Health and Society Research Cluster, School of Social Work, University of Southern California; Dan T. Rosenbaum, Economic Policy Division, Office of Management and Budget; Charles Sallee, New Mexico Legislative Finance Committee, Santa Fe.

Although the reviewers listed above provided many constructive comments and suggestions, they were not asked to endorse the report's conclusions or recommendations, nor did they see the final draft of the report before its release. The review of this report was overseen by Robert A. Moffitt, Department of Economics, Johns Hopkins University, and Greg J. Duncan, School of Education, University of California, Irvine. Appointed by the Academies, they were responsible for making certain that an independent examination of this report was carried out in accordance with institutional procedures and that all review comments were carefully considered. Responsibility for the final content of this report rests entirely with the authoring committee and the institution.

Contents

SUMMARY   **1**

1 INTRODUCTION   **19**
Study Context, 20
Study Charge, 21
Study Approach, 23
Study Scope and Key Definitions, 26
Report Audiences, 34
Guiding Principles, 35
Report Organization, 35
References, 36

2 SETTING THE STAGE   **39**
Methods for Economic Evaluation, 39
Stakeholders of the Production and Use of Economic Evidence, 56
Current Uses of Economic Evaluation to Inform Investments in
    Children, Youth, and Families, 59
Challenges in the Use of Economic Evaluation to Inform
    Investments in Children, Youth, and Families, 65
Economic Evidence as Part of the Evidence Ecosystem, 75
References, 76

3   **PRODUCING HIGH-QUALITY ECONOMIC EVIDENCE TO
     INFORM INVESTMENTS IN CHILDREN, YOUTH, AND
     FAMILIES**   83
     Determining Whether an Intervention Is Ready for Economic
         Evaluation, 86
     Defining the Scope of the Economic Evaluation, 89
     Evaluating Intervention Cost, 95
     Determining Intervention Impacts, 104
     Valuing Outcomes, 109
     Getting to Results: The Development and Reporting of
         Summary Measures, 126
     Handling Uncertainty in Economic Evaluation, 131
     Addressing Equity Considerations, 133
     Recommendations for Best Practices for Producing and
         Reporting High-Quality Economic Evidence, 135
     References, 145

4   **CONTEXT MATTERS**   159
     Alignment of Evidence with the Decision Context, 160
     Other Factors in the Use of Evidence, 171
     Factors That Can Facilitate the Use of Economic Evidence, 182
     Examples of Efforts to Improve the Use of Evaluation
         Evidence, 191
     Recommendations, 200
     References, 202

5   **A ROADMAP FOR IMPROVING THE USE OF
     HIGH-QUALITY ECONOMIC EVIDENCE**   211
     Overview of the Preceding Chapters, 211
     A Roadmap for Success, 212
     Recommendations, 224
     References, 226

APPENDIXES
A   Public Session Agendas   231
B   Biographical Sketches of Committee Members and Staff   235

GLOSSARY   241

List of Boxes, Figures, and Tables

BOXES

S-1 Methods Used to Produce Economic Evidence, 2
S-2 What Consumers and Producers of Economic Evidence Want Each Other to Know, 6

1-1 Statement of Task, 22
1-2 National Academies Efforts Relevant to the Study Charge, 24
1-3 Information-Gathering Process, 25
1-4 Summary of Key Definitions, 27

2-1 Illustrative Example of Cost Analysis (CA), 46
2-2 Illustrative Example of Cost-Effectiveness Analysis (CEA), 48
2-3 Illustrative Example of Benefit-Cost Analysis (BCA), 52
2-4 Concepts of Equity, 55
2-5 The Role of Economic Evidence in Promoting Publicly Funded Home Visiting Programs, 60
2-6 Issues Affecting the Use of Economic Evidence, 68

3-1 Assessing Approaches to Measuring Quality-of-Life Gains, 123

4-1 Building Capacity to Seek and Use Evidence: An Example, 165
4-2 The Importance of Implementation Fidelity: An Example, 168
4-3 The Impetus for Economic Evaluation: Examples, 182

4-4 Illustrative Example of Accountability: No Child Left Behind, 185
4-5 Knowledge Translation Strategies, 192

5-1 Recommendations from Chapter 3, 213
5-2 Recommendations from Chapter 4, 214
5-3 What Consumers and Producers of Economic Evidence Want Each
  Other to Know, 216

FIGURES

3-1 Different types of economic evaluation can be conducted to answer
  different types of questions, 87

4-1 Opportunities for the use of administrative data in economic
  evaluations, 179

TABLES

1-1 Types of Interventions Relevant to This Study, 31
1-2 Outcome Domains of Interventions Relevant to This Study, 33

2-1 Types of Economic Evaluation Methods and Associated Information
  Requirements and Outputs, 42
2-2 Examples of Evidence-Supported Legislation/Programs and Resulting
  Impacts, 66

3-1 Illustrative Valuation of Fixed and Variable Cost in Cost
  Analysis, 102
3-2 Examples of Direct and Linked Economic Impacts in Three Benefit-
  Cost Analysis Studies, 114
3-3 Means and 95 Percent Confidence Intervals of Values of
  Willingness to Pay to Prevent a Homicide, by Study (in millions of
  2014 dollars), 121

Summary

In recent years, the U.S. federal government has invested approximately $463 billion annually in interventions[1] that affect the overall health and well-being of children and youth, while state and local budgets have devoted almost double that amount. The potential returns on these investments may not only be substantial but also have long-lasting effects for individuals and succeeding generations of their families. Those tasked with making these investments face a number of difficult questions, such as:

- What does it cost to implement this intervention in my particular context and what are its expected returns?
- To what extent can these returns be measured in monetary or non-monetary terms?
- Who will receive the returns and when?
- Is this investment a justifiable use of scarce resources relative to other investments?

Ideally, decision makers would have available to them the evidence needed to answer these questions, informing their investments and increasing the investment returns. *Economic evidence*[2] in particular has great

---

[1] The term intervention is used to represent the broad scope of programs, practices, and policies that are relevant to children, youth, and families.

[2] In this context, economic evidence refers to the information produced from cost and cost-outcome evaluations, including cost analysis, cost-effectiveness analysis, and benefit-cost analysis.

BOX S-1
Methods Used to Produce Economic Evidence

The methods used to produce economic evidence, collectively termed *economic evaluations*, encompass the following:

Cost analysis (CA)—Can help answer the question: *What does it cost to fully implement a given intervention for a specified time period?* This evaluation can provide a complete accounting of the economic costs of all the resources used to carry out an intervention.

Cost-effectiveness analysis (CEA)—Can help answer the questions: *What is the economic cost to achieve a unit change in a given outcome from an intervention (e.g., one more high school graduate) or what is the amount of a given outcome obtained for each dollar invested in an intervention?* When comparing two or more interventions, the one that can produce the outcome at lowest cost or the one that can produce the largest gain for each dollar invested would generally be selected. For CEA, outcomes of an intervention are typically measured in nonmonetary terms.

Benefit-cost analysis (BCA)—Can help answer the question: *Is the investment a justifiable use of scarce resources?* This evaluation determines whether the economic value of the outcomes of an intervention exceeds the economic value of the resources required to implement the intervention. Interventions with net value, or total net benefit, greater than zero are considered justifiable from an economic standpoint. For BCA, both outcomes and costs of an intervention are valued in monetary terms.

---

potential to show not just what works but what works within budget constraints. (Box S-1 defines the methods used to produce economic evidence that are the focus of this study.) As the result of a number of challenges, however, such evidence may not be effectively produced or applied. These shortcomings weaken society's ability to invest wisely and also reduce future demand for this and other types of evidence.

In this context, the Institute of Medicine and the National Research Council, in fall 2014, empaneled the Committee on the Use of Economic Evidence to Inform Investments in Children, Youth, and Families. In this report, the committee highlights the potential for economic evidence to support these investments; describes challenges to its optimal use; and offers recommendations whose implementation can promote lasting improvement in its quality, utility, and use.

IMPROVING THE USE OF ECONOMIC
EVIDENCE IN DECISION MAKING

While many decisions about investments in children, youth, and families would be enhanced by stronger evidence, including economic evidence, decision makers face budget constraints, time limitations, and competing incentives that limit their use of such evidence. The committee proposes that to overcome these limitations, both producers and consumers of economic evidence give full consideration to two simple but fundamental guiding principles: (1) *quality counts* and (2) *context matters*.

Quality Counts

The committee identified challenges to the quality of economic evidence that limit its utility and use. For example, high-quality evidence can be difficult to derive because economic evaluation methods are complex and entail many assumptions. Moreover, methods are applied inconsistently in different studies, making results difficult to compare and use appropriately for policy and investment decisions. Furthermore, the evaluation results may be communicated in ways that obscure important findings, are unsuitable for nonresearch audiences, or are not deemed reliable or compelling by decision makers.

Based on its review of the landscape of economic evaluation, the committee produced a set of research conclusions. These conclusions determined that conducting an economic evaluation requires careful consideration of a number of assumptions, decisions, and practices to produce economic evidence that is of high quality. For example, high-quality economic evaluations are characterized by a clearly defined intervention and a well-specified counterfactual; a previously established perspective, time horizon, and baseline discount rate; accurate cost estimates of the resources needed to replicate the intervention; and consideration of the uncertainty associated with the evaluation findings. In addition, the committee concluded that registries can increase uniformity of practice, and that the acknowledgment of equity concerns can enhance the quality and usefulness of economic evaluations.

Context Matters

Economic evidence, even of the highest quality, may not be used effectively to inform investment decisions if it is deemed irrelevant, infeasible, or difficult to interpret by its consumers. Yet, evidence is often produced without considering the end-user's needs, values, and capacity to access and analyze the evidence—that is, the context for evidence use.

From its review of the salient research, the committee drew a set of conclusions about the utility and use of evidence to inform investments in children, youth, and families. For example, the infrastructure for developing, accessing, analyzing, and disseminating research evidence often has not been developed in public agencies and private organizations; interactive, ongoing, collaborative relationships between decision makers and researchers and trusted knowledge brokers are a promising strategy for improving the use of economic evidence; and that growing interest in performance-based financing is likely to increase the demand for economic evidence to inform decisions on investments in children, youth, and families. Moreover, whether evidence is used varies significantly according to the type of investment decision being made and the decision maker's incentives (or lack thereof) for its use. In short, the committee determined that economic evidence has the potential to play an influential role in the decision-making process—if the concerns and interests of decision makers are considered in the development and communication of evidence.

A ROADMAP FOR MOVING FORWARD

Many of the challenges to the quality, use, and utility of economic evidence affect its consumers, producers, and intermediaries[3] alike. Accordingly, the committee formulated a roadmap for promoting improvements in the use and usefulness of high-quality economic evidence. This roadmap highlights the need to foster multi-stakeholder partnerships and build coordinated infrastructure to support the development and use of economic evidence.

The committee concluded that long-term, multi-stakeholder collaborations that include producers, consumers, and intermediaries can provide vital support for the improved use of economic evidence to inform investments in children, youth, and families. Together these stakeholders can play a more impactful role not simply by gathering but also by working together to build a sustainable, coordinated infrastructure that will support the systematic use of high-quality economic evidence. However, investments are vitally needed to help build such an infrastructure. Funders, policy makers, program developers, program evaluators, and publishers engaged in science communication each have unique opportunities to help achieve this advancement, but those opportunities, in turn, will depend in no small part on the incentives offered by the various stakeholders to each other.

Given the crucial need to improve communication among and between stakeholders, sometimes even at the most basic level, the committee identified key messages that producers and consumers of economic evidence

---

[3]Intermediaries are defined as stakeholders who use economic evidence to enhance practice and policy through advocacy, technical assistance, or other avenues.

would like each other to know and take account of before, during, and after the production of economic evidence (see Box S-2).

RECOMMENDATIONS

Based on their research conclusions, the committee formulated recommendations for producing high-quality economic evidence; improving the utility and use of evidence; and actualizing those improvements to better inform investments for children, youth, and families.

Producing High-Quality Economic Evidence

The committee developed a set of best practices to help current and would-be producers of economic evidence understand when an intervention is sufficiently ready for an economic evaluation and what it takes to produce and report high-quality economic evidence so as to achieve transparency, consistency, and usefulness to decision makers. Although these best practices are targeted largely at the producers of evidence, they also should be helpful to consumers of the evidence, particularly with respect to assessing its quality and completeness. It is the committee's hope that these best practices will serve as the basis for long-term improvements to support the production of clear, credible, and applicable economic evidence for decision makers. Such practices depend upon the type of economic evaluation being performed, and range from describing the purpose of an intervention, the alternative with which the intervention is compared, and the time horizon for the analysis; to valuing all the resources needed to implement and sustain the intervention; to determining the extent to which impacts are included; to employing sensitivity analysis. The list is wide ranging and fairly comprehensive and is provided in checklist form at the end of this summary for use particularly by those preparing for and engaging in an economic evaluation of an investment.

> RECOMMENDATION 1: In support of high-quality economic evaluations, producers of economic evidence should follow the best practices delineated in the checklist below for conducting cost analyses, cost-effectiveness analyses, benefit-cost analyses, and related methods. Producers should follow the core practices listed and, where feasible and applicable, the advancing practices as well. Consumers of economic evidence should use these recommended best practices to assess the quality of the economic evidence available to inform the investment decisions they are seeking to make.

BOX S-2
What Consumers and Producers of Economic Evidence
Want Each Other to Know

Five Things Consumers of Economic Evidence Want Producers to Know

1. Many factors other than economic evidence (including political pressures and capacity) influence the decision-making process.
2. The time frames for research outcomes and investment decisions can be very different and affect the value of the evidence.
3. Seldom do all the benefits realized from investment decisions accrue to those who make the decisions or their community.
4. Existing evidence is not always aligned with the evidence needed by the decision maker.
5. Real-world constraints that affect the implementation fidelity and scale-up of an intervention need to be identified before further investments are made.

Five Things Producers of Economic Evidence Want Consumers to Know

1. Better investment decisions can be made with a foundational understanding of precisely what economic evidence is, the ways it can be used, its limitations, and considerations of causality and external validity.
2. Either directly or through intermediaries, consumers need to be able to distinguish between higher- and lower-quality economic evaluations.
3. Clearinghouses reveal only which interventions have attained success, usually relative to some alternative and according to certain specified criteria; accordingly, they cannot and generally should not be considered adequate to indicate which programs are best suited to a particular organization, context, or goal.
4. To support sound investments in children and facilitate high-quality program implementation, investment is required in the infrastructure needed to collect, analyze, and disseminate high-quality economic evidence; crucial here are data tracking children's well-being over time so that future, often not-yet-specified, evaluations can be conducted.
5. Investing in education, training, technical assistance, and capacity building often leads to successful development, analysis, and implementation of interventions.

RECOMMENDATION 2: In support of high-quality and useful economic evaluations of interventions for children, youth, and families, producers of economic evidence should follow the best practices delineated in the checklist below for reporting the results of cost analyses, cost-effectiveness analyses, benefit-cost analyses, and related methods.

Improving the Utility and Use of Economic Evidence

To help improve the utility and use of economic evidence to inform investments for children, youth, and families, the committee developed a set of recommendations addressing the opportunities available to a diverse group of stakeholders. Public and private funders, government agencies, and education providers each hold an influential position with respect to the production and use of economic evidence. It is the committee's hope that stakeholders will implement these recommendations to increase funding, training, and support for the improved use of economic evidence in decisions on investments for children, youth, and families.

RECOMMENDATION 3: If aiming to inform decisions on interventions for children, youth, and families, public and private funders of applied research[4] should assess the potential relevance of proposed research projects to end-users throughout the planning of research portfolios.

RECOMMENDATION 4: To achieve anticipated economic benefits and optimize the likelihood of deriving the anticipated outcomes from evidence-based interventions, public and private funders[5] should ensure that resources are available to support effective implementation of those interventions.

RECOMMENDATION 5: Providers of postsecondary and graduate education, on-the-job training, and fellowship programs designed to develop the skills of those making or seeking to inform decisions related to children, youth, and families should incorporate training in the use of evidence, including economic evidence, in decision making.

RECOMMENDATION 6: Government agencies[6] should report the extent to which their allocation of funds—both within and across programs—is supported by evidence, including economic evidence.

---

[4] "Funders" here might include staff in public agencies (e.g., the Centers for Disease Control and Prevention, the Institute for Education Sciences, and the National Institutes of Health), as well as staff in private, philanthropic, or other organizations.

[5] "Funders" here might include elected officials at the local, state, or federal level; leadership of public grant-making agencies or regulatory bodies; and private funders of programs for children, youth, and families.

[6] The key actors in "government agencies" here would include agency leadership, budget offices, and others with management and budget functions in executive and legislative branches at the federal, state, and local levels.

Actualizing Improvements in the Utility and Use of High-Quality Economic Evidence

To promote lasting improvement in the quality, utility, and use of economic evidence to inform investments for children, youth, and families, the committee determined that both producers and consumers of economic evidence need to engage at several levels beyond simply producing higher-quality and more useful evidence in a single research endeavor. Multiple stakeholder groups—including funders, policy makers, program developers, program evaluators, and publishers engaged in science communication—contribute to the production and use of economic evidence. Each of these groups can either facilitate or impede the production and use of high-quality, high-utility economic evidence. To initiate and sustain process reforms, the committee recommends that efforts be made to foster the development of multi-stakeholder collaborations and partnerships, build and fund coordinated infrastructure, and strengthen incentives for the production and use of better economic evidence.

> RECOMMENDATION 7: Program developers, public and private funders, and policy makers should design, support, and incorporate comprehensive stakeholder partnerships (involving producers, consumers, and intermediaries) into action plans related to the use of economic evidence.

> RECOMMENDATION 8: Multi-stakeholder groups should seek to build infrastructure that (1) supports access to administrative data; (2) maintains a database of estimates of outcome values; (3) archives longitudinal data for multiple purposes, including improved tracking of children and families and the development of better estimates of long-term impacts and shadow prices; (4) educates future producers and consumers of economic evidence; and (5) develops tools for tracking nonbudgetary resource consumption.

> RECOMMENDATION 9: To support sustainable action toward the production and use of high-quality economic evidence, public and private funders should invest in infrastructure that supports (1) the regular convening of producers, consumers, and intermediaries of economic evidence; (2) enhanced education and training in economic evaluation; (3) efforts to attend to progressive data requirements and data-sharing management needs; and (4) the integration of economic evaluations into budget processes.

RECOMMENDATION 10: Public and private funders, policy makers, program developers, program evaluators, and publishers engaged in science communication should strengthen the incentives they provide for the production and use of high-quality economic evidence likely to be of high utility to decision makers.

Checklist of
Best Practices for Producing High-Quality Economic Evidence

For All Economic Evaluation Methods, Report the Following:

— Specify the intervention for the economic evaluation, including a description of the intervention's purpose, its intended recipients, the intensity and duration of services provided, the approach to implementation, the causal mechanisms, and the intended impact(s).

— Specify the context in which the intervention was or will be implemented, such as characteristics of the population served; the time, place, and scale of implementation; and other relevant contextual factors.

— Specify the counterfactual condition, including whether the alternative is no intervention, an alternative intervention, or business as usual. In the case of cost-effectiveness analysis (CEA) and benefit-cost analysis (BCA), ensure that the same counterfactual applies to the cost analysis (CA) and the impacts used for the CEA or BCA.

— Determine the scope of the economic evaluation, including the type of method to be used and the perspective (and any subperspectives) for the analysis; if the societal perspective is not adopted, discuss limitations of the evidence and/or generate results from the societal perspective in a sensitivity analysis.

— Determine the currency and reference year for all monetary values.

— If new taxes will be used to fund the intervention, determine the assumed deadweight loss parameter. If a 0 percent rate is selected (i.e., no deadweight loss), generate results in a sensitivity analysis using loss parameters greater than 0 when accounting for new revenue required to pay for an intervention or for impacts on taxes paid or transfer payments.

— Determine the time horizon for the analysis, and when costs or outcomes accrue over multiple years, the base case discount rate and age or point in time to which to discount (e.g., start of the intervention or a standardized child age). If a 3 percent discount rate is not selected, generate results using a 3 percent discount rate in a sensitivity analysis.

— Determine the method for addressing uncertainty, and apply it to generate standard errors and confidence intervals for all summary measures, such as estimates of total (present-discounted-value [PDV]) costs, total (PDV) benefits, net (PDV) benefits, cost-effectiveness and benefit-cost ratios, and internal rate of return.

— Employ sensitivity analyses to test the robustness of estimates under a variety of assumptions, including alternative discount rates,

deadweight loss parameters, and estimates of the societal perspective if not the main perspective.
— Determine whether equity issues need to be addressed.
— Follow the reporting guidelines on the checklist for best practices for reporting economic evidence below.

For CA

Core Practices:
— Value all resources needed to implement the intervention, including infrastructure needs.
— Use shadow prices to derive an accurate estimate of the value of a resource when a market price is not available.
— Allocate overhead costs based on use.
— Annuitize capital investments.
— Calculate total costs and cost components: fixed, variable, and marginal costs.
— Calculate unit costs (e.g., cost per participant) to facilitate implementation and replication.

Advancing Practices (all core practices plus the following):
— Prospectively plan for cost analyses to be integrated into program evaluation.
— Use micro costing procedures whenever possible to improve the quality of intervention cost estimates and facilitate implementation and replication.
— Define major intervention activities and identify costs associated with each, including who bears those costs.
— Estimate costs for intervention planning, development, and adoption separately from those for intervention implementation.
— Use Monte Carlo methods to evaluate simultaneously the implications of multiple sources of uncertainty.
— Develop or modify budgetary and other management information systems to include relevant cost categories.

For CEA and Related Methods (in addition to best practices for CA)

Core Practices:
— Determine an explicit rationale for including intervention impacts in the CEA and selecting the focal impact that will not be valued in the monetary unit. All included impacts should be attributable to the intervention's theory of change. When available and relevant to the evaluation question(s), use information from well-conducted

systematic reviews and/or meta-analyses to inform intervention impact estimates.
— Determine whether the CEA will use a quality-of-life measure (e.g., quality-adjusted life years, disability-adjusted life years) as the focal impact and what method will be used for scoring that measure.
— Determine whether the CEA will be limited to direct, observable economic impacts, or linked or projected impacts also will be included.
— For impacts valued in the monetary unit (if any), use willingness-to-pay methods to calculate their prices. This may mean using a combination of market prices and shadow prices.
— Calculate the average cost-effectiveness ratio and, where feasible, the incremental cost-effectiveness ratio.

Advancing Practices (all core practices plus the following):
— Conduct CEA only when an intervention has been evaluated using research designs that can produce unbiased causal estimates of impact.
— Conduct CEA from a societal perspective to produce the most comprehensive economic estimates.
— Link or project observed outcomes only when strong causal evidence of the assumed relationship exists.
— Estimate costs and benefits separately by perspective (e.g., participant, agency, government, other beneficiary) and by category (e.g., income, crime, health care).
— Use Monte Carlo methods to evaluate simultaneously the implications of multiple sources of uncertainty.

For BCA and Related Methods (in addition to best practices for CA)

Core Practices:
— Determine an explicit rationale for including intervention impacts in the BCA. All included impacts should be attributable to the intervention's theory of change. When available and relevant to the evaluation question(s), use information from well-conducted systematic reviews and/or meta-analyses to inform intervention impact estimates.
— Determine whether the BCA will be limited to direct, observable economic impacts, or linked or projected impacts also will be included.
— Determine whether the BCA will include intangible as well as tangible economic impacts.

— Use willingness-to-pay methods to calculate prices for impacts. This may mean using a combination of market and shadow prices.
— Estimate linked or projected economic impacts using the strongest available theoretical and empirical literature. When available, use information from well-conducted systematic reviews and/or meta-analyses to inform estimates used for linking and projections.
— Calculate PDV costs, benefits, and net benefits (total and unit). Where relevant, also calculate benefit-cost ratio, return on investment, and internal rate of return.
— When there is concern that impact estimates may be biased (e.g., nonexperimental design, quasi-experimental design), test the robustness of findings to variation in effect size.

Advancing Practices (all core practices plus the following):
— Conduct BCA only when an intervention has been evaluated using research designs that can produce unbiased causal estimates of impact.
— Conduct BCA from a societal perspective to produce the most comprehensive economic estimates.
— Link or project observed outcomes only when strong causal evidence of the assumed relationship exists.
— Generate tangible and intangible values separately.
— Estimate costs and benefits separately by perspective (e.g., participant, agency, government, other beneficiary) and by category (e.g., income, crime, health care).
— Use Monte Carlo methods to evaluate simultaneously the implications of multiple sources of uncertainty.

Checklist of
Best Practices for Reporting Economic Evidence

For All Economic Evaluation Methods, Report the Following:

— The features of the intervention analyzed (e.g., logic model, intended recipients, intensity and duration of services, implementation, and other intervention features)
— The context in which the intervention was or will be implemented (e.g., population served; time, place, and scale of operation)
— The counterfactual (baseline or status quo) with which the intervention is compared
— The perspective for the analysis and any subperspectives examined, with associated results
— The currency and reference year for all monetary values
— The assumed deadweight loss parameter, if one was used
— The horizon for measuring economic values and, when discounting is used, the discount rate and time (or age) to which discounted
— Summary measures of the economic evaluation results (see below for each specific method)
— When relevant, results disaggregated by stakeholder
— The approach for addressing uncertainty, details on how the method was implemented, and the associated standard errors or confidence intervals for all summary measures
— Sensitivity analyses performed and associated results*
— When relevant, any equity considerations

For cost-effectiveness analysis (CEA), benefit-cost analysis (BCA), and Related Methods That Employ Impact Estimates Also Report:

— The evaluation method, the intervention impacts* and their statistical significance,* potential biases in estimates of causal effects, and any adjustments to estimated intervention impacts
— All limitations resulting from the strength of the evidence of causal intervention impacts

In Addition to the Elements for All Methods, for Cost Analysis (CA) and the CA Component of a CEA or BCA Also Report:

— The costing method (e.g., micro costing)
— The inventory of resources used and those that are valued versus not valued in the CA

— The method for obtaining information on how much of each resource is used, any related assumptions made, and how much of each resource is used
— The method for obtaining unit costs, prices, or shadow prices for each type of resource; any related assumptions made; and the resulting values*

CA Results
— Total costs and unit cost (e.g., cost per participant)
— Fixed, variable, and marginal costs
— The implications of methods (e.g., omission of resources, prices applied) for under- or overestimating intervention costs

In Addition to the Elements for All Methods and for CA, for a CEA Also Report:

— Which impacts measured in the evaluation are valued in the CEA and which are not*
— Which impacts are observed versus linked or projected, for whom they are linked or projected, and the linking or projection method
— For the impacts valued in the monetary unit (if any), the prices used,* their derivation, and the geographic or jurisdictional boundary to which the valuations apply*
— If the focal impact is a quality-of-life measure (e.g., quality-adjusted life years, disability-adjusted life years), how that measure was scored

CEA Results
— The average cost-effectiveness ratio and, where feasible, the incremental cost-effectiveness ratio
— The implications of methods (e.g., omission of resources in CA, prices applied in CA, causal evidence on outcomes, linkages or projections of outcomes, valuation for outcomes) for under- or overestimating cost-effectiveness

In Addition to the Elements for All Methods and for CA, for a BCA Also Report:

— Which impacts measured in the evaluation are valued in the BCA and which are not*
— Which impacts are observed versus linked or projected, for whom they are linked or projected, and the linking or projection method

— For each impact valued, the price or shadow price used,* its derivation, and the geographic or jurisdictional boundary to which the valuation applies*

BCA Results
— PDV societal costs, benefits, and net benefits
— Benefit-cost ratio, return on investment, and/or internal rate of return
— The PDV benefits (or costs) of each outcome valued,* with disaggregation by outcomes observed versus projected and, where possible and relevant, by tangible versus intangible benefits (e.g., for crime or child abuse and neglect)
— The implications of methods (e.g., omission of resources in CA, prices applied in CA, causal evidence on outcomes, exclusion of outcomes, linkages or projections of outcomes, valuation for outcomes) for under- or overestimating intervention net benefits

NOTE: An asterisk denotes reporting that may be suitable for a table.

1

Introduction

Societies, both domestic and international, invest substantially in interventions[1] designed to support the well-being of children, youth, and families in such areas as education, health, and social welfare. Often, the success of these interventions varies widely, leading to calls for evidence on how to make more informed investment decisions. Economic evidence— information derived from economic principles and methods—can help meet this need.[2] Economic evidence can be used to determine not just what works, but what works within budget constraints.

Economic *evaluation* is a particular means of producing economic evidence that can be used to calculate and compare the costs and outcomes of an intervention. Unfortunately, economic evaluation is not always executed or applied effectively. These shortcomings may not only weaken society's ability to invest wisely but also reduce the demand for this and other types of evidence. On the other hand, economic evaluation that is of both high quality and high utility—timely, accessible, and relevant within the context or environment in which it can best be used—can significantly improve and increase the returns on investments targeted to children, youth, and families.

This report examines many of the factors that both weaken and

---

[1] Throughout this report, the term intervention is used to represent the broad scope of programs, practices, and policies that are relevant to children, youth, and families.

[2] In the context of this report, economic evidence refers to the information produced by cost and cost-outcome evaluations, including cost analysis, cost-effectiveness analysis, and benefit-cost analysis.

strengthen the effective use of economic evidence. It proposes best practices and makes recommendations to both producers and consumers of economic evidence, as well as those who mediate between the two, for improving the use of such evidence to inform investments for children, youth, and families.

STUDY CONTEXT

In recent years, significant efforts have been devoted to strengthening the use of evidence, as well as performance measurement, for decision making in both the public and private sectors. Building on various efforts to "reinvent government," a movement given momentum by Osborne and Gaebler (1992), Congress passed the Government Performance and Results Act (GPRA) of 1993 to strengthen measures of government performance and use them to guide future actions. The Program Assessment Rating Tool (PART), a 2002 initiative of the George W. Bush administration, was introduced as a diagnostic tool designed to help assess and improve the performance of federal programs. The GPRA of 2010 continued the momentum of these efforts by building on lessons learned and providing examples of agencies that had made use of evidence in planning and assessing their programs and policies. A more recent legislative effort advocating the use of evidence in general in investment decisions is the Evidence-Based Policymaking Commission Act of 2015, first introduced in 2014 by U.S. Senator Patty Murray (D-WA) and Representative Paul Ryan (R-WI), which would establish a commission to determine how best to expand the use of data for evaluating the effectiveness of federal investments. One of the hopes for this bill is to increase the availability and use of data in support of program evaluation.[3]

Additional efforts are evident in a growing number of publicly and privately funded initiatives designed to help implement evidence-based programs and policies, support new and continuous evaluation, and target investments toward what works. Examples include the Bloomberg Foundation's What Works Cities Initiative; the Results First Initiative of the Pew Charitable Trusts and the John D. and Catherine T. MacArthur Foundation; the U.S. Department of Education's Investing in Innovation Fund (i3); Making Results-Based State Government Work, a joint project of the National Conference of State Legislatures and the Urban Institute; Results for America; Pay for Success initiatives; the International Initiative for Impact Evaluation (3iE); and Health Systems Evidence. Additional initiatives to support the use of evidence include the recent efforts of the William T. Grant Foundation, which recently introduced a new research

---

[3] *Evidence-Based Policymaking Commission Act of 2015*, 114th Congress; 1st Session; H.R. 1831 (2015).

focus to support studies aimed at identifying and testing actionable strategies for improving the production and use of "useful" research evidence, and the Laura and John Arnold Foundation, whose new Evidence-Based Policy and Innovation Division will develop and support initiatives that encourage policy makers to use evidence in their decision making.

Although these initiatives have made substantial progress in bringing the use of economic evidence in decision-making to the forefront of investment conversations, not all are not concerned specifically with *economic* evidence, but are focused on evidence more generally. For example, outcomes (e.g., graduation from high school) may be measured with little regard for intervention costs. Policy makers are seeking more information (e.g., from economic evaluations) to determine what works in the most cost-effective manner so that resources can be allocated wisely.

Not surprisingly, evidence is not the only factor influencing decisions. Weiss (1983) notes that ideology, interests, and information are the three major influences on government decisions. A 2012 report of the National Research Council (NRC) titled *Using Science as Evidence in Public Policy* similarly notes that scientific evidence is only one of the many influences on policy decisions, and that in a democracy, the views and interests of citizens and interested groups must be taken into account in formulating policy (National Research Council, 2012). Indeed, democratic processes by their very nature provide a means of making decisions in the absence of certainty. Nevertheless, the report highlights what it terms the "unique voice" of research evidence: It is "governed by systematic and rule-governed efforts that guard against self-deception . . . science is designed to be disinterested" (p. 10). Its procedures also are carefully detailed and circumscribed to allow for replication so that evidence can continually be tested and retested (National Research Council, 2012).

Although decision making clearly is the result of a dynamic process influenced by emotions and values, not just empirical evidence, such evidence—particularly economic evidence—can be used more effectively in investment decisions. Obviously, if the quality of the economic evidence is weak or the context (e.g., timelines or access to relevant data) in which it might be utilized is not carefully considered, the evidence will have limited utility. Given the potential for economic evaluations to influence better investments for children, youth, and families, this report outlines promising strategies for strengthening the evaluations themselves and better incorporating the evidence they produce into the processes used by decision makers.

STUDY CHARGE

In fall 2014, with support from the MacArthur Foundation, the Robert Wood Johnson Foundation, the Jacobs Foundation, the Institute of Medicine and the NRC formed the Committee on the Use of Economic Evidence to Inform Investments in Children, Youth, and Families. The committee was charged with conducting a study of how to improve the use of evidence derived from economic evaluations of costs, benefits, and potential for return on investment to inform policy and funding decisions on investments for children, youth, and families. The committee's statement of task is presented in Box 1-1. Topics related to methodological standards, principles, and practices are covered at length within Chapter 3. The other topics of the charge are discussed throughout the entire report.

The committee's charge at its core was to formulate recommendations for better ensuring that decision-making processes for investments in children, youth, and families are as informed as possible by economic evidence and, closely related, that the processes used by elected officials, researchers, budgeters, agency managers, and individual practitioners can result in better use of such evidence. Other National Academies efforts related to the study charge are highlighted in Box 1-2.

BOX 1-1
Statement of Task

An ad hoc committee under the auspices of the Institute of Medicine (IOM) and the National Research Council (NRC) will study how to improve the use of economic analysis of costs, benefits, and potential for return on investment to inform policy and funding decisions on investments for children, youth, and families. The committee will make recommendations to improve the quality, utility, and use of research, evaluation, and economic evidence about investments in children, youth, and families. The committee will take into consideration the perspectives of and actions that can be taken by prevention researchers, economic researchers, implementation researchers, evaluation scientists, implementers, and those engaged in making decisions about policies and investments. Throughout its information gathering and deliberations, the committee will consider lessons learned from similar economic analyses in other fields.

The committee will

- Review and investigate the current landscape of the design, methods, utility, and use of research and evaluation on effectiveness, costs, benefits, feasibility to implement on a large scale, and potential for return on investment to determine what is being learned about investments in children, youth, and families; who is using the knowledge; and how it is being used.

BOX 1-1 Continued

- Review existing standards or guides for the design, methods, and reporting of cost effectiveness, benefit-cost, return on investment, and budgetary impact analyses.
- Identify areas where widespread adoption of common methodological approaches is needed to ensure both consistent quality (e.g., appropriate choice of methods, validity, rigor) and appropriate utility (e.g., match of research questions to policy and implementation needs, comparability of studies, consistency of reporting).
- Specify common methodological approaches to be adopted in areas where sufficient evidence is available to reach consensus, including articulating options where one fixed standard may not be appropriate or needed.
- Identify and propose principles and processes for arriving at and adopting common methodological approaches over time in areas where consensus is not currently achievable or appropriate.
- Identify and propose processes for ensuring that the research and evaluation community, implementers, and those engaged in decision making are mutually informed and involved in designing studies, evaluations, and economic analyses to answer both important research questions and critical policy questions (e.g., costs, implementation, and effects at scale; components of interventions; portfolios of interventions; timeframe of anticipated outcomes and returns; accrual of benefits and returns to sectors/budgets other than the original expenditure).
- Identify current efforts and propose potential opportunities to support sustained, ongoing use of research, evaluation, and economic evidence in the public, philanthropic, and private sectors to inform investment in children, youth, and families. This includes incorporating evidence into decision-making processes alongside other political and value considerations.

The committee will build on the information gathered in two prior workshops conducted by the IOM and NRC: the 2009 Workshop on Strengthening Benefit-Cost Analysis for Early Childhood Interventions and the 2013 Workshop on Standards for Benefit-Cost Analysis of Preventive Interventions for Children, Youth, and Families.

STUDY APPROACH

To address the study charge, the National Academies appointed a committee whose membership included experts in a variety of disciplines and fields, including public policy, public health, education, social welfare, economics, sociology, developmental psychology, prevention science, program evaluation, and decision science. Members also included practitioners with experience (e.g., legislative, agency) in making decisions on interventions

---

BOX 1-2
National Academies Efforts Relevant to the Study Charge

Workshops
- Strengthening Benefit-Cost Analysis for Early Childhood Interventions (National Research Council and Institute of Medicine, 2009)
- Considerations in Applying Benefit-Cost Analysis to Preventative Interventions for Children, Youth, and Families (Institute of Medicine and National Research Council, 2014)

Reports
- *Bridging the Evidence Gap in Obesity Prevention* (Institute of Medicine, 2010)
- *Using Science as Evidence in Public Policy* (National Research Council, 2012)

Roundtables
- The Communication and Use of Social and Behavioral Science Research (2015)

---

for children, youth, and families. (See Appendix A for public session agendas and Appendix B for biographical sketches of the committee members and staff.) At the end of this report is a Glossary of key terms.

The committee conducted reviews of the peer-reviewed and gray literature (e.g., research reports, online publications) relevant to the topics outlined in the study's statement of task. The committee used this evidence to formulate conclusions and actionable recommendations to inform the research, practice, and policy decisions of prevention researchers, economic researchers, implementation researchers, evaluation scientists, implementers, and budgetary decision makers. The committee's search efforts revealed areas of weakness in economic evaluations, such as gaps in guidance related to cost analysis and other economic evaluation methods. As a result, the committee formulated recommendations for improving future economic evaluations, including some suggested best practices.

Given the many competing influences entailed in decision-making processes, the existing literature provided little explicit evidence on precisely *how* economic evidence in general—much less economic evaluation per se and, still less, high-quality economic evaluations of investments in children, youth, and families—can better be incorporated into those processes. Accordingly, to assess how better use might be made of the results of economic evaluations, the committee found it useful to look beyond the quality issue to studies on the use of research and economic evidence more broadly

---

BOX 1-3
Information-Gathering Process

The committee used various sources to supplement its research efforts. The committee met in person four times and held one half-day virtual meeting. In addition to its closed-session meetings, the committee held three public information-gathering sessions and commissioned three research papers. Participants in these supplemental information-gathering processes included prominent experts such as budgetary decision makers, translators of economic evidence, researchers, statisticians, and implementers representing perspectives from the fields of state and federal government, academia, and foundations and other nonprofit institutions.

Public Information-Gathering Sessions—Discussion Panels
- The Use of Economic Evidence in Decisions
- Facilitating and Overcoming Barriers to the Use of Economic Evidence in Investments
- Bridging the Gap Between Producers and Consumers of Economic Evidence
- Barriers to and Advances in the Use of Administrative Data/Integrated Data Systems

Commissioned Papers
- Drs. Jeff Valentine (University of Louisville) and Spyros Konstantopoulos (University of Michigan) addressed the technical issues surrounding the design, quality, and use of meta-analyses in certain economic analyses.
- Dr. Richard Cookson (University of York) addressed the state of the art and current efforts related to introducing equity issues and outcomes into economic evaluations of social-sector interventions related to children, youth, and families.
- Dr. Donald Moynihan (University of Wisconsin) addressed the nature and use of performance data to provide insight on how to improve the use of economic data.

---

defined, deriving salient information from such fields as public administration. The committee supplemented its literature review with commissioned papers and open-session discussions with outside experts. Throughout the chapters of this report, the reader will find selected statements made during those open-session discussions that support the key messages of this report.[4] Box 1-3 provides detail on the committee's supplemental information-gathering process.

---

[4] The experts quoted throughout the report provided written permission to include their names and testimony.

STUDY SCOPE AND KEY DEFINITIONS

The committee first worked to determine how to define and limit the scope of its work while achieving the study's purpose. Specifically, the committee developed definitions of economic evidence and its use and identified the types of investments in children, youth, and families that were relevant to the study. Throughout this report, for example, the committee elected to use the term *intervention* to represent the broad scope of programs, practices, and policies that are relevant to children, youth, and families. The committee's decisions about definitions and relevance are reviewed in the following sections; at the same time, the committee recognizes that alternative, or broader, definitions of these terms are possible.[5] It should also be noted that several illustrative examples are presented throughout the report, but the committee recognizes that these examples are inadequate to cover the gamut of possible types of investments in children, youth, and families.

Definitions Related to Economic Evidence

Economic evidence broadly defined refers to the various types of information collected using economic principles and methods—all of which are important for decision making. Based on both the statement of task for this study (Box 1-1) and the expertise of its appointed members, however, the committee focused on a particular class of methods for producing economic evidence. These methods formally fall under the rubric of *cost and outcome evaluation* or *economic evaluation* methods but are better known in terms of several specific types of analysis: cost analysis (CA), cost-effectiveness analysis (CEA), and benefit-cost analysis (BCA). For purposes of this report, *cost* is defined as the full economic value of the resources required to implement a given social intervention, and *outcomes* are defined as the causal impacts of an intervention on children, youth, and families (relevant outcome domains are detailed later in this section). Key definitions related to economic evidence are given in Box 1-4. A Glossary of key terms is at the end of this report.

It should be noted that *cost analysis* is sometimes used as a generic term for multiple economic evaluation methods. To avoid confusion, the abbreviation CA is used in this report when cost analysis is being discussed as a specific type of analysis. The objective of a CA is to measure the full economic value of the resources required to implement an intervention relative to the baseline condition (typically the status quo).

---

[5]For example, the Centers for Disease Control and Prevention uses the term program to describe any organized public health action (e.g., research initiatives, infrastructure-building projects, training education services) (Koplan et al., 1999).

BOX 1-4
Summary of Key Definitions

Benefit-cost (or cost-benefit) analysis—a method of economic evaluation in which both costs and outcomes of an intervention are valued in monetary terms, permitting a direct comparison of the benefits produced by the intervention with its costs.

Break-even analysis—a method of economic evaluation that can be used when the outcomes of an intervention are unknown; can be used to complement cost analysis as a way of anticipating potential economic returns.

Budgetary impact analysis—a special case of cost-savings analysis that examines the impact, year-by-year, of a health-related intervention on the government budget for aggregate or specific agencies.

Cost—the full economic value of the resources required to implement a given social intervention.

Cost analysis—a method of economic evaluation that provides a complete accounting of the economic costs of a given intervention over and above the baseline scenario.

Cost-effectiveness analysis—a method of economic evaluation in which outcomes of an intervention are measured in nonmonetary terms. The outcomes and costs are compared with both the outcomes and cost for competing interventions (or an established standard) to determine whether the outcomes are achieved at reasonable monetary cost.

Cost savings analysis—a method of economic evaluation that entails performing a benefit-cost analysis, but only from the perspective of the government sector.

Cost utility analysis—a method of economic evaluation that entails performing a cost-effectiveness analysis using quality-of-life measures.

Counterfactual—the base condition used as the basis for comparison in evaluating an intervention. No treatment, the current situation, or the best proven treatment are common counterfactuals.

Discount rate—a factor used to estimate future costs or the value of future benefits at the current equivalent value.

DALY (disability-adjusted life year)—a general measure of the burden of disease on the quantity of life lived.

Economic evidence—the information produced from cost and cost-outcome evaluations, including cost analysis, cost-effectiveness analysis, and benefit-cost analysis.

Impact—an effect of an intervention, or change in an outcome, that can be attributed to the intervention.

continued

BOX 1-4 Continued

Intervention—in the context of this report, a term used to represent the broad scope of programs, practices, and policies that are relevant to children, youth, and families.

Logic model—a pictorial representation of an intervention's theory of change. Logic models typically show the relationship among resources, or inputs needed to carry out an intervention; major activities involved in the intervention; and the results of the intervention, expressed as outputs, outcomes, and/or impacts.

Outcome—an attitude, action, skill, behavior, etc., that an intervention is intended to causally influence.

QALY (quality-adjusted life year)—a general measure of the burden of disease on the quality and quantity of life lived.

Return-on-investment analysis—a method of economic evaluation used in special cases in which benefit-cost analysis is conducted for a specific stakeholder group.

Shadow price—the estimated true value or cost of the results of a particular decision, as calculated when no market price is available or when market prices do not reflect the true value.

CA provides a foundation for both CEA and BCA.[6] In CEA, outcomes of an intervention are measured in nonmonetary terms, while in BCA, both costs and outcomes of an intervention are valued in monetary terms. CEA and BCA both incorporate the impacts of the intervention, not just its costs. In the case of CEA, for any given outcome affected by an intervention, the cost of attaining a given impact, such as the cost for each additional high school graduate, is calculated. Alternatively, a CEA can identify the amount of an outcome achieved for each dollar of cost. BCA goes one step further to value (ideally) all of the outcomes of an intervention in dollar terms, so that the aggregate value of the outcomes can be compared with the full economic cost of attaining those impacts. A BCA demonstrates whether the value of an intervention's outcomes exceeds the value of the intervention's cost, or whether the ratio of benefits to costs exceeds 1. In principle and in idealized form, a BCA also allows for comparisons across interventions to determine which ones provide the highest ratio of benefits to costs when

---

[6] Related evaluation methods that can be considered special cases of these three approaches include *cost-savings analysis*, *break-even analysis*, *cost-utility analysis*, and *budgetary impact analysis*. These methods are defined in Box 1-4 and described in greater detail in Chapter 2.

available resources are restricted. Illustrative examples of these methods can be found in boxes throughout Chapter 2.

While economic evidence can be quite valuable and fulfill a unique role, it does not dominate other forms of evidence and concerns. In the case of public policy decisions that are highly value-dependent or involve substantial nonquantifiable outcomes because of uncertainty or other reasons (e.g., the death penalty), the extent to which any economic evaluation can or should determine the final decisions made may be limited.

Definitions Related to the Use of Economic Evidence

A key word in the committee's statement of task is *use*. The committee was not asked to determine which method of economic evaluation is best, which studies are most informative, or how recent reports might suggest ways to allocate resources. Instead, the question posed was how best to improve the use of economic evidence, both existing and as it might be developed, to inform decision making on investments in children, youth, and families. In this context, economic evidence per se serves two main purposes: it provides a unique, disinterested voice and a rigor often unavailable elsewhere, and a broader framework for decision making in the presence of limited information. The ideal goal for the use of economic evidence, particularly that derived from BCA, is to maximize the return derived from each additional dollar, moment of time, or other resource expended at each margin. Since there never will be enough evidence to ensure that every dollar or other incremental resource could not be better spent or used elsewhere, the very framework of economic evaluation maintains a balanced focus by calling on those producing or using evidence to look at costs, not just benefits; at margins, not just averages; at every margin, not just one. For instance, a simple evidence framework might reveal that a certain effort succeeds at a certain task, but the economic evidence framework asks additionally whether there might be some better use of the last $100 spent on that effort.

To understand potential drivers of the use of economic evidence, it is important to acknowledge the complexity and variability entailed in decision making, as well as the differing typologies of use that may have distinct influencers (Innvaer et al., 2002; National Research Council, 2012; Pirog, 2009). The following is a nonexhaustive list of the typologies of use:

- *Instrumental use*—Study results are used to make concrete decisions. The decisions may be formative or summative and may be made by many different stakeholders.
- *Imposed use*—Requirements set by government offices or funders

mandate that scientific information be collected or that evidence-based interventions be implemented as a condition for funding.

- *Conceptual or enlightenment use*—This category of use refers to broad changes in how policy makers or stakeholders view an issue over time. Such use can occur when evaluation findings over time affect the conceptual framework that policy makers use to address policy issues.
- *Tactical use*—A decision is made to draw on research evidence to support or refute a specific idea, program, legislative action, or reform effort.
- *Process use*—In practice, evaluations often influence how people in an organization think. Such process use is particularly common when those in the organization are directly involved in a study. As a result of their involvement, they may, for example, begin making more requests for data, increase their use of logic models, or ask for more evidence in planning or making other types of decisions.
- *Symbolic use*—Evaluation results are used for strategic or persuasive purposes, to justify pre-existing positions. Views or decisions of the user do not truly change, but the user's goal is to change the views of others.

It is important that typologies of use are considered by those seeking to make economic evidence more useful. Illustrative examples of instrumental use, imposed use, and conceptual use of economic evidence are described in Chapter 2.

Relevant Investments for Children, Youth, and Families

The committee's charge focused specifically on *investments* in children, youth, and families, and should not be viewed as being related to spending on families more broadly defined. Not all spending, public or private, represents investment. The term *investment* normally implies less, not more, consumption today to promote more well-being and consumption tomorrow. The corresponding notion that an investment produces a rate of return is incorporated explicitly into economic evaluations by the way in which they sum and compare costs and benefits over time. A classic case is education, which entails a return tomorrow for investments made today.

As a result, although many types of spending or other efforts may be beneficial to children, youth, and families, they do not necessarily provide the types of return on investment that would be identified by evidence from economic evaluation. Table 1-1 summarizes the types of interventions that fall within the relevant policy domains of this study. Of course, such categorizations are somewhat arbitrary. Many social interventions may fall

TABLE 1-1 Types of Interventions Relevant to This Study

Domains	Examples of Interventions
Early Childhood	Home visiting, parent education, early learning, and other inventions that serve parents or children from the prenatal period to kindergarten entry through services delivered in the home, in centers, or through other providers (e.g., pediatricians)
K–12 Education	School-based interventions that serve children during the K–12 years, as well as school- or community-based out-of-school-time learning programs (i.e., before- or after-school or summer learning)
General Youth Development	School- or community-based programs that serve adolescents to promote positive youth development (e.g., mentoring, sports)
Child Welfare	Home- or community-based programs designed to prevent abuse or neglect or to intervene with children and families in the child welfare system
Health Promotion or Prevention	School- or community-based programs for parents or children designed to promote general physical and mental health or to prevent specific health problems, including disease
Safety Promotion and Injury Prevention	Home-, school-, or community-based programs designed to promote safety or prevent injury
Wellness	Home-, school-, or community-based programs for children and families focused specifically on nutrition and physical activity
Mental Health	School- or community-based programs for parents, youth, and children designed to diagnose and treat mental health or substance use conditions
Teen Pregnancy Prevention	School- and community-based programs for children and youth designed to promote sexual health and prevent teenage childbearing
Crime/Violence Prevention	School- and community-based programs for children and youth designed to prevent delinquency, crime, and violence
Homelessness Prevention and Supports	Programs providing housing support to prevent homelessness or providing supportive services for those that are homeless
Employment, Training, and Welfare	Training, employment, and income or in-kind assistance programs for families with children

SOURCE: Adapted from http://www.rand.org/content/dam/rand/pubs/technical_reports/2008/RAND_TR643.pdf [March 2016].

into more than one category, as many interventions have multiple objectives. For example, some early childhood interventions could be regarded either as child welfare interventions when they focus on prevention of abuse and neglect or as crime/violence prevention interventions when that is an eventual outcome. Likewise, interventions designed as general youth development programs may also be considered substance abuse prevention programs or teen pregnancy prevention programs if those are domains of behavior in which they have impacts. In general, the committee classifies interventions based on the primary outcomes they are designed to effect, even when there is overlap with other domains. Further, although many of the examples in Table 1-1 come from the U.S. experience, the committee also reviewed international practices and provides examples of economic evaluation of major development topics, such as disease prevention interventions.

The intervention types listed in Table 1-1 share a focus on children and youth, either directly or through their intervention with parents. Interventions of interest for this study include those that start as early as the prenatal period and extend through early childhood, the elementary school ages, and adolescence toward adulthood (given that returns on investment can extend throughout a child's life). Interventions often may center on the parent-child dyad or adopt a two-generation focus, with differential services centered on the child(ren) and the parents. Interventions of interest include those that deliver services in the home, as well as those that reach children and parents through a childcare or early learning program, a medical provider, a school, or some other community-based setting. The interventions listed in Table 1-1 may be made available universally or on a targeted basis according to specific indicators of risk, such as low income, health risks, or developmental delays.

The findings and recommendations presented in this report concern a broad range of interventions addressing children, youth, and families. The interventions may be at the federal, state, regional, or local level and in the United States or other countries. They may vary in intensity, frequency, duration, and cost and be financed by governmental or nonprofit entities or other actors. Finally, in addition to the types of interventions listed in Table 1-1, of relevance are regulatory policies, whether established by legislatures or agencies, designed to affect child and family well-being. For instance, safety promotion and injury prevention often are accomplished through specific legislation or regulations regarding products in the marketplace or safety practices, such as the use of safety belts or child seats in vehicles.

Relevant Outcome Domains

Although some interventions, such as those within the early childhood education field, may focus on the child, others, such as those related to housing, focus on the family; moreover, benefits to one family member often redound to others. Table 1-2 lists some of the outcome domains that the interventions in Table 1-1 would be expected to affect and for which economic evaluations need to account. As organized here, the outcome domains are divided into one set measured for children and youth and another measured for adults. Table 1-2 reveals a wide-ranging set of outcome areas that need to be considered, many of which may not typically be examined in economic evaluations, often because data are inadequate. Broadly speaking, these areas cover all aspects of child development—cognitive, social, emotional, behavioral, and physical—as well as similar domains of well-being

TABLE 1-2 Outcome Domains of Interventions Relevant to This Study

Domains	Examples
	Child and Youth Outcome Areas
Behavioral/Emotional	Behavior problems, school discipline (suspension, expulsion), social-emotional functioning (e.g., emotional regulation, executive function), mental health (e.g., depression, anxiety, stress, other psychological dysfunction)
Cognitive	IQ, other cognitive development measures
Education	Achievement tests and other education outcomes through high school (e.g., attendance, grades, grade repetition, special education use, high school graduation/dropping out)
Physical Health	Physical health, reproductive health (e.g., teen pregnancy, contraceptive use), health care utilization
Antisocial/Risky Behavior	Delinquency, crime, substance abuse, sexual activity, bullying
	Adult Outcome Areas
Family Functioning	Parent-child relationships, child abuse and neglect, healthy relationships
Education	Postsecondary education outcomes
Economic	Labor market outcomes, use of social welfare programs
Health	Physical health, mental health, reproductive health (e.g., childbearing, contraceptive use), health care utilization
Crime and Substance Abuse	Criminal activity; arrests and convictions; recidivism; use of tobacco, alcohol, and drugs

SOURCE: Adapted from http://www.rand.org/content/dam/rand/pubs/technical_reports/2008/RAND_TR643.pdf [March 2016].

in adulthood. The adult outcomes also encompass economic outcomes, including those related to labor and the use of welfare interventions, both for parents and for children as they age.

Although many conclusions about the use of economic evidence might well apply to any intervention, why place special focus on children, youth, and families? First, much spending on children and youth is aimed at improving their long-term well-being into adulthood and for decades to come (Hahn, 2014). Those concerned with long-term advancement for both individuals and society often turn their attention to the early stages of life—a critical period in cognitive, social, behavioral, and neurological development (Doyle et al., 2009). Second, relative to many other forms of spending, such as retirement support, much of government spending on children does take the form of investment, as evidenced by the share of spending on children going to education (Hahn, 2014). Of note, investment is especially amenable to economic analysis both in framing interventions and in providing evidence of success. Finally, it simply turns out that a good deal of recent effort devoted to providing economic evidence (see examples above) has focused on ways of providing services that would help children advance (Hahn, 2014).

REPORT AUDIENCES

To guide its deliberations, the committee considered the audiences for this report—those who produce evidence (including economic evidence) and those whose decisions ultimately affect whether and how well the evidence is used. These audiences can be divided broadly into the producers and consumers of evidence, with intermediaries often called upon to bridge the gap between them. Stakeholder groups for which this report may be relevant include prevention, economic, and implementation researchers; evaluators; implementers; knowledge translators; technical assistance providers; federal, state, and local agencies and policy makers; budget offices; and public, private, and nonprofit funding agencies. Additionally, many of the key messages of this report were designed to be applicable to stakeholders in both domestic and international contexts.

Researchers generally produce or provide economic evaluations, although those who gather the data used in such studies often determine what studies can be performed and what costs and benefits can be assessed. Both government entities (legislative and executive branches at the local, state, and federal levels) and philanthropies can finance economic evaluations and in that role affect what is studied and how results are disseminated. Of course, they simultaneously determine much of what is demanded and naturally serve as primary consumers of the evidence they demand. Within those institutions are individuals who provide, consume, and mediate the evidence resulting from economic evaluations, including elected officials and agency leaders with the power both to allocate resources to produce the evidence and to make use of the evidence to reallocate resources. Such power varies widely from person to person and field to field. For instance, a welfare budget may be determined by a legislature, but vaccination decisions may be made by an administrator or, more likely, a service provider (e.g., a nurse or physician in concert with parents).

Advocates for children, youth, and families or for particular subgroups, such as children with diabetes or in charter schools, are among those who exercise influence over public policy choices. At the broadest level, of course, society in general and, more specifically, families themselves serve as consumers of economic evidence, often deciding through private spending and voting just how such evidence will be used in allocating societal resources.

GUIDING PRINCIPLES

To support efforts to make better investment decisions for children, youth, and families through the use of economic evidence, it is critical that stakeholders, across sectors and systems, recognize the complexities surrounding the production, use, and utility of the evidence. For those stakeholders seeking ways to improve the use of economic evidence in decision making on investments in children, youth, and families, the committee proposes that they give substantial attention to two simple guiding principles: (1) *quality counts*, and (2) *context matters*. That is, it is not enough simply to require the use of evidence without also addressing issues of the quality and utility of the evidence. Failure to address quality issues weakens not just individual reports but also the acceptance of evidence more broadly by decision makers. In turn, context always matters: failure by researchers conducting economic evaluations to address the values and concerns of decision makers practically ensures that the resulting evidence will be weakly used, if at all. These two principles provide the framework for this report and support the committee's overall conclusion that the greatest promise for improving the use of economic evidence lies in producing high-quality and high-utility economic evidence that fits well within the context in which decisions will be made.

REPORT ORGANIZATION

The remainder of this report details the key messages framed by the above two guiding principles. Chapter 2 provides background for the succeeding chapters, summarizing the methods commonly used in economic evaluation. It identifies the relevant stakeholders in the production, use, and support of economic evidence; highlights current uses of economic evidence and common challenges to its use; and examines the untapped potential of economic evidence to inform investments in children, youth, and families. Chapter 3 describes the procedural steps in producing high-quality economic evidence. It also provides recommendations, including best practices, for the production and reporting of the results of high-quality economic evaluations of interventions for children, youth, and families, while also describing some related emerging issues. Chapter 4 acknowledges the vital importance of context in considering how quality economic evidence can best be used, highlights the broader influential factors that affect investment decisions, and offers related recommendations. Chapter 5 consolidates the key messages conveyed within Chapters 3 and 4, presenting a roadmap with a multipronged strategy for promoting improvements in the use of high-quality economic evidence. The recommendations offered in Chapter 5 present potential opportunities for stakeholders in economic evidence to partner to resolve some of the most pressing, cross-cutting issues (e.g., infrastructure, incentives, and funding) that must be addressed to promote more optimal use of economic evidence to inform investment decisions.

The committee's hope is that the recommendations and best practices presented in this report will help bridge the gap between the needs and interests of the consumers and producers of economic evidence and stimulate improvements, such as long-term partnerships and advanced development of data, in the ways in which economic evidence informs investments in children, youth, and families.

REFERENCES

Doyle, O., Harmon, C.P., Heckman, J.J., and Tremblay, R.E. (2009). Investing in early human development: Timing and economic efficiency. *Economics & Human Biology*, 7(1), 1-6.

Hahn, H. (2014). *Kids' Share 2014: Report on Federal Expenditures on Children Through 2013*. Washington, DC: Urban Institute.

Innvaer, S., Vist, G., Trommald, M., and Oxman, A. (2002). Health policy-makers' perceptions of their use of evidence: A systematic review. *Journal of Health Services Research & Policy*, 7(4), 239-244.

Institute of Medicine. (2010). *Bridging the Evidence Gap in Obesity Prevention: A Framework to Inform Decision Making*. S.K. Kumanyika, L. Parker, and L.J. Sim (Eds). Committee on an Evidence Framework for Obesity Prevention Decision Making. Food and Nutrition Board. Washington, DC: The National Academies Press.

Institute of Medicine and National Research Council. (2014). *Considerations in Applying Benefit-Cost Analysis to Preventive Interventions for Children, Youth and Families: Workshop Summary*. S. Olson and K. Bogard (Rapporteurs). Board on Children, Youth, and Families. Washington, DC: The National Academies Press.

Koplan, J.P., Milstein, R., and Wetterhall, S. (1999). Framework for program evaluation in public health. *Morbidity and Mortality Weekly Report: Recommendations and Reports*, 48(RR-11), 1-40.

National Research Council. (2012). *Using Science as Evidence in Public Policy.* Committee on the Use of Social Science Knowledge in Public Policy. K. Prewitt, T.A. Schwandt, and M.L. Straf (Eds.). Division of Behavioral and Social Sciences and Education. Washington, DC: The National Academies Press.

National Research Council and Institute of Medicine. (2009). *Strengthing Benefit-Cost Analysis for Early Childhood Interventions: Workshop Summary.* A. Beatty (Rapporteur). Committee on Strengthening Benefit-Cost Methodology for the Evaluation of Early Childhood Interventions. Board on Children, Youth, and Families. Division of Behavorial and Social Sciences and Education. Washington, DC: The National Acadmies Press.

Osborne, D., and Gaebler, T. (1992). *Reinventing Government: How the Entrepreneurial Spirit is Transforming the Public Sector.* Reading, MA: Addison-Wesley.

Pirog, M. (Ed.). (2009). *Social Experimentation, Program Evaluation, and Public Policy* (Vol. 1). Chicago, IL: John Wiley & Sons.

Weiss, C.H. (1983). Ideology, interests, and information: The basis of policy positions. In D. Callahan and B. Jennings (Eds.), *Ethics, the Social Sciences, and Policy Analysis* (pp. 213-245). New York: Plenum.

2

Setting the Stage

Thishis chapter provides a foundation for the remainder of the report. It begins by reviewing common methods used for economic evaluation, including the types of questions that can be answered by using these methods and the methods' limitations. It then identifies the stakeholders who produce and consume the economic evidence resulting from these evaluations, as well as those who serve as intermediaries in the economic evaluation process. The next two sections provide selected examples of the current uses of economic evidence to inform investments in children, youth, and families and highlight the challenges involved in these efforts, particularly with respect to the quality, usefulness, and use of the evidence. The final section describes the important role of economic evidence within the broader evidence ecosystem. Many of the topics summarized in this chapter are discussed in greater depth in subsequent chapters.

METHODS FOR ECONOMIC EVALUATION

For purposes of this study, the discussion here focuses on several types of economic evaluation that are classified collectively as cost and outcome analysis methods (Boardman et al., 2001; Gramlich, 1997; Karoly et al., 2001; Zerbe and Bellas, 2006). (See Chapter 1 for definitions of key terms used in this discussion.)

Questions Economic Evaluation Methods Can Answer

As shown in Table 2-1, there are three main methods that can be applied for the economic evaluation of social interventions: cost analysis (CA); cost-effectiveness analysis (CEA) and related methods of cost-utility analysis; and benefit-cost analysis (BCA) (also known as cost-benefit analysis [CBA]) and several related methods, including return-on-investment (ROI) analysis (also known as cost-savings analysis in the case of government stakeholders), budgetary impact analysis (BIA) (a special case of cost-savings analysis), and break-even analysis. Each of these methods addresses a somewhat different question. They all share the need for a comprehensive measure of the full economic cost of the intervention of interest, but they differ as to whether they require measurement of intervention outcomes or impacts and whether those impacts are monetized. In all cases, when costs and outcomes are measured, the measurement is always in reference to a baseline condition (or counterfactual), which may be the status quo or some other scenario. In addition, all of the methods can be used to conduct an economic evaluation of an intervention that has been implemented (and evaluated)—often referred to as an ex post or retrospective analysis. In such instances, the analysis will be based on measured results for program cost and, in the case of CEA and BCA, program outcomes. These methods also can be applied to an intervention that has yet to be implemented but for which the resources required and the expected impacts can be estimated (perhaps based on a similar program or one implemented at a smaller scale), and the potential cost, cost-effectiveness, or benefit-cost results can be calculated—typically called a prospective or ex ante analysis. Ultimately, which economic evaluation method is most appropriate depends on the question being addressed and the information on costs and outcomes that is available; what is feasible also depends on the resources available to support the research. The following subsections briefly describe and illustrate these methods. Further detail on these methods and their use is provided in Chapter 3.

Cost Analysis (CA)

CA is quite simple conceptually, although potentially complex in practice. It is used to address the question: What is the full economic value of the resources used to implement the intervention of interest over and above the baseline scenario? In effect, CA captures the "cost" of a program serving children, youth, and families. When a stand-alone CA is performed, it is not necessary to have measures of program impact; when a CA is part of a CEA or BCA, measures of program impact are required to capture the return on the resources invested. The output of a CA is straightforward: a comprehensive measure of the program costs. Box 2-1 describes an illustrative CA for the PROSPER (PROmoting School-Community-University Partnerships to Enhance Resilience) program. This example illustrates how CA can inform the implementation of an intervention, support planning for its replication, and provide the foundation for a CEA or BCA. The issues involved in CA are taken up in more depth in Chapter 3.

Both CEA and BCA and their related methods build on the results of a CA and incorporate intervention impacts, thereby capturing the return on the investment. For all of these methods, this requires an estimate of the causal impact of the intervention on its intended outcome or outcomes. Issues involved in deriving such an estimate as an input to economic evaluation are reviewed in Chapter 3. For now, it is assumed that a rigorous measure of intervention impacts is available as input to a CEA or BCA. The difference between CEA and BCA lies in the way they measure program impact: CEA uses natural units[1] (or another nonmonetary unit), while BCA converts outcomes into a monetary value. The methods related to BCA (see Table 2-1) examine investment and return from different perspectives, such as the government in the case of a cost-savings analysis or BIA or the private sector in the case of ROI analysis. BCA investments and returns can also be examined from the perspectives of the participant or of others who are not participants but are impacted by the intervention in some way. Break-even analysis focuses on the time period over which the return occurs.

Cost-Effectiveness Analysis (CEA) and Related Methods

In CEA, selected intervention impacts are measured in their natural units. Given a measure of the full economic cost of an intervention, CEA is used to determine the cost (possibly net of impacts on market costs) to achieve one more unit of the outcome, such as one more year of schooling. Alternatively, when meaningful, one can calculate the reverse ratio to determine the amount of a given outcome that is generated per dollar of cost, such as a gain of a certain number of scale points on an achievement test per dollar spent. As illustrated in Box 2-2, CEA can be a powerful tool for demonstrating the economic benefit of investing in an intervention and for comparing the relative cost-effectiveness of different interventions. The example in Box 2-2 further illustrates that CEA can be informative for investments in children, youth, and families in less developed, not just more developed, countries.

One issue that arises with CEA relates to its use of natural units to measure outcomes. Social interventions typically have multiple outcomes,

---

[1] Natural units are nonmonetary measures, such as a change in an achievement test scale score or in the number of years of schooling.

TABLE 2-1 Types of Economic Evaluation Methods and Associated Information Requirements and Outputs

Type of Evaluation	Questions Addressed	Requirements for Cost	Requirements for Outcomes	Outputs of Analysis
		Cost Analysis		
Cost analysis (CA)	• What is the full economic value of the resources used to implement a given intervention?	• Comprehensive measure of the intervention's economic costs from a societal perspective (may be disaggregated by stakeholder)[a]	—	• Cost of the intervention
		Cost-Effectiveness Analysis and Related Methods		
Cost-effectiveness analysis (CEA)	• What is the cost for an intervention to achieve a unit change in a given outcome? • What is the amount of a given outcome generated per dollar spent to implement an intervention?	• Comprehensive measure of the intervention's economic costs from a societal perspective (may be disaggregated by stakeholder)[a]	• Measures of the intervention's impact at a given point in time in natural units • Optionally, the monetary valuation of market outcomes • Examination of one (or more) unmonetized outcome(s) at a time in a given natural unit	• For a given outcome, the net cost per unit change in that outcome • For a given outcome (or outcomes in the same natural units), the amount of that outcome achieved per dollar spent

Method	Questions	Economic Costs	Measures/Inputs	Outputs
CEA using a quality-of-life measure (also known as cost-utility analysis)	• What is the cost for an intervention to achieve a unit change in a given measure of quality of life? • What is the amount of quality of life (e.g, quality-adjusted life years [QALYs] or disability-adjusted life years [DALYs]) generated per dollar spent to implement an intervention?	• Comprehensive measure of the intervention's economic costs (may be disaggregated by stakeholder)[a]	• Measures of the intervention's impact at a given point in time in natural units • Conversion of outcomes to a measure of quality of life (e.g., QALYs or DALYs)	• For a given measure of quality of life (e.g., QALYs or DALYs), the net cost per unit change in that outcome • For a given measure of quality of life, the amount of that outcome achieved per dollar spent

Benefit-Cost Analysis and Related Methods

Method	Questions	Economic Costs	Measures/Inputs	Outputs
Benefit-cost (or cost-benefit) analysis (BCA or CBA)	• Does the economic value[b] to society of the outcomes affected by an intervention exceed the economic value to society of the resources used to implement the intervention?[c]	• Comprehensive measure of the intervention's economic costs to society (may be disaggregated by stakeholder)[a]	• Measures of the intervention's impacts at each point in time in natural units • Market prices or "shadow prices" of the value to society of all outcomes (may be disaggregated by stakeholder)	• Net benefits to society, inclusive of all impacts[a] • Ratio of benefits to costs • Internal rate of return to society

continued

TABLE 2-1 Continued

Type of Evaluation	Questions Addressed	Requirements for Cost	Requirements for Outcomes	Outputs of Analysis
Return-on-investment (ROI) analysis (also known as cost-savings analysis in the case of government stakeholders)	• Does the economic value to the stakeholder(s) (e.g., private sector/government) of the outcomes affected by an intervention exceed the economic value to the stakeholder(s) of the cost to implement the intervention?	• Comprehensive measure of the intervention's economic costs to the stakeholder(s)	• Measures of the intervention's impacts at each point in time in natural units • Market prices or "shadow prices" of the value to the stakeholder(s) of all outcomes	• Net benefits to the stakeholder(s), inclusive of all impacts • Ratio of benefits to costs for the stakeholder(s) • Internal rate of return to the stakeholder(s)
Budgetary impact analysis (BIA) (a special case of cost-savings analysis)	• What is the impact, of an intervention, year-by-year, on the government budget (revenues and expenditures), in the aggregate and for specific budget components?	• Comprehensive measure of the intervention's economic costs to the government sector	• Measures of the intervention's impacts at each point in time in natural units • Market prices or "shadow prices" of the value to the government sector of all outcomes	• Net effect, year-by-year, on the government budget in the aggregate and for specific budget components
Break-even analysis	• How great would the impacts of an intervention have to be in order to break even, i.e., to pay back the intervention's cost?	• Comprehensive measure of the intervention's economic costs to society or to the stakeholder(s)	• Market prices or "shadow prices" of the value to society or to the stakeholder(s) of all outcomes	• Magnitude of impacts required on any one outcome or combination of outcomes to break even

NOTES: All measures of intervention cost and impact are relative to a baseline condition.

[a] Although societal perspective is a desirable goal, other perspectives need to be considered as well, including the perspectives of program participants, other nonparticipants affected by the program, and/or the government or public sector. BCA results can be particularly informative when the societal perspective is disaggregated to show these sub-perspectives. See the section in Chapter 3 on Defining the Scope for more discussion on this topic.

[b] When costs and/or benefits accrue over multiple time periods, the dollar streams are discounted to a given point in time to reflect the time value of money. Thus, the relevant outcome is net present-value savings or benefits or the ratio of present values.

[c] The broadest stakeholder for BCA is society as a whole. Society as a whole may be subdivided into specific stakeholders, typically defined as the government sector (or individuals as taxpayers), program participants (as private individuals), and the rest of society (program nonparticipants as private individuals).

SOURCE: Adapted from http://www.rand.org/content/dam/rand/pubs/technical_reports/2008/RAND_TR643.pdf [March 2016].

BOX 2-1
Illustrative Example of Cost Analysis (CA)

Rigorous CA can provide important information about the resources required to deliver an evidence-based intervention serving children, youth, and families. The comprehensive CA conducted by Crowley and colleagues (2012) for the PROSPER (PROmoting School-Community-University Partnerships to Enhance Resilience) community-based prevention delivery system illustrates the value of investigating the full economic cost of an intervention as part of a larger program evaluation. In particular, the study employed the Cost-Procedure-Process-Outcome Analysis model developed by Yates (1996, 2009) and differentiated between total economic costs—accounting for the value of all resources used—and financial costs—those resources used by the implementing organization, in this case the PROSPER system. As seen in the table below, the full economic costs, whether measured in the aggregate or per youth served, exceeded the financial costs by about 50 percent. In addition, the analysis demonstrated that it is essential to recognize the system-level or infrastructure costs associated with the implementation of specific school-based, evidence-based prevention interventions.

The study further examined how costs evolved over time as the model was developed and implemented in the community. Separate identification of the costs of adoption, implementation, and sustainability demonstrated the differential time path of activities required to deliver PROSPER in a given community and the associated resource requirements over the 5-year demonstration project. Such information is valuable for interpreting intervention impacts derived from an outcome evaluation, but also for planning for replication in other communities.

Cost Estimates for PROSPER Delivery System

	Low Estimate (in millions of $)	High Estimate (in millions of $)
Aggregate Cost		
Total economic cost	$4.34	$5.21
Total financial cost	$2.66	$3.53
Average Cost per Youth Served		
Total economic cost	$486	$580
Total financial cost	$311	$405

NOTE: The study further examined how separate costs evolved over time as the model was developed and implemented in the community.
SOURCE: Adapted from Crowley et al. (2012, Table 2).

and except for those outcomes that are naturally measured in the same unit or can be converted to the same unit (e.g., converted to a monetary value), it is not possible to aggregate them.[2] Thus, CEA typically focuses on one unmonetized outcome only, such as achievement score gains, years of schooling achieved, or number of crimes averted. If the same program that reduces crime also increases schooling, the latter will not be taken into account in a CEA. This is one drawback for CEA in the context of social interventions, which often have impacts on multiple outcomes, typically measured in different units. The ability of interventions or agencies to work together on the total well-being of children and youth is limited when each measures cost-effectiveness along a single dimension. Another major limitation of CEA is that it does not allow for the comparison of uses of resources for directly enhancing the well-being of children and youth with other uses of resources (e.g., infrastructure investments).

In the health policy field, the issue of multiple outcomes with CEAs has been somewhat mitigated by the development of several measures of quality of life, such as quality-adjusted life years (QALYs) or disability-adjusted life years (DALYs).[3] These indices often combine two outcome measures: health-related quality of life and length of life (or survival). With this common metric, researchers can use the CEA methodology to measure the net cost of an intervention per QALY or DALY or the gain in QALYs or DALYs per dollar of cost. Current guidance for the field in the conduct of cost-utility analysis was provided almost two decades ago by the consensus Panel on Cost-Effectiveness in Health and Medicine (Gold et al., 1996; Weinstein et al., 1996) and is currently being updated by the 2nd Panel on Cost-Effectiveness in Health and Medicine.[4]

Although medical and health-services interventions cover much that is beyond the scope of this report, QALYs and DALYs have been used for economic evaluation of social and behavioral interventions. In other fields, such as education, attempts have been made to combine multiple outcomes using value weights on outcomes derived from key stakeholders, loosely following the tenets of the utility theory underlying the use of QALYs and

---

[2]For a CEA, it may be possible to aggregate the impacts across more than one outcome if the different outcomes are measured in the same natural unit, such as impacts on subdomains of an achievement test where a scale point on each test has the same meaning. Aggregation may also be possible when impact estimates can be converted to another common metric other than a monetary unit. This is the case, as discussed next, with the quality-of-life measures used in the health policy field.

[3]The validity of the QALY and DALY measures is based on utility theory developed by von Neumann and Morgenstern (with application to health and QALYs; see Pliskin and colleagues [1980]). Hence, the application of CEA using QALYs or DALYs is also known as cost-utility analysis.

[4]See http://2ndcep.hsrc.ucsd.edu [May 2016].

BOX 2-2
Illustrative Example of Cost-Effectiveness Analysis (CEA)

The evidence-based policy movement extends to developing countries' efforts to promote child and family well-being. The growing number of randomized controlled trial evaluations provides a basis for conducting economic evaluation; CEA in particular has been a useful approach for comparing the gains in key outcomes per dollar spent.

For example, Dhaliwal and colleagues (2013) from the Jameel Poverty Action Lab (J-PAL) assembled the evidence for the educational impact of 12 intervention models implemented and evaluated in Africa, Asia, and Latin America that were designed to increase students' school attendance. With the addition of information about program cost and using a standardized approach, the researchers estimated the additional years of schooling obtained per $100 spent. As shown in the table below, the results indicated that the greatest educational gain per dollar spent was associated with an intervention implemented in Madagascar to provide information to parents about the returns to education, with the aim of influencing their children's educational investment. The next most cost-effective strategy was an intervention evaluated in Kenya to deworm students through their primary schools. The other programs examined had considerably smaller cost-effectiveness ratios. The table in this box illustrates that each program generated a range of cost-effectiveness ratios given the uncertainty in the estimates of program impact.

The authors examined the sensitivity of their relative rankings of the cost-effectiveness of the alternative education interventions to several methodological choices, such as accounting for the time costs of program participants, the treatment of transfers in measuring intervention cost, and the choice of the discount rate. Regardless of these choices, the top two interventions listed in the table continued to dominate in terms of their cost-effectiveness.

Comparative Cost-Effectiveness Estimates for 12 Interventions

Intervention Model (Country)	Additional Years of Education per $100 Spent		
	Lower Bound	Point Estimate	Upper Bound
Information Session for Parents on Returns to Education (Madagascar)	1.0	20.6	40.2
Deworming Through Primary Schools (Kenya)	5.1	12.5	19.9
Free Primary School Uniforms (Kenya)	0.33	0.71	1.09
Merit Scholarships for Girls (Kenya)	0.07	0.16	0.24
Conditional Cash Transfers for Girls—Average Transfer Amount (Malawi)	0.03	0.07	0.12
Unconditional Cash Transfers for Girls (Malawi)	0.00	0.02	0.04
Iron Fortification and Deworming in Preschools (India)	0.10	2.7	5.4
Building Village-Based Schools (Afghanistan)	1.0	1.5	3.0
Camera Monitoring of Teachers' Attendance (India)	—	—	—
Computer-Assisted Learning Curriculum (India)	—	—	—
Remedial Tutoring by Community Volunteers (India)	—	—	—
Menstrual Cups for Teenage Girls (Nepal)	—	—	—
Information Session for Boys on Return to Education (Dominican Republic)	0.08	0.24	0.40

NOTE: — = no significant impact of the intervention.
SOURCE: Adapted from Dhaliwal et al. (2013), reprinted with permission.

DALYs (Levin and McEwan, 2001). For example, Levin and McEwan (2001) discuss a cost-utility framework whereby multiple measures of effectiveness for an education intervention are weighted by their importance to parents, administrators, or some other audience. Weights are estimated subjectively or more rigorously using techniques similar to those applied in the field of health. See Chapter 3 for additional discussion of this topic.

When multiple interventions have multiple outcomes, another alternative is to conduct CEAs for each outcome of interest and compare their results to determine whether one intervention dominates the others across the outcomes examined. For example, Levin and colleagues (1987) compared the costs and impacts of four education interventions: cross-age tutoring, computer-assisted instruction, reduced class size, and increased instructional time. They found that for achievement in math, peer tutoring was most cost-effective, followed by class size reduction; for achievement in reading, they found that peer tutoring was most cost-effective, followed by computer-assisted instruction. As in this example, the rank ordering of the cost-effectiveness of interventions may depend on which outcome is being considered.

Benefit-Cost Analysis (BCA) and Related Methods

With BCA, all outcomes, in theory, can be accounted for in the economic analysis because an economic value is assigned to each outcome, so they are all measured in the same monetary unit (e.g., dollars). Thus all outcomes can be aggregated into their total monetary value to society, which can then be compared with the monetary value of the intervention's costs to society. This approach is particularly useful in the context of social interventions, which as noted above often affect multiple outcomes. As illustrated in the BCA example in Box 2-3, early childhood interventions, for example, may have effects on the child in terms of school readiness, health, or service utilization (e.g., emergency room visits) while at the same time affecting the mother or father in terms of their employment or use of social welfare programs. In a BCA, the economic values attached to each of these outcomes can be aggregated as a total measure of the benefit of an intervention to compare against its cost. The results of the BCA are then expressed in terms of net benefits (typically net present-value benefits when costs and benefits occur over time), a benefit-cost ratio, or a measure of the internal rate of return. With BCA, of course, the challenge is assigning a monetary value to each outcome. This and other methodological issues associated with BCA (e.g., the use of discount rates, accounting for uncertainty, the appropriate summary metrics) are addressed in greater detail in Chapter 3.

BCA is conducted from a societal perspective, although its results can be disaggregated to portray costs and benefits from the perspective of specific stakeholders, such as the government, program participants, and other members of society that are not participants. This additional detail can be very useful to decision makers, as it can show whether all stakeholders gain from an intervention or whether costs and benefits are distributed quite differently across stakeholder groups. For example, an intervention that is cost-beneficial overall but leads to losses or only small gains to participants may be less appealing to funders than an intervention that shares net benefits more equitably across stakeholders.

As noted above and in Table 2-1, a number of methods can be considered special cases of BCA.[5] In ROI analysis, the BCA is conducted from a specific perspective, such as the funding agency of the provider. In cost-savings analysis, the BCA is conducted from the perspective of government—the federal government, a particular state or local government, or potentially all levels of government combined. Thus in an ROI or cost-savings analysis, costs are limited to those that are paid for by the specific stakeholder(s) targeted, and the values attached to outcomes are those that apply to the targeted stakeholder(s) as well (e.g., the effect of outcomes in terms of government revenues or expenditures). For some outcomes, the only economic values included are private values that apply to the individuals participating in the intervention or to other members of society who experience private gains. But many such outcomes have a public-sector component. Examples include interventions that increase individual earnings, a portion of which will be paid to the government in taxes; that reduce the need for special education, thereby also lowering the cost of providing public education; or that reduce crime, effectively lowering the costs of the criminal justice system.

BIA can likewise be viewed as a special case of cost-savings analysis that examines the impact, year by year, of a health-related intervention on the government budget, both revenues and expenditures, in the aggregate or for specific agencies. Since BIA takes the government perspective, costs are measured specifically for the relevant government sector, and outcomes are also valued in terms of the impact on government revenues and expenditures, and ultimately the net budgetary impact. While the typical cost-savings analysis may entail calculating summary metrics such as a cost-savings ratio, the primary objective of BIA is to present the net program impact, year by year, on the government budget.

Finally, break-even analysis is an option when intervention outcomes

---

[5]These special cases are sought frequently. However, when they are used, it is important to state that results do not reflect a comprehensive assessment of costs and benefits to all stakeholders. Therefore, conclusions may differ from what would be found using a societal perspective. For example, an intervention that is cost-beneficial from a societal perspective may not yield favorable ROI or BIA results. The opposite can also be true. An intervention that yields favorable ROI or BIA results may not be cost-beneficial from a societal perspective.

BOX 2-3
Illustrative Example of Benefit-Cost Analysis (BCA)

In the field of early childhood interventions, the series of BCAs for the Perry Preschool Program has been highly influential in making an economic argument for investing in high-quality early learning interventions. Perry Preschool was a 1- or 2-year part-day center-based preschool program that served a small number of children with low income and low IQ scores in Ypsilanti, Michigan. The program was evaluated using a randomized controlled trial (RCT) for several cohorts of children from 1962 to 1965, with a total of 123 children in the treatment and control groups. After showing favorable effects on school readiness, the children in the evaluation were followed to assess educational and other life-course outcomes through the school-age years and again at ages 19, 27, and 40 (see Schweinhart et al., 2005, for the findings as of age 40, as well as earlier years).

The table in this box summarizes the benefit-cost ratios from the series of BCAs conducted for the Perry Preschool Program, starting with the follow-up data available through age 19 and continuing through the age 40 follow-up. One series of studies, those marked with an asterisk, was conducted by the High Scope team that implemented Perry Preschool and their collaborators. These studies showed an initial estimated return of $3.56 for every dollar of cost based on the age 19 follow-up impact estimates, a return that reached $16.14 for every dollar invested based on the results as of the age 40 follow-up. Two other BCAs were conducted by independent research teams. For the most part, the High Scope-sponsored studies used a similar methodology over time, so the increasing estimated returns with each successive follow-up study are attributable to greater precision in the estimated benefits in terms of the observed improvements in labor market earnings, levels of crime, and other areas of social gain. For any given follow-up age, the independent studies showed somewhat different results largely because of different choices regarding the outcomes to value and the economic values as-

are unknown—for example, because an evaluation has not yet been conducted. If the cost of the intervention can be assessed and its potential outcomes identified and valued in dollar terms, one can then infer how large the impacts would have to be for the intervention to pay back its costs. This can be done considering either a single or multiple outcomes. A break-even analysis can be a useful complement to a stand-alone cost analysis, prior to an impact evaluation, as a way of anticipating whether an intervention is likely to show a favorable economic return.

signed to each given outcome. For example, Karoly and colleagues (1998) did not include the intangible costs of crime (e.g., pain and suffering of victims), in contrast to the High Scope analysis, also conducted with follow-up data as of age 27 (Barnett, 1993, 1996; Schweinhart et al., 1993). Studies also varied in the discount rate applied. Despite these differences, the series of BCAs for Perry Preschool consistently shows a benefit-cost ratio that is substantially larger than 1.

Benefit-Cost Ratios from BCAs of the Perry Preschool Program

BCA Study	Follow-up Age	Benefit-Cost Ratio
Berrueta-Clement et al. (1984)	Age 19 follow-up	3.56
Karoly et al. (1998)	Age 27 follow-up	4.11[a]
Barnett (1993, 1996), *Schweinhart et al. (1993)	Age 27 follow-up	8.74[b]
Belfield et al. (2005), *Nores et al. (2005), *Belfield et al. (2006)	Age 40 follow-up	16.14[b]
Heckman et al. (2010)	Age 40 follow-up	7.1–12.2 [b,c]

NOTES: The benefit-cost ratios are the ratio of the present discounted value of total benefits to society as a whole (participants and the rest of society) divided by the present discounted value of program costs. The discount rate is 3 percent unless otherwise noted. The value of reducing intangible crime victim costs is excluded unless otherwise noted.
[a]Discount rate is 4 percent.
[b]Includes value of reduced intangible crime victim costs.
[c]Reported range of estimates under alternative assumptions regarding the economic cost of crime.

Additional Principles and Values That Drive Investment Decisions

"The most important factor that influences people in their decision making is their existing belief system."
—Jerry Croan, senior fellow, Third Sector Capital, in the committee's open session discussion on March 23, 2015.

The economic evaluation methods summarized in Table 2-1 have the potential to play an important role in helping decision makers understand the economic value of the resources required to implement an intervention, the cost to achieve a given impact, or the economic value of outcomes from the intervention relative to the costs of implementation. However, the questions shown in the table are not the only ones of interest to decision makers considering investments in children, youth, and families. Rather, these methods contribute important information to be considered along with other factors in making such decisions. This section highlights several such factors that influence investment decisions.

Equity Considerations

Among the most prevailing concerns in both public and private policy making is equity. Issues of equity enter the discussion throughout this report since, while not the focus of this study, they remain a consideration in all policy choices.

Equity principles described in Box 2-4 and examined in detail in a paper commissioned for this study (Cookson, 2015) can be divided roughly into three categories: (1) equal justice or equal treatment of equals, or horizontal equity; (2) progressivity, or vertical equity; and (3) individual equity (the right to the rewards from one's own efforts and, consequently, to ownership of property properly acquired). Each of these principles has a long tradition and is considered meritorious to some degree by philosophers and citizens alike. Seldom is any policy considered without attention to each of these three equity principles, which, along with administrative considerations and the efficiency considerations inherent in economic evaluation, form much of the landscape for decision making on investments in children, youth, and families.

Equity plays a role in allocating scarce resources across interventions. Within each intervention for children, youth, and families, the question arises of whether resources should be distributed equally, progressively, where they efficiently produce the highest return, or some combination thereof. For instance, should investments in children be increased not simply if they are good investments but as a way of trying to achieve equality of opportunity? Should each child have equal access to quality early childhood education? And do increased costs justify imposing additional taxes on the earnings of others? As discussed further in Chapter 3, economic evaluation methods are tools to support efficiency in the allocation of scarce resources, but typically are not employed to address concerns about equity. Nonetheless, as discussed in Chapter 4, the relevance of evidence derived from economic evaluation is likely to be enhanced when equity considerations are incorporated in the analysis or when implications for equity are discussed.

Other Considerations

The United States is a pluralistic society with diverse political views, cultural norms, and values. Evidence from economic evaluations is one of

BOX 2-4
Concepts of Equity

Equal Justice or Horizontal Equity

In many ways the queen of principles, equal justice applies to almost all policies: equal punishment for equal crimes, equal taxes for those with equal net income or other measure of a tax base, equal right to vote, and so forth. The challenge here is often determining just who are "equals." For instance, does income define those who deserve some equal level of child benefit, or should one also take into account family size, large medical expenses, or other factors?

Progressivity or Vertical Equity

Progressivity usually requires that those with greater means pay more and those with greater needs receive more. Although highly controversial in application, at some level the principle almost follows from some concept of natural law. That is, one does not expect children in a family to pay their fair share of costs, nor does one hold such expectations in larger society for those too severely disabled to work. Those with no income or assets cannot pay income tax, which automatically makes the system progressive at that level. Attempts to means test interventions often are favored by conservatives as well as liberals, since means testing costs less than more universal programs while progressively distributing benefits. But means testing has its own consequences, such as high effective tax rates when benefits are phased out as income rises. Foundations, in turn, typically do not make grants that subsidize the rich as much as or more than the poor. One complication here and the source of much controversy is that no principled standard exists for just how progressive any system should be.

Individual Equity

The right to the returns from one's own labor and to ownership of property derived from one's saving effectively restricts the extent to which government can tax or engage in "takings" without due compensation. This principle arises most commonly with respect to taxation, although it also leads to requirements for due compensation when government exercises, say, the power of eminent domain. In taxation, adherence to this principle aligns closely with the notion of benefit taxation (taxation according to benefit received) versus ability-to-pay taxation (taxation according to ability to pay, which aligns more closely with progressivity).

NOTE: For the purposes of this report, poverty alleviation is considered a special method of improving vertical equity.
SOURCE: Cookson (2015).

several factors for policy makers to weigh as they make difficult choices among competing priorities. In addition to the equity considerations just referenced, decision makers may take into account other values or moral judgments when weighing policy options. Political considerations also may enter into the decision-making process. Thus even when evidence from economic evaluations is of the highest quality and is made available to those making decisions about resource allocation, a range of factors in addition to or even instead of economic considerations will likely influence those decisions.

STAKEHOLDERS OF THE PRODUCTION
AND USE OF ECONOMIC EVIDENCE

In most markets, producers devote considerable resources to understanding the needs of consumers. They conduct research to attain an in-depth understanding of consumers' desires, preferences, and constraints and design their products accordingly. In the realm of interventions for children, youth, and families, by contrast, the research and development systems and incentives needed to ensure that research results are supplied to policy makers and practitioners (the consumers) in a way that addresses their needs and constraints are lacking. Stakeholders tend to talk to their peers (researchers to other researchers, practitioners to other practitioners), with few individuals bridging the divide. Before considering how this divide can be addressed, it is important to understand the different groups involved and how their needs and incentives vary.

Producers of Economic Evidence

The economic evaluation methods listed in Table 2-1 have long been used by economists to examine costs and outcomes in a wide array of policy arenas. As their use has grown, however, the community of producers has expanded as well. In the context of investments in children, youth, and families, producers of economic evidence may be researchers and policy analysts affiliated with the following types of institutions:

- university academic departments or affiliated research centers;
- think tanks, foundations, and other nonacademic organizations;
- executive or legislative branch agencies at the federal, state, or local level;
- international agencies, development banks, and country-specific government agencies; and
- advocacy, consumer rights, and victim support organizations.

This group of stakeholders also includes consultants who may conduct economic evaluations alone or in collaboration with other analysts.

When it comes to economic evidence for a particular intervention, producers of the evidence may or may not be independent of the intervention evaluators. In the example provided earlier of the BCAs of the Perry Preschool Program (Box 2-3), the analyses have been conducted by individuals associated with the team that implemented and evaluated the program, as well as by research teams at universities and think tanks that were not previously affiliated with the program.

The results of economic evaluations may appear in peer-reviewed outlets such as journals or research reports. They also may be released as studies under the imprint of a particular organization, such as a foundation, think tank, or advocacy group.

Consumers of Economic Evidence

A wide array of individuals might be considered consumers or users of evidence from economic evaluations. Under the broadest definitions, users can include the researchers themselves, their funders, and others who may use the evidence to apply for new funding or inform research agendas. For purposes of this report, the committee focused primarily on the use of research for applied purposes—that is, to develop or improve policy and practice. Thus, the focus here is on users who are in a position to translate research results into policy or practice.

Even within this more restricted category of users, however, many different types of actors may benefit from economic evidence. Elected officials and their staff may decide what policies and strategies should have priority and be included in budgets. Civil servants may use economic evidence to guide a range of decisions within a specific public program, such as how to emphasize more effective strategies in their budgets, grant making, regulations, and technical assistance. At the practice level, individuals in nongovernmental organizations may use economic evidence in selecting interventions to implement and in structuring their organizations for effective implementation.

In addition to those who make policy and practice decisions, a large array of intermediary organizations may use economic evidence to enhance policy and practice through advocacy, technical assistance, and other avenues. For instance, advocacy organizations may use economic evidence to argue for increased funding in a given area, such as early childhood (Christeson et al., 2013; Committee for Economic Development, 2012). Think tanks and research organizations may use economic evidence to highlight particular strategies for decision makers at the federal, state, or local level (Karoly et al., 2005). And technical assistance providers may use economic evidence to determine how best to inform and support individual organizations or groups of organizations, public or private, in selecting and implementing evidence-based strategies.

Finally, a growing number of organizations have an explicit mission of helping to translate evidence (including but not specific to economic evidence) into policy or practice. For instance, several relatively young organizations have developed with a mission of scaling up evidence-based practices and interventions (for example, Bridgespan Group, the Coalition for Evidence-Based Policy [now part of the Laura and John Arnold Foundation], Results First, and Results for America). Finally, philanthropic organizations play a large role in connecting evidence to practice, and many have specific portfolios (or a more general mission) to aid in that process.

In addressing how better use of economic evidence can be supported, the committee considered the needs of these many different types of users and the many different decisions for which they might bring economic evidence to bear. The key question here is how relevant the evidence is to the type of decision being made. For instance, evidence about the cost-effectiveness of a broad area of policy—such as early education for young children or teenage pregnancy prevention—is most relevant to decisions about how to allocate public or private resources across different areas of policy and practice. On the other hand, information on effective implementation of a given intervention is most relevant to those charged with the intervention's implementation (such as a nongovernmental organization or other implementing organization) or those charged with supporting and overseeing implementation (such as a government agency or technical assistance provider). Relevance applies both to the types of decisions for which the evidence is most suited and to the ways that evidence can be used to influence those decisions (Neuhoff et al., 2015).

Other Intermediaries

The set of stakeholders with interest in the production and use of evidence from economic evaluations extends to other intermediaries that play various roles, often in combination with their roles as producers and/or consumers. Such intermediaries include organizations in the public and private sectors that fund the evaluation research underlying economic evaluations or fund the economic evaluations themselves. Such organizations typically serve as consumers of economic evidence as well. Another type of intermediary sets standards for best practices in the application of economic evaluation, a role often played by professional associations, government agencies or research arms, and foundations, among others. Professional associations, along with institutions of higher education and other independent groups, also contribute to the field through involvement in capacity building and training, typically focused on producers, but in some cases appropriate for consumers as well. Other organizations perform the critical function of aggregating and translating the findings from economic evaluations, whether through centralized repositories, syntheses, or other strategies for dissemination. Chapter 4 provides additional discussion of the roles of intermediaries.

CURRENT USES OF ECONOMIC EVALUATION TO INFORM INVESTMENTS IN CHILDREN, YOUTH, AND FAMILIES

As discussed above and in greater detail in Chapter 3, high-quality economic evaluations are based on *credible* evidence of intervention impact. The importance of this point cannot be overstated in the context of how economic evidence is used. For example, when intervention impacts are credible and economic savings are identified, legislators may appropriate funds for specific interventions based on that evidence, pass legislation requiring practitioners to use a particular intervention, or reduce or eliminate funding for existing interventions. As both the quantity and quality of economic evidence have expanded, professionalization of the field has grown, and interest in and funding support for economic evaluation has increased. In this context, the discussion now turns to the variety of ways in which economic evidence is currently used and the implications for decision making.

Chapter 1 introduces a typology for characterizing different uses of evidence more generally, which is applied here to the use of economic evidence. The discussion focuses in particular on the ways in which economic evidence has been used for three of the use categories: instrumental use, imposed use, and conceptual use. The discussion is not intended to be exhaustive of all the ways in which economic evidence has been and is being used to inform decision making. Rather, specific examples are cited to illustrate the point that economic evidence may be used in various ways—both productive and unproductive—in policy debates regarding investments in children, youth, and families.

Instrumental Use

In the face of growing public pressure for accountability and efficiency, employees in public and nonprofit settings increasingly are being called upon to collect, analyze, and interpret data on the effectiveness of specific interventions. Similarly, policy makers and funders are expected to make use of economic evidence in making decisions. In particular, evidence of cost-effectiveness from a CEA or of a positive economic return from a BCA can make the case even stronger for investing resources in an intervention that has demonstrated favorable impacts. The addition of economic evidence to existing evaluation evidence can elevate an intervention from being just "evidence-based" to being a "good investment," thereby attracting resources and other support needed to keep the intervention operating or extend it into other localities.

An excellent example of the complementarity between program evaluation and economic evaluation is the Nurse-Family Partnership (NFP), a home visiting program that has been evaluated extensively through a series of randomized controlled trials (RCTs) and has also been subjected to several economic evaluations. As noted in Box 2-5, on the strength of the evaluation evidence, this program's reach has been significantly expanded across the United States. At the same time, the absence of evidence of effectiveness or cost-effectiveness is not always the end of the line for publicly funded interventions. For example, federally funded abstinence-only programs, designed to delay sexual activity until marriage as a way of reducing

---

BOX 2-5
The Role of Economic Evidence in Promoting Publicly Funded Home Visiting Programs

The 2010 Patient Protection and Affordable Care Act included $1.5 billion in new funds to allow states to experiment with and adopt evidence-based models for home visiting with families with pregnant women and children ages 0-5. The Maternal, Infant, and Early Childhood Visiting (MIECHV) Program[a] requires that 75 percent of grant funding be spent on proven home visiting models. Arguably the most visible program on the list of 17 approved "evidence-based models" is the Nurse-Family Partnership (NFP) Program.[b]

The NFP began as a demonstration program in Elmira, New York, known then as the Prenatal/Early Infancy Project (PEIP). David Olds and colleagues designed the program to provide economically disadvantaged first-time mothers with a series of home visits by registered nurses who were trained in and delivered a structured curriculum designed to promote healthy maternal behaviors during pregnancy and postpartum, parental caregiving, and maternal life-course development. An average of 9 home visits occurred during pregnancy, and another 23 visits on average took place during the next 2 years until the child turned age 2. To evaluate the program, a group of eligible pregnant women were recruited starting in 1977 and randomly assigned to the treatment group ($N = 116$) or a control group ($N = 184$). Mothers and children were followed during pregnancy and every 4-6 months for 4 years. A later follow-up occurred when the children reached ages 15 and 19. Published findings from the experimental evaluation showed favorable effects on maternal and child outcomes in multiple domains, including pregnancy outcomes, health-related behaviors, utilization of health services, welfare use,

BOX 2-5 Continued

and criminal activity, particularly for a higher-risk sample of unmarried mothers of low socioeconomic status (Eckenrode et al., 2010; Olds, 1996; Olds et al., 1986a, 1986b, 1988, 1994, 1997a, 1997b, 2002, 2004a, 2004b).

A cost-savings analysis by the evaluation team, based on findings 2 years after the program ended when the children were age 4, showed that government savings just exceeded program costs for low-income families, but net savings to government were negative for the sample as a whole (Olds et al., 1993). With the additional follow-up data through age 15, when other outcomes such as reduced crime and delinquency for mothers and children were measured, a BCA by researchers at RAND estimated net benefits to society per higher-risk family of $30,766 (in 1996 dollars using a 4 percent discount rate) or a benefit-cost ratio of about $5 to $1 (Karoly et al., 1998). For lower-risk families, the benefits to society just exceeded the costs of the program. Likewise, net savings to government were estimated to be positive for the higher-risk population served but negative for the lower-risk group. Given that the NFP was focused on targeting higher-risk first-time mothers, the evidence of a favorable economic return to society and to government was taken to indicate that the program was a worthwhile investment, and also indicated where such resources were likely to produce the highest returns. Subsequent BCAs of the program, based either on the Elmira results or including the findings from replication trials in Memphis, Tennessee (in 1988) and Denver, Colorado (in 1994) have also concluded that net benefits to society are positive, with benefit-cost ratios ranging from 2.89 to 6.20 (Karoly et al., 2005; Miller, 2013; Washington State Institute for Public Policy, 2015).

On the basis of both the evaluation of impacts and the evidence of economic returns, the NFP began to expand its reach, first with replications in Ohio and Wyoming in 1996 and with additional sites soon thereafter in California, Florida, Missouri, and Oklahoma, funded by the U.S. Department of Justice. Pennsylvania was one of the first states with statewide implementation. The opportunity for public funding was greatly expanded with the advent of the 2010 MIECHV program. As a result, NFP programs are now found in 43 states, as well as the U.S. Virgin Islands and six tribal communities (Nurse-Family Partnership, 2015). Estimates provided by Miller (2015) indicate that the nearly 180,000 pregnant women enrolled in NFP programs from 1996 to 2013 will generate government savings from reduced expenditures on Medicaid, Temporary Assistance to Needy Families, the Supplemental Nutrition Assistance Program of $3.0 billion (present-value 2010 dollars), well in excess of the program's $1.6 billion cost. This budgetary impact analysis does not fully incorporate the benefits to society from the array of improved maternal and child outcomes projected by Miller (2015) to include 500 fewer infant deaths, 10,000 fewer preterm births, 15,000 fewer childhood injuries, 42,000 fewer cases of child maltreatment, and 90,000 fewer violent crimes by youth.

---

[a]For more information, visit Health Resources and Services Administration Maternal and Child Health at http://mchb.hrsa.gov/programs/homevisiting [March 2016].

[b]For more information, visit Nurse Family Partnership at http://nursefamilypartnership.org [March 2016].

teenage pregnancy, at one time received strong federal support (doubling from slightly less than $100 million in 2000 to $200 million in 2009[6]), although there was virtually no evidence of such programs' effectiveness, and in fact some indication that they could contribute to higher levels of teenage pregnancy (Stranger-Hall and Hall, 2011). In such cases, values and moral judgment may simply trump the evidence from program and economic evaluations; however, the research also may compel supporters to amend their approaches, re-examine the details behind their theory of change, and essentially attempt different intervention designs.

While the NFP illustrates the use of economic evidence to support investments in a single intervention, the Washington State Institute of Public Policy (WSIPP) (a research institution described in more detail in Chapter 4) has developed a BCA model that supports the use of economic evaluation to assess the costs, benefits, and net benefits of multiple interventions within a domain (e.g., early childhood or youth development interventions), and potentially across domains. Based on a survey of the 50 states as part of the Pew-MacArthur Results First Initiative, however, the impressive WSIPP model is the exception rather than the rule (Pew Charitable Trust and MacArthur Foundation, 2013). While state policy makers recognize the potential value of CEAs and BCAs, and there is some forward momentum toward increased production and use of such economic evidence, states vary considerably in the production and use of evidence from high-quality economic evaluations. While all states conducted at least one BCA between 2008 and 2011, the majority of the nearly 350 analyses identified were carried out in just 12 states. Slightly more than half (29) of the states reported that BCAs had informed one or more decisions on the part of the legislative or executive branch to fund or eliminate interventions (Pew Charitable Trust and MacArthur Foundation, 2013).

Economic evidence also has contributed to the rapidly evolving pay for success (PFS) movement—also known by various other names, such as social impact bonds, outcome-based financing, and pay-for-performance and payment-by-results models.[7] The PFS financing tool leverages private investment to support preventive services that lead to public savings (Liebman and Sellman, 2013). In essence, the underlying premise of PFS and related financing mechanisms is that there is potential for a positive economic return from investing in an effective government intervention. When a PFS contract is successful, the private investors receive back their

---

[6] Sexuality Information and Education Council of the United States, see http://www.siecus. org [May 2016].

[7] In this context, these terms are used to refer to financing instruments. The terms are used differently in some contexts. In international development, for example, outcome-based financing and pay-for-performance more often refer to incentive-based payment mechanisms.

initial capital outlay that supported service delivery, as well as a percentage return, while the public sector benefits from the remaining cost aversion or savings (often in the form of reduced service utilization). This financing structure makes PFS contracts of particular interest for interventions that target developmental processes that otherwise lead to downstream costs (Finn and Hayward, 2013; Golden, 2013).

Since a 2010 pilot program was launched in the United Kingdom,[8] several U.S. municipalities and states have initiated PFS arrangements to fund interventions with an empirical record of reducing recidivism among juvenile offenders, emergency care costs for children with asthma, and special education utilization for at-risk youth (Brush, 2013; Olson and Phillips, 2013). Interest in PFS interventions is increasing at the federal and state levels—especially for those interventions targeting early childhood, whose return on investment may be the greatest (Currie and Widom, 2010; Heckman et al., 2010; Office of Management and Budget, 2011; Walters, 2014). As of August 2015, PFS projects had been launched in 6 states and were being explored in 27 others (Nonprofit Finance Fund, 2015). The benefits and challenges of the PFS model are discussed in Chapter 4.

Imposed Use

The federal government has a long history of requiring the use of economic evaluation to justify action in some policy domains. The 1992 Office of Management and Budget (OMB) Circular No. A-94, for example, establishes guidelines for the use of economic evaluation "to promote efficient resource allocation through well-informed decision making by the Federal Government" (Office of Management and Budget, 1992). While the circular includes in its scope "benefit-cost or cost-effectiveness analysis of Federal programs or policies," in practice federally funded programs serving children, youth, and families typically are not subjected to CEA or BCA, nor are the many "programs" that operate through the tax code, such as the earned income tax credit, child credit, or exclusion from tax for employer-provided health insurance. At the same time, under the Obama administration, there has been a push to expand the use of evidence of effectiveness in making resource allocation decisions. As catalogued in

---

[8] In March 2010, the United Kingdom's Ministry of Justice (MOJ) and Social Finance, a not-for-profit organization created in 2007, launched a pilot program aimed at reducing recidivism among prisoners released from the Peterborough prison. The key feature of this pilot was its financial arrangement: private parties, mainly charitable trusts and foundations, provided approximately £5 million to fund the program, while MOJ agreed to pay them up to £8 million after 7 years, accordingly to observed recidivism among program participants. Furthermore, if the program failed to achieve a reduction in recidivism of 7.5 percent, investors would lose their money (Disley et al., 2011; Nicholls and Tomkinson, 2013).

Haskins and Margolis' (2014) *Show Me the Evidence*, the federal government had six evidence-based social policy initiatives under way as of 2015 to allocate resources in such areas as early care and education, home visiting, K-12 education, teen pregnancy prevention, employment and training, and community-based programs. Notably, while these evidence-based initiatives require at least a preliminary level of evidence of impact and a commitment to further evaluation to add to the evidence base, they have not required economic evaluation as part of the justification for new or expanded funding. Several state-specific initiatives summarized in Table 2-2 share this feature of emphasizing "research-based" or "evidence-based" programs but not requiring evidence from economic evaluation to support funding decisions.

Conceptual Use

With the growing emphasis on results-based accountability, evidence from economic evaluation has served to provide a larger framework within which to view policy choices concerning interventions serving children, youth, and families. Perhaps the best example of this type of conceptual use has occurred in the framing of investments in early childhood interventions. In particular, results of BCAs for specific early childhood interventions such as the Perry Preschool Program (Box 2-3) and Nurse-Family Partnerships (Box 2-4) have been used to frame such interventions as investments: these interventions require an up-front investment in return for a stream of future dividends in the form of lower public-sector costs, higher levels of economic and social well-being for participants, and gains for the rest of society from reduced crime and other social ills. The investment framework has been used to appeal to the business community, in which such concepts as ROI resonate strongly (Christeson et al., 2013; Committee on Economic Development, 2012; Institute for a Competitive Workforce, 2010; Pepper, 2014). Investments in early childhood interventions also have been framed as an economic development strategy, one with an even higher rate of return than such traditional community investment strategies as building a sports arena or attracting businesses to relocate to a new community (Bartik, 2011; Rolnick and Grunewald, 2003).

At the same time that economic evidence is contributing to a conceptualization of early childhood programs as an investment with a high rate of return, the evidence has sometimes been simplified and misused. For example, the Perry Preschool finding of a return as high as $16 for every dollar invested (Box 2-3) applies to a small-scale demonstration preschool program implemented in the 1960s in one midwest city, considered to be of high quality, and serving a highly disadvantaged population of African-American children and families. Yet that result often is cited to suggest that any preschool program—including a universal program that would be available to both low- and high-income children—would generate such favorable returns. This application of the evidence reflects little recognition of the context within which Perry Preschool was implemented and how that context affects the generalizability of the findings for that one program to the range of early childhood programs being implemented today. For example, returns may be lower if programs are not delivered with the same level of quality and intensity of services as the Perry Preschool Program.

In his 2013 State of the Union address, President Obama referenced a somewhat smaller $7 return for every dollar invested in high-quality preschool in making the case for expanding access to high-quality preschool to every 4-year-old (Obama, 2013). That estimate is closer to the benefit-cost ratio estimated for the Chicago Child-Parent Centers Program, operated by the Chicago Public Schools and targeted to low-income children (Karoly, 2012). While the 7-to-1 ratio may be more realistic for a scaled-up program operating in real-world conditions, it is not clear that this return would apply to a universal program. A more universal program, depending on its design, might not only include more children with fewer needs but also lead to greater shifts from privately to publicly financed education. Notably, the WSIPP model shows a benefit-cost ratio of about 4-to-1 for publicly funded district and state preschool programs for 4-year-olds, based on a meta-analysis of the evaluation literature (Washington State Institute for Public Policy, 2015).

The Perry Preschool example is a reminder that all economic evaluations of existing interventions provide the most information about the economics of that intervention in relation to the alternative, which may be no intervention or some alternative program. The Perry Preschool example is also a reminder about the importance of context. Whether the economic evidence can be applied to decisions to fund other interventions or even the same intervention in a new setting requires careful consideration of the contextual factors of the interventions. The greater the similarity between the context of the new intervention and the context in which the evidence was generated, the more likely economic estimates are to apply. The importance of conveying information about the context of an intervention in an economic evaluation is discussed in Chapter 3, and issues pertaining to valid use of existing evidence are taken up in Chapter 4.

CHALLENGES IN THE USE OF ECONOMIC EVALUATION TO INFORM INVESTMENTS IN CHILDREN, YOUTH, AND FAMILIES

Interest in improving the use of different types of evidence (e.g., scientific, economic) in the social and medical sciences has increased, but its impact on public policy making and decision making has remained limited

TABLE 2-2 Examples of Evidence-Supported Legislation/Programs and Resulting Impacts

Type of Action	Example Legislation/Programs	Impact	State
Require the use of evidence- or research-based programs	The Public Safety and Offender Accountability Act (2011) mandates use of evidence-based programs for supervision, treatment, and intervention for the pretrial population, inmates, and those on probation and parole.	• 75% of program funding expected to come from prison savings by 2016 • $13.9 million invested in evidence-based education, training, and treatment programs during fiscal year (FY) 2012 • 5% increase in pretrial release rates • 40% increase in defendants participating in Monitored Conditional Release Program • Program that facilitates reentry into society was mandated by legislation	Kentucky
Dedicated funding for evidence- or research-based programs	State agencies are required to demonstrate that an increased percentage of funds is dedicated to evidence-based substance use and mental health treatment and to adult recidivism and juvenile crime prevention programs.	• Funds used to support evidence-based programs increased from 25% to 75% • Significant reduction in recidivism • Alternative Incarceration Program (AIP) was introduced in the bill, allowing sentence reduction for inmates completing research-based treatment programs • AIP returns $2.86 for every $1.00 spent	Oregon
Financial incentives for evidence-based interventions	The Treatment Alternatives and Diversion Program provides counties with grants to fund alternatives to incarceration for nonviolent offenders with substance use disorders.	• Incarceration days reduced by 231,533 • 57% of participants not convicted of a new crime 3 years after discharge from the program • Offenders successfully completing treatment and monitoring had significantly lower 3-year rate of recidivism (14%) compared with those who did not complete the program (24%)	Wisconsin

| Categorization of funded programs by effectiveness | A bill requires the creation of standards for program effectiveness, including evidence of cost-effectiveness where possible, and an inventory of programs meeting these standards in child welfare, mental health, and juvenile justice. | • Department of Social and Health Services can now track:
  – Number of people served in evidence-based programs
  – Percentage of funds directed to evidence-based programs
  – Number of eligible people who did not receive services
• Juvenile justice system was able to:
  – Identify eight programs meeting evidence standards
  – Ascertain that 67% of treatment funds were being spent on evidence-based programs | Washington |

SOURCE: Data from Pew Charitable Trust and MacArthur Foundation (2015).

(National Research Council, 2012). Research has shown that decision makers across sectors and levels of government do not consistently utilize scientific evidence, and that economic evidence is even less likely to inform decisions about the allocation or prioritization of resources (Eddama and Coast, 2008; National Research Council, 2012; Nutbeam and Boxall, 2008; Orton et al., 2011; van Dongen et al., 2013). Numerous factors—methodological, individual, organizational, and contextual—affect why and how certain types of evidence are brought to bear in determining the value of investments in children, youth, and families (Bowen and Zwi, 2005; Lessard et al., 2010).

The committee's information-gathering processes led to the two guiding principles articulated in Chapter 1: *quality counts* and *context matters*. Box 2-6 highlights the key issues identified with regard to the use of economic evidence in decision making—issues identified in the literature,

---

BOX 2-6
Issues Affecting the Use of Economic Evidence

Quality of Inputs
- Cost data are not collected prospectively; cost estimates are incomplete.
- Rigorous program evaluation evidence is not available; results are based on research designs that do not provide causal evidence.
- Available evaluation results often are for demonstration programs that may be less effective when scaled up.
- Many outcomes relevant for children, youth, and families do not have economic values for use in benefit-cost analysis.
- Limitations on access to data (particularly administrative data) preclude evaluation and valuation of outputs.

Quality of Outputs
- In the absence of standards, producers apply methods differently, and at times inappropriately or not comprehensively.
- No standards exist for reporting results of economic evaluation.

Usefulness of Economic Analyses
- Weighing alternatives is difficult because results are based on different methods, making them difficult to compare.
- Results are presented in a manner that obscures their relevance to investment decisions.
- Questions of interest to policy makers may not be understood or incorporated in research studies.
- Economic analyses may not be available in the time frame relevant for decision making.

as well as through the committee's information-gathering sessions with key stakeholders and other informants. Several of the specific issues pertain to aspects of quality: the quality of the inputs that go into producing economic evidence and the quality of the resulting output. Other issues are more germane to aspects of the context in which evidence from economic evaluation is used (or not used) to inform decision making. Some issues are most relevant for the producers of economic evidence identified earlier, while others are more closely aligned with the consumer side of the equation. Notably, there also are cross-cutting issues pertaining to incentives, capacity, and infrastructure that are faced by both producers and consumers, along with the intermediaries who transfer and interpret information among them.

Use of Economic Analyses

- Information needs to come from a known and trustworthy source, and such relationships may be lacking.
- Economic evidence is not available to inform decisions (poor data availability).
- Methods are complex and can be difficult to understand (reporting and communication issues).
- Results may be misinterpreted or misapplied by advocates.
- A lack of understanding of the policy and funding worlds may impede the ability to harness findings to meet decision-makers' needs.
- The organizational culture around the use of economic evidence may be weak.

Incentives, Capacity, and Infrastructure

- Funding for quality economic evaluations is lacking or insufficient.
- The cadre of trained professionals needed to conduct economic evaluations is lacking.
- Government agencies often lack the capacity to conduct economic evaluations or the expertise to use them well.
- There is a shortage of professionals trained to translate and use the evidence from economic evaluation and move the science forward.
- Systematic processes for assessing the quality of economic evidence, including specific guidance in funding announcements, are lacking.
- There are few incentives to use economic evidence in decision making.
- Incentives for researchers to conduct economic evaluations are insufficient.

Challenges Related to Quality

"The purpose of economic evidence is to be an input in the process. The better we can make the input, the better off the outcomes will be."
—Jerry Croan, senior fellow, Third Sector Capital, in the committee's open session discussion on March 23, 2015.

Box 2-6 enumerates several issues related to the quality of the available economic evidence pertaining to investments in children, youth, and families.[9] Some of these issues can be categorized as affecting the quality of the inputs to economic evaluations. As noted earlier, CA is a tool that provides valuable information on its own and also provides the foundation for CEA and BCA. While program administrators regularly estimate the costs of services for budgeting purposes, evaluation-oriented CAs remain rare for many interventions that impact children, youth, and families (Goldhaber-Fiebert et al., 2011). The committee reviewed a convenience sample of 1,294 articles relating to RCTs of interventions for children, youth, and families published in 2012-2015. Only 36 reported the cost of the intervention.[10] The committee's literature review also revealed that almost no articles address the factors that need to be taken into account when one is attempting to estimate the costs of interventions operating at scale compared with their costs in trials. This gap in information on intervention costs as part of program evaluation means that those conducting a CA, CEA, or BCA often try to reconstruct the required information retrospectively and may miss key cost components altogether or derive biased estimates.

Other issues are more relevant to the quality of the inputs required for CEA and BCA. In particular, both methods require evidence of intervention impact, preferably from a rigorous evaluation design such as an RCT or a quasi-experimental method that supports causal inference.[11] However, many interventions serving children, youth, and families may have been evaluated not at all or only using weaker evaluation designs— reflecting in part the costs in terms of time and other resources to conduct high-quality evaluations. While there has been support for implementing lower-cost RCTs and other designs using administrative data (Coalition for

---

[9] These issues are explored in length in Chapter 3.

[10] SCOPUS database search using key terms: "child," "children," "youth," "families," "randomized trial," "program," intervention," "cost-benefit," "benefit-cost," "cost-effectiveness," "cost analysis," published > year 2012.

[11] Causal inference is one of many factors that are relevant to the validity of a study or set of studies for any given decision. It can be challenging to address certain factors beyond causal inference because they are often dependent upon concerns that the researcher cannot reasonably foresee or control (e.g., the generalizability of the study context).

Evidence-Based Policy, 2015), the simple lack of data because of previous inattention to what might be required for later evaluations of new or existing interventions, as well as the lack of access to existing data, precludes wider application of such designs. When evaluations are conducted, another challenge is the absence of economic values (shadow prices) for many of the relevant outcomes, especially outcomes for young children, such as measures of school readiness, academic performance, and social and emotional development (Karoly, 2008). Here, too, better development of and access to administrative data could play a role in helping to calculate valid shadow prices. And even where the required evaluation evidence is strong and shadow prices exist, those who conduct economic evaluations may follow different practices with respect to key methods, which limits the comparability of results (Karoly, 2012).

One potential reason for these shortfalls in the quality of the inputs to economic evaluation and the resulting outputs is that the literature provides little guidance on best practices in general or specific to interventions for children, youth, and families. With a few notable exceptions (Children's Bureau et al., 2013; Gorsky, 1996; Yates, 1996), most guidance for CA comes from texts, primers, or government documents on how to conduct BCA and CEA, with chapters/text devoted to assessing program costs (Drummond et al., 2005). Recognizing this issue, the 2013 Institute of Medicine (IOM)/ National Research Council (NRC) workshop on Considerations in Applying Benefit-Cost Analysis to Preventive Interventions for Children, Youth, and Families (Institute of Medicine and National Research Council, 2014) identified four areas pertaining to cost analyses that could benefit from standardization: (1) identify essential cost categories that all cost analyses should strive to include; (2) develop guidelines for appropriate handling of costs that are not reflected in program budgets; (3) establish minimum levels of sensitivity analyses to explore uncertainty in cost estimates; and (4) ensure consistent reporting of cost estimates to enhance transparency and utility. There is a similar lack of guidance regarding the conduct and reporting of BCAs for interventions serving children, youth, and families although some resources exist for specific policy areas (see, for example, Karoly, 2012, for early childhood programs). Just as expert guidance exists for standardized methodology pertaining to CEA (Gold et al., 1996), CA and BCA could benefit from greater standardization from the field. Based on its review of the literature and expert guidance, the committee recommends in Chapter 3 a set of best practices that would enhance the production of, availability of, or opportunity to conduct high-quality economic evaluations of interventions for children, youth, and families.

Challenges Related to Usefulness and Use

"Talking about uncertainty and 95-percent confidence intervals can be difficult to communicate to legislators."
—Stephanie Lee, senior research associate, Washington
State Institute for Public Policy, in the committee's
open session discussion on March 23, 2015.

"How and what you evaluate really matters. We have to pick the right tools to generate the best evidence about a very particular set of issues that we are trying to solve. Contextualizing your tools for the problems you are solving is extraordinarily important."
—Nadya Dabby, assistant deputy secretary for innovation
and improvement, U.S. Department of Education, in the
committee's open session discussion on March 23, 2015.

Numerous factors beyond the quality of the evidence for the effectiveness of or economic return on an intervention can drive choices about what investments in children, youth, and families will be made in a community.[12] Research on the usefulness and use of evidence in general has helped illuminate some pressing issues, many of which also help explain why economic evidence is not well utilized. These issues include the timeliness and relevance of the evidence (Innvaer et al., 2002; Oliver et al., 2014), access to the evidence and sufficient time to review it (Merlo et al., 2015; O'Reilly, 1982), and the perceived credibility of the evidence (Jennings and Hall, 2011; Lorenc et al., 2014), all of which have impacted the extent to which leaders have relied on scientific evidence in the past. Jennings and Hall (2011) suggest that knowing the degree of conflict within an agency (e.g., competing pressures and demands, scientific capacity) also helps in understanding why some agencies are more or less likely to use evidence-based approaches.

A lack of connection between researchers and policy makers breeds a mistrust that can undermine the success of both parties (Innvaer et al., 2002; Oliver et al., 2014). Administrators have been known to blend related funding so as to maximize the reach or depth of available services or to design comprehensive approaches to complex social problems. The drive to meet the needs of the greatest number of eligible residents often is at odds with an administrator's desire to best serve each child or intervention. This often limits the analysis conducted and the conclusions that can be drawn from it.[13]

---

[12] These issues are explored at length in Chapter 4.

[13] Observation made at the committee's open session of June 1, 2015, Panel 2; see Appendix A.

Whether one can expect the impact or cost-effectiveness of an intervention to be as successful as previous research suggests depends on the quality of the intervention's implementation, including the depth of the monitoring performed, the number of local resources committed, and other important contextual factors.[14] Historically, researchers have placed greater emphasis on the internal than on the external validity of studies (Brownson et al., 2009; Kemm, 2006), yet the assessment of fit between intervention and context is a powerful indicator of long-term adoption and long-term investment. Influential factors external to the individual decision maker include the organizational culture around the use of evidence, the role of leadership, the prevailing political ideological and budgetary context, and the strength of advocacy agendas (Armstrong et al., 2014; Brownson et al., 2009). A number of studies have found that government leaders may perceive the influence and usefulness of local data, public opinion, and organizational capacity as more important than scientific evidence (Armstrong et al., 2013, 2014; Atkins et al., 2005; McGill et al., 2015). In addition, values and belief systems play a large role in which interventions garner public support and are funded.

The ways in which data are collected, measured, and regulated vary greatly across states and localities. Furthermore, limited communications between and within agencies, as well as the significant challenges faced in transferring data across agencies, undermine confidence in the available data and affect how well they can be used in establishing an evidence base or determining best practices in the implementation of interventions.[15]

Cross-cutting Issues Regarding Incentives, Capacity, and Infrastructure

"The more evidence that is made available, the more informed the end decision maker will be. We have heard several agencies tell us that they've done internal evaluations, but that these data are available to those inside their county or state, and not necessarily to other potentially applicable audiences. I think that appropriate infrastructure needs to be in place to support the sharing of data and evaluations. That is definitely something that could actually be done in the short term."
—Danielle Berfond, consultant, The Bridgespan Group, in the committee's open session discussion, June 1, 2015.

Box 2-6 lists a remaining set of cross-cutting issues that affect both producers and consumers of economic evidence, as well as other intermediaries involved in supporting the production and dissemination of the evidence.

---

[14] Observation made at the committee's open session of June 1, 2015, Panel 1; see Appendix A.

[15] Observation made at the committee's open session of June 1, 2015, Panel 2; see Appendix A.

Many of these issues were cited in the committee's information-gathering sessions, while others have been identified in the literature.

In terms of incentives, one challenge is that funding often is not available to support quality economic evaluations.[16] Funders may wish to see evidence of favorable impact before deciding to support an economic evaluation such as a CEA or BCA. This "wait-and-see" approach is one reason why the data required for cost analysis are not collected routinely as part of program evaluation: study teams simply were not given the resources to collect the required data. Funding gaps mean that program evaluators have little incentive to integrate economic evaluation into the program evaluation's agenda and design. If economic analyses are not called for in funding announcements and economists are not included on review panels, the incentives for conducting economic evaluation are further diminished. Even a lack of interest on the part of publishers, such as those that produce peer-reviewed field-specific journals (e.g., in the areas of child development, youth development, and prevention science) could signal that economic evidence is not valued as part of building the evidence base. On the consumer side, in the absence of imposed use of economic evidence (such as the initiatives discussed earlier), there may be little incentive to use the evidence from economic evaluation to support resource allocation decisions, especially if the evaluation results are not presented in an accessible way and the analysis is not provided by a trusted source.

Capacity issues also affect producers, consumers, and other intermediaries. On the producer side, no well-established cadre of trained professionals is available to conduct economic evaluations—a precondition for more widespread use of such evidence. While economists may have a working knowledge of economic evaluation issues as part of their academic training, few specialize in such analyses. Such training is not always routine in policy programs or in fields outside of economics. The establishment of the Society for Benefit-Cost Analysis (SBCA) in the last 5 years has helped raise the visibility of economic evaluation and provide a forum for developing interest in the area, encouraging new researchers to enter the field, and sharing the latest developments in methods and findings.

On the consumer side, many agencies at the federal, state, or local level lack the caacity to produce economic evaluations, and their staff do not necessarily possess the expertise required to be knowledgeable users of the evidence that is available (Pew Charitable Trust and MacArthur Foundation, 2013). The problem has two facets: users ideally would know what economic evaluation both can and cannot do. In addition, there is a shortage of professionals available to serve as intermediaries between the producers and consumers of economic evidence—individuals who could

---

[16] See Chapter 3 for discussions of cost components of quality economic evaluations.

help assemble the available evidence and translate it in ways that are useful for decision makers.

Finally, infrastructure gaps affect many of the intermediaries identified earlier. At present, for example, there are no centralized repositories of economic evidence for interventions serving children, youth, and families (Neumann, 2009). Those seeking to fund economic evaluations lack access to guidelines that could be used to establish requirements or standards for high-quality economic evaluations.

Chapters 4 and 5 provide additional discussion of the issues of incentives, capacity, and infrastructure that affect the usefulness and use of economic evidence.

ECONOMIC EVIDENCE AS PART OF THE EVIDENCE ECOSYSTEM

Despite some of the high-profile examples cited earlier, a great deal of unrealized potential remains for incorporating evidence from economic evaluation into decision making regarding investments in children, youth, and families. The factors relating to the quality of economic evidence outlined above are elaborated in Chapter 3, while those relating to the context in which this evidence is developed and used—and hence to its usefulness and use—are discussed in detail in Chapter 4.

The ultimate objective of this study was to determine what steps can be taken to ensure that evidence from economic evaluations contributes— along with results of program evaluations and other information—to decisions about investments in children, youth, and families. Ideally, consideration of economic evidence is incorporated into an overall evaluation framework addressing important questions at each stage of planning, documenting, and testing an intervention. At the earliest stages of a process or implementation study, the information required for CA can be collected as part of understanding the intervention model and how to implement it with fidelity, a point at which there are opportunities for quality improvement. When evaluations turn to assessing the impact of an intervention, the choice of which outcomes to measure can be guided both by the underlying logic model or theory of change and by a delineation of which outcomes are most amenable to evaluation using CEA, BCA, or related methods. Once information needs have been met, the goal is to ensure the production of high-quality economic evidence that is accessible, relevant, and used appropriately by decision makers who understand both the value of the economic evaluation methods employed and their limitations.

REFERENCES

Armstrong, R., Waters, E., Dobbins, M., Anderson, L., Moore, L., Petticrew, M., Clark, R., Pettman, T.L., Burns, C., Moodie, M., Conning, R., and Swinburn, B. (2013). Knowledge translation strategies to improve the use of evidence in public health decision making in local government: Intervention design and implementation plan. *Implementation Science, 8*, 121.

Armstrong, R., Waters, E., Moore, L., Dobbins, M., Pettman, T., Burns, C., Swinburn, B., Anderson, L., and Petticrew, M. (2014). Understanding evidence: A statewide survey to explore evidence-informed public health decision-making in a local government setting. *Implementation Science, 9*(1), 188.

Atkins, D., Slegel, J., and Slutsky, J. (2005). Making policy when the evidence is in dispute: Good health policy making involves consideration of much more than clinical evidence. *Evaluating Evidence, 24*(1), 102-113.

Barnett, W.S. (1993). Benefit-cost analysis of preschool education: Findings from a 25-year follow-up. *American Journal of Orthopsychiatry, 63*(4), 500-508.

Barnett, W.S. (1996). *Lives in the Balance: Benefit-Cost Analysis of the Perry Preschool Program through Age 27.* Monographs of the High/Scope Educational Research Foundation. Ypsilanti, MI: High/Scope Press.

Bartik, T.J. (2011). *Investing in Kids: Early Childhood Programs and Local Economic Development.* Kalamazoo, MI: W.E. Upjohn Institute.

Belfield, C., Nores, M., Barnett, W., and Schweinhart, L. (2005). Updating the benefit-cost analysis of the High/Scope Perry Preschool Programme through age 40. *Educational Evaluation and Policy Analysis, 27*(3), 245-262.

Belfield, C.R., Nores, M., Barnett, S., and Schweinhart, L. (2006). The High/Scope Perry Preschool Program. *Journal of Human Resources, XLI*(1), 162-190.

Berrueta-Clement, J.R., Schweinhart, L.J., Barnett, W S., Epstein, A.S., and Weikart, D.P. (1984). *Changed Lives: The Effects of the Perry Preschool Program on Youths through Age 19.* Monographs of the High/Scope Educational Foundation Research Foundation, No .8. Ypsilanti, MI: High/Scope Press.

Boardman, A.E., Greenberg, D.H., Vining, A.R., and Weimer, D.L. (2001). *Cost-Benefit Analysis: Concepts and Practice* (2nd Edition). Upper Saddle River, NJ: Prentice Hall.

Bowen, S., and Zwi, A.B. (2005). Pathways to "evidence-informed" policy and practice: A framework for action. *PLoS Medicine, 2*(7), 0600-0605.

Brownson, R.C., Fielding, J.E., and Maylahn, C.M. (2009). Evidence-based public health: A fundamental concept for public health practice. *Annual Review of Public Health, 30*, 175-201.

Brush, R. (2013). Can pay for success reduce asthma emergencies and reset a broken health care system? *Community Development Investment Review*, 115-125. Available: http://www.frbsf.org/community-development/files/pay-for-success-reduce-asthma-emergencies-reset-broken-health-care-system.pdf [March 2016].

Children's Bureau, Administration for Children and Families, U.S. Department of Health and Human Services. (2013). *Cost Analysis in Program Evaluation: A Guide for Child Welfare Researchers and Service Providers.* Washington, DC: Calculating the Costs of Child Welfare Services Workgroup.

Christeson, W., Bishop-Josef, S.J., Taggart, A.D., and Beakey, C. (2013). *Georgia Report: A Commitment to Pre-Kindergarten is a Commitment to National Security: High-Quality Early Childhood Education Saves Billions While Strengthening Our Military and Our Nation.* Washington, DC: Mission: Readiness.

Coalition for Evidence-Based Policy. (2015). *Low-Cost RCT Competition.* Available: http://coalition4evidence.org/low-cost-rct-competition [March 2016].

Committee for Economic Development. (2012). *Unfinished Business: Continued Investment in Child Care and Early Education is Critical to Business and America's Future.* Washington, DC: Committee for Economic Development.

Cookson, R. (2015). *The Use of Economic Evidence to Inform Investments in Children, Youth, and Families.* Commissioned Paper on the Methods for Incorporating Equity into Economic Evaluation of Social Investments. Available: http://iom.nationalacademies.org/Activities/Children/EconomicEvidence.aspx [May 2016].

Crowley, D.M., Jones, D.E., Greenberg, M.T., Feinberg, M.E., and Spoth, R.L. (2012). Resource consumption of a diffusion model for prevention programs: The PROSPER delivery system. *Journal of Adolescent Health, 50*(3), 256-263.

Currie, J., and Widom, C.S. (2010). Long-term consequences of child abuse and neglect on adult economic well-being. *Child Maltreatment, 15*(2), 111-120.

Dhaliwal, I., Duflo, E., Glennerster, R., and Tulloch, C. (2013). Comparative cost-effectiveness analysis to inform policy in developing countries: A general framework with applications for education. In P. Glewwe (Ed.), *Education Policy in Developing Countries* (Ch. 8) (pp. 285-338). Chicago, IL: University of Chicago Press.

Disley, E., Rubin, J., Scraggs, E., Burrowes, N., and Culley, D.M. (2011). *Lessons Learned from the Planning and Early Implementation of the Social Impact Bond at HMP Peterborough.* Santa Monica, CA: RAND.

Drummond, M.F., Sculpher, M.J., Claxton, K., Stoddart, G.L., and Torrance, G.W. (2005). *Methods for the Economic Evaluation of Health Care Programmes.* New York: Oxford University Press.

Eckenrode, J., Campa, M., Luckey, D.W., Henderson, C.R., Cole, R., Kitzman, H., Anson, E., Sidora-Arcoleo, K., Powers, J., and Olds, D. (2010). Long-term effects of prenatal and infancy nurse home visitation on the life course of youths: 19-year follow-up of a randomized trial. *Archives of Pediatrics & Adolescent Medicine, 164*(1), 9-15.

Eddama, O., and Coast, J. (2008). A systematic review of the use of economic evaluation in local decision-making. *Journal of Health Policy, 86*(2-3), 129-141.

Finn, J., and Hayward, J. (2013). Bringing success to scale: Pay for success and housing homeless individuals in Massachusetts. *Community Development Investment Review, 9*(1). Available: http://www.frbsf.org/community-development/files/bringing-success-scale-pay-for-success-housing-homeless-individuals-massachusetts.pdf [December 2015].

Gold, M.R., Siegel, J.E., Russell, L.B., and Weinstein, M.C. (Eds.). (1996). *Cost-Effectiveness in Health and Medicine.* New York: Oxford University Press.

Golden, M. (2013). *Using Pay for Success Financing to Improve Outcomes for South Carolina's Children.* Greenville, SC: Institute for Child Success.

Goldhaber-Fiebert, J.D., Snowden, L.R., Wulczyn, F., Landsverk, J., and Horwitz, S.M. (2011). Economic evaluation research in the context of child welfare policy: A structured literature review and recommendations. *Child Abuse & Neglect, 35*(9), 722-740.

Gorsky, R.D. (1996). A method to measure the costs of counseling for HIV prevention. *Public Health Reports, 111*(Suppl. 1), 115-122.

Gramlich, E.M. (1997). *A Guide to Benefit-Cost Analysis* (2nd Edition). Long Grove, IL: Waveland Press.

Haskins, R., and Margolis, G. (2014). *Show Me the Evidence: Obama's Fight for Rigor and Results in Social Policy.* Washington, DC: Brookings Institution Press.

Heckman, J.J., Moon, S.H., Pinto, R., Savelyev, P.A., and Yavitz, A. (2010). The rate of return to the Highscope Perry Preschool Program. *Journal of Public Economics, 94*(1-2), 114-128.

Innvaer, S., Vist, G., Trommald, M., and Oxman, A. (2002). Health policy-makers' perceptions of their use of evidence: A systematic review. *Journal of Health Services Research & Policy, 7*(4), 239-244.

Institute for a Competitive Workforce. (2010). *Why Business Should Support Early Childhood Education*. Washington, DC: U.S. Chamber of Commerce.

Institute of Medicine and National Research Council. (2014). *Considerations in Applying Benefit-Cost Analysis to Preventive Interventions for Children, Youth, and Families: Workshop Summary.* S. Olson and K. Bogard (Rapporteurs). Board on Children, Youth, and Families. Washington, DC: The National Academies Press.

Jennings, E.T., Jr., and Hall, J.L. (2011). Evidence-based practice and the uses of information in state agency decision making. *The Journal of Public Administration Research and Theory, 22,* 245-255.

Karoly, L.A. (2008). *Valuing Benefits in Benefit-Cost Studies of Social Programs.* Technical Report. Santa Monica, CA: RAND.

Karoly, L.A. (2012). Toward standardization of benefit-cost analysis of early childhood interventions. *Journal of Benefit-Cost Analysis, 3*(1).

Karoly, L.A., Greenwood, P.W., Everingham, S.S., Hoube, J., Kilburn, M.R., Rydell, C.P., Sanders, M., and Chiesa., J. (1998). *Investing in Our Children: What We Know and Don't Know about the Costs and Benefits of Early Childhood Interventions.* Santa Monica, CA: RAND.

Karoly, L.A., Kilburn, M.R., Bigelow, J.H., Caulkins, J.P., and Cannon, J.S. (2001). *Assessing Costs and Benefits of Early Childhood Intervention Programs: Overview and Application to the Starting Early Starting Smart Program.* Seattle, WA: Casey Family Programs and Santa Monica, CA: RAND.

Karoly, L.A., Kilburn, M.R., and Cannon, J.S. (2005). *Early Childhood Interventions: Proven Results, Future Promise.* Santa Monica, CA: RAND.

Kemm, J. (2006). The limitations of "evidence-based" public health. *Journal of Evaluation in Clinical Practice, 12*(3), 319-324.

Lessard, C., Contandriopoulos, A.P., and Beaulieu, M.D. (2010). The role (or not) of economic evaluation at the micro level: Can Bourdieu's theory provide a way forward for clinical decision-making? *Social Science & Medicine, 70*(12), 1948-1956.

Levin, H.M., and McEwan, P.J. (2001). *Cost-Effectiveness Analysis: Methods and Applications* (Vol. 4). Thousand Oaks, CA: Sage.

Levin, H.M., Glass, G.V., and Meister, G.R. (1987). Cost-effectiveness of computer-assisted instruction. *Evaluation Review, 11*(1), 50-72.

Liebman, J., and Sellman, A. (2013). *Social Impact Bonds: A Guide for State and Local Governments.* Cambridge, MA: Harvard Kennedy School Social Impact Bond Technical Assistance Lab.

Lorenc, T., Tyner, E.F., Petticrew, M., Duffy, S., Martineau, F.P., Phillips, G., and Lock, K. (2014). Cultures of evidence across policy sectors: Systematic review of qualitative evidence. *European Journal of Public Health, 24*(6), 1041-1047.

McGill, E., Egan, M., Petticrew, M., Mountford, L., Milton, S., Whitehead, M., and Lock, K. (2015). Trading quality for relevance: Non-health decision-makers' use of evidence on the social determinants of health. *BMJ Open, 5*(4), e007053.

Merlo, G., Page, K., Ratcliffe, J., Halton, K., and Graves, N. (2015). Bridging the gap: Exploring the barriers to using economic evidence in healthcare decision-making and strategies for improving uptake. *Applied Health Economics and Health Policy, 13*(3), 303-309.

Miller, T.R. (2013). *Nurse-Family Partnership Home Visitation: Costs, Outcomes, and Return on Investment.* Beltsville, MD: Pacific Institute for Research and Evauation.

Miller, T.R. (2015). Projected outcomes of nurse-family partnership home visitation during 1996-2013, USA. *Prevention Science, 16*(6), 765-777.

National Research Council. (2012). *Using Science as Evidence in Public Policy*. Committee on the Use of Social Science Knowledge in Public Policy. K. Prewitt, T.A. Schwandt, and M.L. Straf (Eds.). Division of Behavioral and Social Sciences and Education. Washington, DC: The National Academies Press.

Neuhoff, A., Axworthy, S., Glazer, S., and Berfond, D. (2015). *The What Works Marketplace: Helping Leaders Use Evidence to Make Smarter Choices*. Boston, MA: The Bridgespan Group.

Neumann, P.J. (2009). Costing and perspective in published cost-effectiveness analysis. *Medical Care, 47*(Suppl. 1), S28-S32.

Nicholls, A., and Tomkinson, E. (2013). *The Peterborough Pilot Social Impact Bond*. Oxford, UK: Oxford University, Saïd Business School.

Nonprofit Finance Fund. (2015). *Pay for Success U.S. Activity*. Available: http://payforsuccess. org/pay-success-deals-united-states [March 2016].

Nores, M., Belfield, C.R., Barnett, W.S., and Schweinhart, L. (2005). Updating the economic impacts of the High/Scope Perry Preschool Program. *Educational Evaluation and Policy Analysis, 27*(3), 245-261.

Nurse-Family Partnership. (2015). *Nurse-Family Partnership: Program History*. Available: http://www.nursefamilypartnership.org/about/program-history [March 2016].

Nutbeam, D., and Boxall, A.-M. (2008). What influences the transfer of research into health policy and practice? Observations from England and Australia. *Public Health, 122*(8), 747-753.

Obama, B. (2013). *Remarks by the President in the State of the Union Address*. Presented at the United States Capitol, February, Washington, DC.

Office of Management and Budget. (1992). *Circular No. A-94 Revised: Guidelines and Discount Rates for Benefit-Cost Analysis of Federal Programs*. Available: https://www. whitehouse.gov/omb/circulars_a094#1 [March 2016].

Office of Management and Budget. (2011). *OMB Circular A-133 Compliance Supplement 2011*. Available: https://www.whitehouse.gov/omb/circulars/a133_compliance_supplement_2011 [March 2016].

Olds, D.L. (1996). *Reducing Risks for Childhood-Onset Conduct Disorder with Prenatal and Early Childhood Home Visitation*. Paper presented at the APHA Pre-Conference Workshop, Prevention Science and Families, Mental Health Research and Public Policy Implications, November, New York.

Olds, D.L., Henderson, C.R., Tatelbaum, R., and Chamberlin, R. (1986a). Improving the delivery of prenatal care and outcomes of pregnancy: A randomized trial of nurse home visitation. *Pediatrics, 77*(1), 16-28.

Olds, D.L., Henderson, C.R., Chamberlin, R., and Tatelbaum, R. (1986b). Preventing child abuse and neglect: A randomized trial of nurse home visitation. *Pediatrics, 78*(1), 65-78.

Olds, D.L., Henderson, C.R., Tatelbaum, R., and Chamberlin, R. (1988). Improving the life-course development of socially disadvantaged mothers: A randomized trial of nurse home visitation. *American Journal of Public Health, 78*(11), 1436-1445.

Olds, D.L., Henderson, C.R., Phelps, C., Kitzman, H., and Hanks, C. (1993). Effect of prenatal and infancy nurse home visitation on government spending. *Medical Care, 31*(2), 155-174.

Olds, D.L., Henderson, C.R., and Kitzman, H. (1994). Does prenatal and infancy nurse home visitation have enduring effects on qualities of parental caregiving and child health at 25 to 50 months of life? *Pediatrics, 93*(1), 89-98.

Olds, D.L., Eckenrode, J., Henderson, C.R., Kitzman, H., Powers, J., Cole, R., Sidora, K., Morris, P., Pettitt, L.M., and Luckey, D. (1997a). Long-term effects of home visitation on maternal life course and child abuse and neglect: Fifteen-year follow-up of a randomized trial. *Journal of the American Medical Association, 278*(8), 637-643.

Olds, D.L., Kitzman, H., Cole, R., and Robinson, J. (1997b). Theoretical foundations of a program of home visitation for pregnant women and parents of young children. *Journal of Community Psychology, 25*(1), 9-25.

Olds, D.L., Robinson, J., O'Brien, R., Luckey, D.W., Pettitt, L.M., Henderson, C.R., Ng, R.K., Sheff, K.L., Korfmacher, J., Hiatt, S., and Talmi, A. (2002). Home visiting by paraprofessionals and by nurses: A randomized, controlled trial. *Pediatrics, 110*(3), 486-496.

Olds, D.L., Robinson, J., Pettitt, L., Luckey, D.W., Holmberg, J., Ng, R.K., Isacks, K., Sheff, K., and Henderson, C.R. (2004a). Effects of home visits by paraprofessionals and by nurses: Age 4 follow-up results of a randomized trial. *Pediatrics, 114*(6), 1560-1568.

Olds, D.L., Kitzman, H., Cole, R., Robinson, J., Sidora, K., Luckey, D.W., Henderson, C.R., Hanks, C., Bondy, J., and Holmberg, J. (2004b). Effects of nurse home-visiting on maternal life course and child development: Age 6 follow-up results of a randomized trial. *Pediatrics, 114*(6), 1550-1559.

Oliver, K., Invar, S., Lorenc, T., Woodman, J., and Thomas, J. (2014). A systematic review of barriers to and facilitators of the use of evidence by policymakers. *BMC Health Services Research, 14*, 2.

Olson, J., and Phillips, A. (2013). Rikers Island: The first social impact bond in the United States. *Community Development Investment Review*, 97-101. Available: http://www.frbsf.org/community-development/files/rikers-island-first-social-impact-bond-united-states.pdf [December 2015].

O'Reilly III, C.A. (1982). Variations in decision makers' use of information sources: The impact of quality and accessibility of information. *Academy of Management Journal, 25*(4), 756-771.

Orton, L., Lloyd-Williams, F., Taylor-Robinson, D., O'Flaherty, M., and Capwell, S. (2011). The use of research evidence in public health decision making processes: Systemic review. *PLoS One, 6*(7), 1-10.

Pepper, J. (2014). Business case for early childhood investments. *Chamber Executive, Fall 2014*. Available: http://www.acce.org/magazine-archive/fall-2014/the-business-case-for-early-childhood-investments [March 2016].

Pew Charitable Trust and MacArthur Foundation. (2013). *States' Use of Cost-Benefit Analysis: Improving Results for Taxpayers*. Philadelphia, PA: Pew Charitable Trust.

Pew Charitable Trust and MacArthur Foundation. (2015). *Legislating Evidence-Based Policymaking: A Look at State Laws that Support Data-Driven Decision-Making*. Available: http://www.pewtrusts.org/~/media/assets/2015/03/legislationresultsfirstbriefmarch2015.pdf [March 2016].

Pliskin, J.S., Shepard, D.S., and Weinstein, M.C. (1980). Utility functions for life years and health status. *Operations Research, 28*(1), 206-224.

Rolnick, A., and Grunewald, R. (2003). Early childhood development: Economic development with a high public return. *The Region, 17*(4), 6-12.

Schweinhart, L.J., Barnes, H.V., and Weikart, D.P. (1993). *Significant Benefits: The High-Scope Perry Preschool Study through Age 27*. Monographs of the High/Scope Educational Research Foundation, No. 10. Ypsilanti, MI: High/Scope Press.

Schweinhart, L.J., Montie, J., Xiang, Z., Barnett, W.S., Belfield, C.R., and Nores, M. (2005). *Lifetime Effects: The High/Scope Perry Preschool Study through Age 40*. Monographs of the High/Scope Educational Research Foundation, No. 14. Ypsilanti, MI: High/Scope Press.

Stranger-Hall, K.F., and Hall, D.W. (2011). Abstinence-only education and teen pregnancy rates: Why we need comprehensive sex education in the U.S. *PLoS One 6*(10), e24658.

van Dongen, J.M., Tompa, E., Clune, L., Sarnocinska-Hart, A., Bongers, P.M., van Tulder, M.W., van der Beek, A.J., and van Wier, M.F. (2013). Bridging the gap between the economic evaluation literature and daily practice in occupational health: A qualitative study among decision-makers in the healthcare sector. *Implementation Science, 8*(57), 1-12.

Walters, C. (2014). *Inputs in the Production of Early Childhood Human Capital: Evidence from Head Start.* Cambridge, MA: National Bureau of Economic Research.

Washington State Institute for Public Policy. 2015. *Nurse Family Partnership for Low-Income Families: Benefit-Cost Estimates Updated July 2015.* Available: http://www.wsipp.wa.gov/BenefitCost/Program/35 [March 2016].

Weinstein, M.C., Siegel, J.E., Gold, M.R., Kamlet, M.S., and Russell, L.B. (1996). Recommendations of the panel on cost-effectiveness in health and medicine. *Journal of the American Medical Association, 276*(15), 1253-1258.

Yates, B.T. (1996). *Analyzing Costs, Procedures, Processes, and Outcomes in Human Services: An Introduction* (Vol. 42). Thousands Oak, CA: Sage.

Yates, B.T. (2009). Cost-inclusive evaluation: A banquet of approaches for including costs, benefits, and cost-effectiveness and cost–benefit analyses in your next evaluation. *Evaluation and Program Planning, 32*(1), 52-54.

Zerbe, R.O., and Bellas, A.S. (2006). *A Primer for Benefit-Cost Analysis.* Northhampton, MA: Edward Elgar.

3

Producing High-Quality Economic Evidence to Inform Investments in Children, Youth, and Families

Three of the major economic evaluation methods that can be applied to interventions[1] serving children, youth, and families identified in Chapter 2 are cost analysis (CA), cost-effectiveness analysis (CEA), and benefit-cost analysis (BCA). These methods can be used to address a number of important questions relevant to decisions about intervention investments. For example, What does it cost to fully implement a given intervention? If an investment is made, what can be expected to be gained in return (e.g., outcomes, dollars, or overall better quality of life)? Is the investment a justifiable use of scarce resources relative to other investments?

Economic evidence generated by these methods can inform investment decisions, but barriers to using this evidence exist. As noted in Chapter 2, some of these barriers relate to the quality of the economic evidence produced. High-quality economic evidence can be difficult to derive because economic evaluation methods are complex and entail many assumptions (Crowley et al., 2014; Lee and Aos, 2011; Vining and Weimer, 2009a). Moreover, methods are often applied inconsistently in different studies, making results difficult to compare and use appropriately in policy and investment contexts (Drummond and Sculpher, 2005; Foster et al., 2007; Institute of Medicine and National Research Council, 2014; Karoly, 2012; Weinstein et al., 1997). Results also may be communicated in a way that obscures important findings or is not suited for nonresearch audiences, or a way in which decision makers may not deem them reliable or compelling

---

[1] As noted in Chapter 1, the term intervention is used to represent the broad scope of programs, practices, and policies that are relevant to children, youth, and families.

(National Research Council and Institute of Medicine, 2009; Oliver et al., 2014; Pew-MacArthur Results First Initiative, 2013). Shortcomings in these areas may not only limit decision makers' use of economic evidence but also reduce their demand for such evidence, as well as other types of evidence, in the future.

The primary aim of this chapter is to examine issues associated with the quality of economic evidence, and thus to address the first of this study's two guiding principles, as described in Chapter 1: *quality counts*. As noted in Chapter 2, the quality of economic evidence is essential to its utility and ongoing use. Thus, a major goal of this chapter is to help current and would-be producers of economic evidence understand when interventions are ready for economic evaluation and what it takes to produce and report high-quality economic evidence. In several instances, the chapter identifies emerging issues—such as the importance of incorporating the impact of intervention investments on participants' quality of life—that merit further investigation to determine their applicability to economic evaluation of investments in children, youth, and families.[2]

In focusing on the quality of economic evidence, the committee drew on the literature and the expertise of its members to identify best practices that can both support high-quality economic evaluation and potentially lead to greater standardization of evaluation methods. Standardization is particularly important because decisions to invest in interventions for children, youth, and families typically involve weighing alternatives in the face of limited budgets; other constraints; and, perhaps, competing values. The use of differing methods to estimate the costs and benefits of alternative investments impedes understanding the economic trade-offs involved and limits the utility of the evidence. At the same time, it is important to recognize the potential disconnect between ideal practice and the real-world analytic issues and constraints that producers of economic evidence encounter. Where possible, this chapter provides strategies for addressing such practical limitations. In addition, the best practices for producing high-quality evidence recommended at the end of the chapter are divided into those that can be viewed as "core" and readily implemented in most circumstances and those the committee characterizes as "advancing," to be pursued when feasible.

The focus of this chapter extends to highlighting best practices for re-

---

[2]In this chapter, the committee discusses at some length both the strengths and limitations of economic evaluations and the economic evidence produced. The committee recognizes that, based on the current state of the field, there is no perfect solution for every issue that is discussed herein. Although economic evidence has its limitations, the hope is that stakeholders, to the extent possible, follow good practices, are transparent about these practices, and understand—whether they are producers or consumers—what can and cannot be derived from economic evaluations.

porting the results of economic evaluations in a consistent and transparent manner. Findings need to be communicated in ways that facilitate understanding, acknowledge limitations, and support their appropriate use in investment decisions. Achieving such transparency and utility is not a small task given the complexity, multiple assumptions, and various sources of uncertainty entailed in the use of economic evaluation methods. Nonetheless, the chapter offers guidelines that in the committee's view can enhance the utility and use of economic evidence while maintaining scientific rigor.

It should be noted that a well-established literature on best practices in the conduct and reporting of CAs provided a solid foundation for the CA-related conclusions and recommendations offered in this chapter. Best practices in CEA in health and medicine, initially established in 1996 (Gold et al., 1996), are currently under review by the 2nd Panel on Cost-Effectiveness Analysis in Health and Medicine.[3] In addition to the best practices pertinent to CEA identified in this chapter, interested readers are encouraged to turn to this panel's recommendations when they are available. Best practices in the application of BCA to investments in children, youth, and families have just begun to appear in the literature, so the committee's conclusions and recommendations on this method are based on the consensus view of the committee members, incorporating perspectives from the available literature and papers and panels sponsored for this study.

Finally, although much of this chapter is directed at producers of economic evidence, its content should also be of interest to consumers of the evidence. Consumers can benefit from understanding the analytic issues associated with planning for and conducting economic evaluations, the best practices for the production and reporting of economic evidence, and the limitations of economic evaluation methods. Similarly, producers of the evidence would benefit from understanding the issues raised in Chapter 4, which deals with how consumers use the economic evidence they receive, even if it is of the highest quality, and the context in which investment decisions are made.

The first two sections of this chapter outline issues pertinent to all types of economic evaluation: determining whether an intervention is ready for economic evaluation and defining the scope of the evaluation. Next is a discussion of issues specific to evaluating intervention cost (relevant to CA), and by extension, CEA and BCA, determining intervention impacts (relevant to CEA and BCA), and valuing outcomes (relevant particularly to BCA and related methods). Sections then follow on the development and reporting of summary measures for the results of CA, CEA, and BCA; how the uncertainty intrinsic to economic evaluations can be handled; and how equity

---

[3] For more information on this effort, see http://2ndcep.hsrc.ucsd.edu/list.html [March 2016].

considerations can be addressed. The chapter closes with the committee's recommendations regarding best practices for producing and reporting high-quality economic evidence.

DETERMINING WHETHER AN INTERVENTION IS READY FOR ECONOMIC EVALUATION

As discussed in Chapter 2, economic evaluation encompasses an array of methods used to answer questions about the economic value of the resources required to implement an intervention, alone or with reference to the intervention's impact, measured in terms of the outcomes affected or the economic value of those outcomes. Determining whether an intervention is ready for economic evaluation and if so, which evaluation method to use, depends on the question(s) of interest and the information available. This section highlights the requirements for undertaking a high-quality economic evaluation, beginning with the most general requirements and then focusing on those that are specific to different economic evaluation methods. Figure 3-1 provides a decision tree used to guide the discussion.

Intervention Specificity, Counterfactual, and Other Contextual Features

For all types of economic evaluation, whether ex post or ex ante, two essential requirements are that the intervention be clearly defined and the **counterfactual** condition be well specified (Figure 3-1).

Intervention specificity means that the intervention's specific purpose, intended recipients, approach to implementation, causal mechanisms, and intended impact can be described in sufficient detail. For an ex post analysis, this specificity means that others can replicate the intervention or apply it in new settings or with new populations (Calculating the Costs of Child Welfare Services Workgroup, 2013; Foster et al., 2007; Gottfredson et al., 2015). For an ex ante analysis, it means that consumers of the analysis understand the nature of the intervention being analyzed.

In the context of an ex post analysis, a **logic model** describing the intervention's theory of change, or mechanisms by which its impact is achieved, is useful in establishing specificity, as are written curricula, manuals, detailed policy plans, and other documents outlining how the intervention is to be implemented and how staff implementing it are to be trained and supported in carrying it out effectively. Many interventions meet this requirement and have published manuals and logic models or explicit theories of change (Gill et al., 2014; Hawkins et al., 2014; Hibbs et al., 1997; Smith et al., 2006). Guidelines for developing logic models where they do not exist are also readily available (Centers for Disease Control and Prevention, 2010; W.K. Kellogg Foundation, 2004).

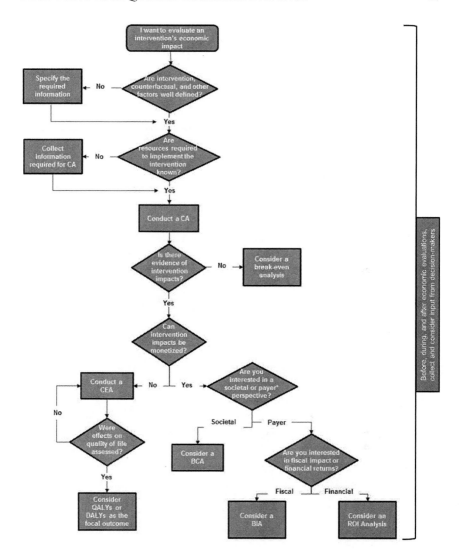

FIGURE 3-1 Different types of economic evaluation can be conducted to answer different types of questions.
NOTES: This decision tree highlights the major types of economic evaluation based on how the estimate will inform the intervention investment and the available information. BCA = benefit-cost analysis, BIA = budgetary impact analysis, CA = cost analysis, CEA = cost-effectiveness analysis, DALY = disability-adjusted life year, QALY = quality-adjusted life year, ROI = return on investment.
*Payers may include employers, government, the health care system, or recipients of the intervention.

The second key requirement is defining the counterfactual, the alternative with which the intervention is being compared in the economic evaluation, whether the evaluation is an ex post or ex ante CA, CEA, or BCA. In the context of program evaluation, this is usually referred to as the control, status quo or baseline, or comparison condition. The counterfactual condition may be no intervention, the status quo, or business as usual (e.g., an existing intervention), or it may be a less intensive version of the intervention of interest. For example, a school-based teen pregnancy prevention intervention might be evaluated in a community where there was no current intervention, where there was an existing intervention (school- or community-based), or where there was an intervention that provided information materials only but no other services. Defining the counterfactual is key, as a CA will be based on measuring the resources used to implement the intervention relative to the counterfactual condition. If a CEA or BCA is to be performed, intervention impacts should be measured relative to the same counterfactual condition as that used for the CA.

Clarifying other aspects of the context in which the intervention has been or will be carried out is necessary for interpreting the results of economic evaluation. Additional contextual details—such as the sociodemographic characteristics of the population targeted and served; the time, place, and scale of implementation; and other elements detailed in Consolidated Standards of Reporting Trials (CONSORT) guidelines (Schulz et al., 2010)—can also aid interpretation, help consumers understand the circumstances under which economic evidence is likely to apply, and guide appropriate use of the evidence in decision making. Without a clear understanding of the base case, the counterfactual, and other contextual factors—"what is delivered for whom, under what conditions, and relative to what alternative"—interpretation of the results of economic evaluation will be muddy.

Other Requirements for Economic Evaluation

Provided that an intervention is well defined and the counterfactual and other contextual factors can be specified, a CA can be performed to understand the economic cost of the resources required for implementation or to provide the foundation for a CEA or BCA. As discussed later in this chapter, conducting a CA, CEA, or BCA requires estimates of the resources used in intervention implementation and the economic values to attach to those resources (Figure 3-1). Later in the chapter, in the discussion of CA as a stand-alone analysis or as a component of CEA or BCA, best practices for measuring the resources used and their values are reviewed.

When investors have more complex questions than cost, such as which interventions are expected to yield the greatest impact for a given investment or which investments are likely to generate positive returns, evidence of intervention impact also is needed so that CEA or BCA can be performed (Figure 3-1) (Jamison et al., 2006; Lee and Aos, 2011; Levin and McEwan, 2001). Issues related to the nature of the evidence of impact are considered later in this chapter. When CA is possible but evidence of intervention impact is not available, Figure 3-1 shows that a break-even analysis can be performed to determine how large impacts would need to be for an intervention to be deemed cost-effective or cost-beneficial, provided that potential intervention impacts can be monetized. When intervention impacts are available and the impacts can be monetized, Figure 3-1 indicates that a BCA can be conducted; otherwise, a CEA is a feasible alternative.

CONCLUSION: *Key requirements for all types of economic evaluation are that the intervention can be clearly defined, the counterfactual well specified, and other contextual features delineated. To conduct cost analysis, cost-effectiveness analysis (CEA), and benefit-cost analysis (BCA), information on the resources used to implement the intervention is required. For CEA or BCA, credible evidence of impact also is needed.*

DEFINING THE SCOPE OF THE ECONOMIC EVALUATION

Once it has been determined that an economic evaluation is feasible, an essential next step is to define key elements of the evaluation's scope. These include the perspective for the analysis, the **time horizon** and **discount rate**, and several other analytic features.

Perspective

The perspective for an economic evaluation is determined by the question(s) to be answered and the audience(s) for the analysis (Figure 3-1). The broadest perspective is the societal perspective, which captures the public and private sectors and includes individuals who may be the focus of the intervention, as well as those who may be affected only indirectly. CA, CEA, and BCA all can be conducted from a societal perspective, with all costs being captured regardless of who bears them, and the economic values associated with all outcomes accounting for all who gain or lose. An economic evaluation conducted from the societal perspective can be disaggregated to consider the results from the perspective of specific stakeholder groups: the individuals who are targeted or served by the intervention; other individuals in society who are not targeted or served by the intervention; and the public sector at all levels of government combined or further disaggregated to consider the federal, state, and local levels separately or even different agencies at a given level. The public sector can also be viewed as representing the costs and benefits borne by individuals as taxpayers. Providing this detail is particularly useful in showing how costs and benefits of an intervention are distributed to various interested parties. For example, an intervention with a small but positive net benefit could mask losses to participants that were offset by public sector savings. Though a favorable investment overall, an intervention with such a distribution of costs and benefits may not be appealing to investors valuing gains to participants over government savings. Further discussion of perspectives is included later in this chapter in the section on best practices for conducting cost analyses.

For some economic evaluations, the primary focus may reflect mainly or solely a government perspective, which is just one component of the societal perspective. As noted in Chapter 2, cost-savings analysis is a BCA from the government perspective (Figure 3-1). The government perspective may be even more narrowly focused, such as for a specific government agency or level of government (e.g., federal, state, or local). Economic evaluations also can be conducted from the private perspective of a specific stakeholder, such as a business, philanthropy, or private investor. When an analysis is conducted for a specific stakeholder, its conclusions will reflect that stakeholder's perspective but may fail to capture the full range of costs and benefits of the intervention being analyzed, and the excluded costs and benefits may be substantial. For example, focusing on the government perspective may fail to provide important information about how an inter-vention impacts the participants involved, in terms of costs borne or gains received from participating in the intervention. In contrast, the advantage of the societal perspective is that in the ideal, it provides a comprehensive accounting of all costs and benefits.

At the same time, when the societal perspective is adopted, it is im-portant to disaggregate societal costs and benefits into those that accrue to the private sector (e.g., to intervention participants and other members of society) and those that accrue to the public sector (e.g., to the govern-ment as a whole or subdivisions of the public sector). The justification for public-sector investments in children, youth, and families is strongest when there are positive net benefits to the public sector and the rest of society, in addition to any private returns to the individual participants. Private indi-viduals may underinvest in those areas (e.g., health, education) where the private returns are less than the social returns (i.e., there are also returns to the public sector or other members of society). Conversely, if the only returns to an investment are private, there is little justification for a public-sector investment.[4]

---

[4]Disaggregating can show how costs, benefits, and net benefits are distributed to different stakeholders, both in total as well as over the time period of interest (e.g., annual costs and

Time Horizon and Discounting

One feature of investments in children, youth, and families is that an intervention may take place over multiple years, and its impact may extend over long periods of time, sometimes covering the entire life course and even affecting future generations. For this reason, it is important to define the time horizon that will be applied to the economic evaluation and whether the stream of future values associated with the resources used to implement the intervention and the outcomes that result will be discounted.

Establishing the time horizon is relatively straightforward. At a minimum, the time horizon will typically include the period over which the intervention is implemented. For discrete interventions, such as an early childhood or youth development program, implementation will occur over a fixed number of years. Depending on the length of the follow-up period, outcomes may be observed only during the intervention period, or they may extend further into the future if participants are followed after the intervention ends. There may also be interest in projecting outcomes beyond the period when outcomes were last measured. Such projections may extend over an individual's lifetime or even to future generations. As discussed later in the chapter, such projections introduce additional uncertainty into the results of an economic evaluation.

The issue of discounting arises because economists often assume that individuals and society place a higher value on costs and outcomes occurring in the present than on those that will occur in the future. Two common arguments to justify this assumption are (1) that money and other resources available today can be invested or used in some way to enjoy more benefits later on than would be realized if the same resources were available only in the future, and (2) that having those resources today eliminates any uncertainty of having them in the future (Miller and Hendrie, 2013).

Discounting is a technique used in economic evaluations to adjust costs and outcomes to account for this premium placed on benefits accrued closer to the present. For economic evaluations focused on children, youth, and families, the social discount rate is appropriate (Boardman and Greenberg, 1998). The standard approach to discounting is analogous to the process of compounding interest: a stream of costs or outcomes is reduced to its present value by applying a compounded discount rate to future streams.

---

benefits to each stakeholder from intervention's start through year 5). Stakeholders included in the analysis should be meaningful to the program and/or policy question. For example, costs and benefits to participants and to taxpayers who may finance and also benefit from the intervention are often included in stakeholder analysis, and there may be additional groups to incorporate as well. It is important to align the stakeholder groups on the cost and benefit sides of the analysis. That is, both the costs and benefits to each stakeholder group of interest should be estimated.

Because higher discount rates lead to higher valuation of outcomes occurring in the present relative to those occurring in the future, the discount rate is a key choice in economic evaluation, especially for interventions with significant impacts over long periods of time. The discount rate used in studies reflects the value of a dollar today versus that of a dollar tomorrow at a particular margin, determined largely by what return is required to attract the last dollar of saving. A discount rate also may vary by whether one uses a risky or riskless return. Discount rates used in economic evaluation have varied widely, although recommendations in recent years appear to be settling in the range of 3-7 percent (Drummond et al., 2005; Gold et al., 1996; Haddix et al., 2003; Hunink et al., 2001; Office of Management and Budget, 2003; Washington State Institute for Public Policy, 2015). A later section of this chapter describes the practice of using a base discount rate and then assessing the sensitivity of the results of the economic evaluation using a range of alternative discount rates.

Although there is little disagreement on the validity of discounting intervention costs, more controversy is associated with the issue of whether other outcomes—health in particular—should be discounted, and at what rate. One argument in favor of discounting health outcomes focuses on uncertainty: individuals would prefer to postpone illness because (1) they may not even be alive in the future, and (2) future medical progress could reduce the negative effects of the same illness occurring today (Miller and Hendrie, 2012). Some argue, moreover, that health outcomes should be discounted at the same rate as costs to avoid a paradox that arises when health is discounted at a lower rate than costs: the economic performance of an intervention may sometimes be improved by delaying its implementation, since the same health benefits could be achieved at a lower (discounted) cost simply by waiting (Gold et al., 1996; Keeler and Cretin, 1983; Weinstein and Stason, 1977). As noted by Drummond and colleagues (2005, p. 111), most guidelines for economic evaluation of health interventions, including those of the U.S. Panel on Cost-Effectiveness in Health and Medicine and the World Health Organization, recommend discounting of both costs and health outcomes using the same rate. For example, if an obesity prevention intervention is conducted when children are 10 years old and the expected impacts are expected to reduce the probability of cardiovascular disease (CVD) in the 50th future year, then the benefits of the intervention—either in natural units in a CEA, in cases of CVD avoided, or in monetary benefits in a BCA—are valued at benefit/$(1 + \text{discount rate})^{50}$. At a 10-percent discount rate, $1,000 spent today would be worth $9; at a 3 percent rate, $228. Note that future health costs and outcome benefits are discounted at the same rate as the cost saving and outcome benefit. For obesity prevention, for example, costs and benefits will be the same for people of different ages.

With investments in health interventions for children, of course, most benefits accrue over time, as in better educational and then work outcomes due to better health. It is the accumulation of all those benefits over time that is typically to be compared with current costs. For many studies, the danger is more that the future benefits simply are not estimated or cannot easily be estimated—less an issue than that long-term benefits are discounted too heavily.

A related and more complex ethical issue arises from discounting any intervention with impacts that affect future generations, or comparing benefits for a younger generation with costs to an older one. Miller and Hendrie (2013, pp. 356-357) give the example of a hypothetical environmental regulation targeting global climate change, which could affect outcomes of today's children and of children centuries into the future. Even using a low discount rate, outcomes just a century away would have present values so low that an economic evaluation would likely favor investments that would avoid even small sacrifices in the present, at the cost of potentially significant harm for future generations.

Part of the complication here is that discount rates assume investments apply at the margin, so that an extra benefit (valued in dollar terms) may be worth less to a future generation, expected to be richer, than to the current one. But if comparisons are made with respect to the value of a life today versus a life tomorrow, then the implicit assumption that the calculation applies at the margin no longer obtains. Put another way, there is no case for valuing a life tomorrow less than a life today, even if an extra lifetime dollar is worth more to the older of two generations.

Solutions suggested for avoiding this problem include starting the "discounting clock" when those affected are born, using a zero discount rate, and eliminating the need for discounting by assuming an explicit social utility function (Cowen and Parfit, 1992; Miller and Hendrie, 2013; Schelling, 1995). A broader suggestion, acknowledging that there is no satisfactory solution to this issue, is to consider moral obligations to future generations separately from the question of discounting practice (Institute of Medicine, 2006).

Finally, Karoly (2012) highlights an issue especially relevant to early childhood. Early programs can start at various child ages, from before birth up to age 5. If discounting originates at the age a program starts, some studies will discount to birth, while others will discount to as late as age 4. In such cases, present-value estimates will not be comparable across studies. The same concern applies in comparing interventions at other stages of development. Unless interventions are discounted to the same age, present-value estimates will not be comparable.[5]

Other Analytic Features

Two other analytic features to determine at the outset of an economic evaluation are (1) the monetary unit and year in which all economic values will be denominated, and (2) whether to account for the deadweight cost of taxation.[6] For the United States, economic evaluations typically use dollars as the currency measure, but any currency is feasible provided resources used and the value of intervention outcomes can be denominated in that currency. To adjust for changes in prices over time, economic evaluations measure the **opportunity cost** of resources and the economic value of outcomes in inflation-free monetary units, using a base year as reference. Thus, prices of resources used or outcome values before the base year are *inflated* using changes in relevant price indices (e.g., the consumer price index or employment cost index in the United States), and prices of resources used or outcome values in the future are held constant at the base year levels. The year of measurement may be specific to the point in time at which costs and outcomes were measured, or monetary values may be inflated to a more recent year so that findings can be expressed in current monetary values. As discussed later in this chapter in the section on reporting, the year for which monetary units are valued—whether intervention costs or the value of intervention outcomes—needs to be clearly stated.

When interventions for children, youth, and families involve new taxes for financing the intervention or produce impacts that affect taxes (e.g., an increase in taxes because of higher earnings or a reduction in welfare payments because of reduced welfare participation), there is a corresponding change in the deadweight cost associated with the distortionary effects of taxes on economic behavior and the costs associated with administering the tax—i.e., the dollars of welfare loss per tax dollar (Vining and Weimer, 2010). Producers of economic evidence may account for this deadweight

---

[5]Maynard and Hoffman (2008) highlight another approach in their analysis of teen pregnancy prevention: assuming that an intervention had been fully implemented (from birth to adulthood for everyone) and then providing a steady-state analysis.

[6]Every dollar of government revenue raised through taxes typically costs society more than one dollar in resources because taxes induce changes in behavior (e.g., reduced work effort) that represent an opportunity cost to society and because of the administrative costs of tax collection. The deadweight loss (also known as excess burden) measures those costs and is usually expressed as a percentage of the revenue raised. Although the costs of administering government-transfer payment programs conceptually can be viewed as a deadweight loss, such changes in administrative costs are best handled as costs or benefits in the cost-outcome equation.

cost of taxation as an additional cost when taxes are increased to pay for an intervention or when taxes rise as a result of an intervention. Conversely, the deadweight loss is reduced when the intervention produces a reduction in taxes. While economic evaluations often assume no deadweight loss, a few recent evaluations have produced results assuming different levels of deadweight loss as part of a **sensitivity analysis** (e.g., as in Heckman et al. [2010] and Washington State Institute for Public Policy [2015], in which deadweight costs are assumed to be 0 percent, 50 percent, and 100 percent).

CONCLUSION: *Once an intervention has been determined to be ready for an economic evaluation, an essential next step entails establishing the perspective; the time horizon for capturing costs (all types of analyses) and outcomes (cost-effectiveness analysis and benefit-cost analysis); the baseline discount rate; the monetary unit and reference year; and the assumed magnitude of the deadweight loss parameter, if deadweight loss will be evaluated.*

EVALUATING INTERVENTION COST

A systematic CA gives stakeholders important insight into the operation of interventions that impact children, youth, and families, including the overall cost of implementing and sustaining an intervention, costs for specific intervention activities, and costs per intervention participant (Crowley et al., 2012; Foster et al., 2007; Haddix et al., 2003). Beyond assessing actual costs, a CA may serve to facilitate planning, maximizing the efficiency of resource use, replication, dissemination, and implementation of efficacious and effective interventions. Chapter 2 describes the place of CA within evaluation and economic evaluation frameworks. CA relies on information about an intervention's implementation, such as the specific programmatic activities, the types and quantities of resources used in delivering intervention services, the number and characteristics of providers delivering and individuals or families receiving services, and the intensity or dosage of services provided. This information on intervention inputs is also the focus of process evaluation, which answers the questions of "what is done," "when," "by whom," and "to whom."

In addition, as discussed in Chapter 2, CA establishes the foundation for other types of economic evaluation, such as CEA and BCA. As detailed later in this chapter, CEA examines the relationship between an intervention's costs and a relevant unit of intervention effectiveness, while BCA quantifies intervention benefits in monetary terms and assesses whether they exceed intervention costs. The precision of these analyses depends, in part, on accurate analysis of intervention costs.

When a consistent and accurate approach is used to collect and analyze cost data, CA also can support comparisons of costs across services, interventions, and agencies. Increasingly, federal agencies require that evaluations of the interventions they fund include cost analyses. For example, a number of program announcements of the Administration for Children and Families requires that applicants propose a reasonable cost evaluation design that (1) allows for analyses of personnel and nonpersonnel resources among cost categories and program activities, (2) allows for analyses of direct services and of management and administrative activities, (3) includes both case-level and aggregate data that can reasonably be obtained and tracked, and (4) identifies anticipated and potential strategies for addressing these issues.

Similarly, at the Department of Education, Office of Innovation and Improvement, applicants for Investing in Innovation funding are required to provide detailed information about how they will evaluate whether their proposed projects are cost-effective when implemented.[7] This evaluation may include assessing the cost of comparable or alternative approaches. To receive competitive preference points, applicants addressing this priority must provide a detailed budget, an examination of different types of costs, and a plan for monitoring and evaluating cost savings, all of which are essential to improving productivity.

Best Practices for Conducting Cost Analyses

The goal of a CA is to quantify the full economic value of the resources required to implement an intervention relative to the status quo or control condition. The characteristics of a high-quality CA necessarily include (1) defining the purpose and scope of the analysis, (2) defining the intervention, (3) providing comprehensive and valid cost estimates, (4) applying widely accepted best practices in the field, and (5) acknowledging the limitations of the analysis. The discussion of best practices in this section draws on a review and synthesis of guidelines for conducting CA in the literature. In so doing, it provides additional support for practices discussed earlier in the chapter that are relevant to economic evaluation methods in general, such as defining the purpose and scope of the analysis and the intervention to be analyzed. This section addresses these issues specifically in the context of CA and the best practices identified in the literature.

---

[7]Notice 80 FR 32229. For additional information, see: https://federalregister.gov/a/ 2015-13673 [March 2016].

Defining the Purpose and Scope of a Cost Analysis

According to the U.S. Children's Bureau guide for assessing the costs of child welfare programs (Calculating the Costs of Child Welfare Services Workgroup, 2013), internal and external stakeholders should be engaged prior to the CA to (1) clarify the goals and audience for the analysis, (2) clearly define the intervention to be analyzed, and (3) specify the time period to be covered. The goals of the study help define who needs the CA (audience) and the intended uses of its results. This information in turn determines the perspective for the analysis, dictating which cost categories to consider. The perspective selected for the study guides all subsequent decisions around how best to estimate intervention costs. Many guidelines in the existing literature do not offer recommendations for a specific study perspective, but rather state that it should arise from the interests of the stakeholders or audience for the analysis and/or the research question (Detsky and Naglie, 1990; Drummond and Jefferson, 1996; European Commission, 2008; Graf von der Schulenburg and Hoffman, 2000; Hjelmgren et al., 2001; Honeycutt et al., 2006; Task Force on Community Preventive Services, 2005; Vincent et al., 2000). If a study perspective is recommended, it is most commonly the societal perspective (Barnett, 2009; Capri et al., 2001; Haddix et al., 2003; Honeycutt et al., 2006, Graf von der Schulenburg and Hoffmann, 2000; Hjelmgren et al., 2001; Laupacis et al., 1992; Luce et al., 1996; Ontario Ministry of Health and Long-Term Care, 1994; Pritchard and Sculpher, 2000; Suter, 2010; Task Force on Community Preventive Services, 2005; World Health Organization, 2012). Further, guidelines state that economists prefer the societal perspective (Chatterji et al., 2001; Drummond and Jefferson, 1996; Gray et al., 2010), and almost always recommend this perspective for BCAs (Calculating the Costs of Child Welfare Services Workgroup, 2013; Commonwealth of Australia, 2006; European Regional Development Fund, 2013; Treasury Board of Canada Secretariat, 2007; World Health Organization, 2006).

When the societal perspective is used to guide the CA, additional information is often gained by disaggregating overall costs into subperspectives showing how costs are borne by various stakeholders. Subperspectives may reflect the potential investors in an intervention (agencies, private organizations, taxpayers) or those impacted by the intervention (e.g., participants, potential victims). For CEAs of interventions provided by the health care sector, for example, several guidelines additionally recommend a health system or payer perspective (Academy of Managed Care Pharmacy, 2012; Graf von der Schulenburg and Hoffmann, 2000; Haute Autorité de Santé, 2012; Hjelmgren et al., 2001; Institute for Quality and Efficiency in Health Care, 2009; Marshall and Hux, 2009; National Institute for Health and Care Excellence, 2013; Walker, 2001). If the full societal costs of an intervention are not estimated, however, the subperspective may provide only a partial picture of the value of all resources required to implement an intervention. Indeed, multiple perspectives for an analysis are often preferred and expected. From a provider perspective, for example, the costs of an intervention may equate to actual monetary expenditures. From a societal perspective, however, the value of all resources required to implement an intervention is included in the analysis regardless of to whom they accrue, so that, for instance, costs would include in-kind donations in addition to monetary expenditures. They might also include the cost to participants of spending their time on program activities instead of alternatives, such as work or leisure.

Defining the Intervention

Defining the intervention to be delivered is another critical step in the analysis that needs to include stakeholders who know the intervention model well. Many options exist for analyzing intervention costs as part of broader evaluation efforts (Yates, 2009), and the collection and analysis of cost data are more likely to be successful if included in evaluation planning from the outset. Logic models are a convenient evaluation tool that can help delineate intervention inputs with a bearing on the CA.

Specifying the time period over which cost data will be collected is also important (Brodowski and Filene, 2009). CAs may cover a time horizon of several years to provide information on how costs vary over time, or they may focus on a single year that is considered to be representative of the intervention's typical operating state. Evaluators also need to specify the intervention's stage of implementation during the CA because costs are likely to differ between a startup or planning period (preimplementation) and a period of steady-state implementation, when the intervention is operating at or near full capacity (Miller and Hendrie, 2015). The potential existence of **economies of scale** implies that differences in output level need to be taken into account in comparing operating efficiency across intervention sites, and cost projections may be inaccurate if they fail to take into account the decrease in average cost that occurs as output expands (Mansley et al., 2002).

> CONCLUSION: *The societal perspective is the most commonly recommended perspective for researchers conducting cost analysis (CA). Subperspectives can be used to tailor cost estimates to specific audiences, but do not necessarily provide a comprehensive estimate of costs and may be inadequate for supporting intervention replication. In addition, CA requires carefully defining the intervention and identifying any of its activities that consume its resources. Best practice further requires that the time horizon for the CA be clearly defined.*

Providing Comprehensive and Valid Cost Estimates

Developing accurate estimates of the cost of an intervention for children, youth, and families requires carefully quantifying and valuing the resource needs to replicate intervention effects. There are a number of methods for costing an intervention (Barnett, 2009; Calculating the Costs of Child Welfare Services Workgroup, 2013; Gray et al., 2010; Haddix et al., 2003; Honeycutt et al., 2006; Luce et al., 1996; Muenning and Khan, 2002; Yates, 1996). These methods represent one of two general approaches. The first is a macro, top-down approach that uses total public spending (or individual site budget or expenditure) data to provide gross average estimates of intervention costs.[8] The other is a bottom-up approach known as micro costing that relies on identifying all resources required to implement an intervention and then valuing those resources in monetary units to estimate intervention costs. The methods used for micro costing—ingredients- and activity-based allocation—are generally considered the methods of choice because, relative to the macro approach, they are more accurate and provide investors with greater detail about intervention costs so that resource needs for success can be projected. This detail includes robust estimates of the marginal and steady-state (average) costs of the intervention (see the section later in this chapter on "Getting to Results" for additional information on summary measures for CA), which allow for estimation of the intervention's per-unit cost (e.g., per family or child served). However, micro costing can be more difficult and time-consuming to implement than other costing methods (Levin and Belfield, 2013), requiring that an infrastructure be in place with which to collect data on resource use at the unit level.[9]

To fully understand resource needs and to ensure that all stages of implementation are covered, combining logic models with the micro costing approach is a good solution to avoid **"hidden"** costs (e.g., for adoption, development, training, technical assistance, and sustainability). Hidden

---

[8]Budgetary information can be a useful data source for conducting cost analyses, but estimating the economic costs of interventions requires more than a simple accounting of budgetary expenditures. Specifically, while budgets can be used to estimate the quantity of some resources consumed to implement an intervention, it should not be assumed that they reflect all the resources needed to adopt, implement, and sustain an intervention. Further, the price information that can be extracted from a budget may be representative only of local market prices. Adjustments may be needed to estimate intervention costs in new settings or for national dissemination.

[9]Many resources are available that can provide comprehensive and field-specific listings of types of costs. For instance, the new Costing-Out tool from Columbia's Center for Benefit-Cost Analyses of Education can be used for interventions delivered in educational settings; the Drug Abuse Treatment Cost Analysis Program (DATCAP) can be used for interventions for children, youth, and families delivered in social service and clinical settings; and the Children's Bureau offers a free Guide for Child Welfare Researchers and Service Providers (Cost Analysis in Program Evaluation).

costs of an intervention also may include resources required beyond the intervention to ensure full implementation. A CA conducted from the societal perspective, for example, may need to include the value of systems-level resources required for implementation, beyond those resources required only at the local level. Considering implementation costs is especially important when comparing differing approaches to intervention. For example, implementation costs are quite different for passing an underage drinking law and issuing regulations to implement it and for adopting a school-based alcohol education program.

Cost Categories Typical cost categories for consideration in micro costing are personnel, space, materials, and supplies. The categorization of costs may be strengthened by consideration of these major cost categories within specified activities associated with an intervention. It may be helpful, for example, to consider an intervention's costs within the broad categories of the preimplementation and implementation phases of intervention delivery, or startup versus ongoing maintenance costs. It may also be useful to consider direct versus indirect costs. Direct costs may refer to those resources required to provide services directly to participants, such as classroom time for a bullying prevention curriculum or home visits to prevent child maltreatment. When estimating costs at the level of the unit of the participant, a CA may need to allocate more resources to the estimation of direct personnel time (Yates, 1996). Indirect costs typically denote overhead costs related to administrative functions of an intervention or to services not provided directly to but on behalf of the participants. Often these costs are shared by more than one intervention or used to create more than one output, or may be defined as expenses that directly benefit the agency (American Humane Association, 2009; Calculating the Costs of Child Welfare Services Workgroup, 2013; Capri et al., 2001; Chatterji et al., 2001; Cisler et al., 1998; Derzon et al., 2005; European Regional Development Fund, 2013; Federal Accounting Standards Advisory Board, 2014; Foster et al., 2003; Graf von der Schulenburg and Hoffmann, 2000; Haute Autorité de Santé, 2012; Institute for Quality and Efficiency in Health Care, 2009; Leonard, 2009; National Center for Environmental Economics, 2010; Pritchard and Sculpher, 2000; Suter, 2010; Task Force on Community Preventive Services, 2005; Treasury Board of Canada Secretariat, 2007).

The consensus in the literature is that analysts should include program and administrative or overhead costs for programmatic CAs (Barnett, 2009; Calculating the Costs of Child Welfare Services Workgroup, 2013; Greenberg and Appenzeller, 1998; Her Majesty's Treasury, 2003; Office of Management and Budget, 2004a, 2004b; World Health Organization, 2012). Indirect costs can be distributed using the proportion of time spent in direct delivery of each service. Once the fraction of time devoted by each staff member to various activities is known, this information can readily be monetized by multiplying the fractions by the staff members' compensation (salaries and other benefits) over an appropriate time period, such as 1 year (Greenberg and Appenzeller, 1998). Alternatively, the total annual expenditures on each indirect cost (e.g., support staff salaries, supervisors' salaries, computers, rental space, telephone, electricity, water, maintenance) can be multiplied by the fraction of the organization's total staff costs devoted to each activity (Greenberg and Appenzeller, 1998; World Health Organization, 2012). However, it is important to assume that not all management tasks are indirect costs (Calculating the Costs of Child Welfare Services Workgroup, 2013); some are directly related to an intervention, and managers may be able to estimate the amount of time they spend on such tasks.

Another important consideration in CA is fixed versus variable costs, particularly when the evaluator is interested in an intervention's marginal and steady-state (average) costs. **Fixed costs** are the value of those resources required only occasionally for the intervention, which do not vary with the number of participants served. Typical fixed costs—such as costs to train providers and to buy furniture—occur in the preimplementation phase of an intervention. By annualizing costs of capital equipment over their useful life, it is possible to allocate a fair portion of those costs to each person served. **Variable costs** are the value of those resources required for each person served by the intervention. Table 3-1 (Ritzwoller et al., 2009) shows a typical valuation of fixed and variable costs in a CA.

Unit Prices The most important determinant of the comprehensiveness of a CA is how well the resources required to implement an intervention are inventoried and then valued. That is, the costing of an intervention is really a function of resources (Q) and their prices (P). But what unit prices should be used? Budget sheets that show intervention expenditures for a given fiscal year include similar resource categories and are often a convenient, but perhaps incomplete, way to value the resources. Stakeholders also may play a role in determining the appropriate unit prices to use, based on the audience for the analysis. If a national intervention is being valued, for example, unit prices may need to reflect national averages for such costs as wage rates, space rental, and supply purchases. Local interventions may need to rely on local unit prices. Either way, transparency of unit prices is critical for replicability of a CA across sites. Moreover, within any analysis, the use of a consistent set of prices (e.g., state, local, federal) and a common reference year is important.

Nearly all recommendations for conducting CAs suggest that resources be valued by their opportunity cost. Often, the market price for a resource is a good approximation for its opportunity cost. However, when a market price does not exist or is suspected not to reflect the opportunity cost, one

TABLE 3-1 Illustrative Valuation of Fixed and Variable Cost in Cost Analysis

Cost Element	Variable ($)	Fixed ($)	Total ($)
Recruitment			
Project staff			
Mailings	1,908		1,908
E-mail	3,990		3,990
Overhead[a]		24,912	24,912
Subject identification		1,470	1,470
Telephone interviewers			
Training		3,046	3,046
Enrollment/eligibility calls	8,104		8,104
Supplies	776		776
Total Recruitment	14,778	29,428	44,206
Intervention Components			
Tailored news letters	10,102		10,102
Interviewers training and supervision		23,865	23,865
Phone counseling/data management		11,872	11,872
Project meetings and e-mail		5,667	5,667
Equipment and materials		2,890	2,890
Personnel management		9,643	9,643
Overhead[a]		4,603	4,603
3-Month Intervention	21,974	46,668	68,642
Total Recruitment plus 3-Month Intervention			112,848

[a]Overhead includes office tasks, such as printing, copy making, unscheduled staff meetings, phone conversations, intervention preparation time, commute to the intervention site where calls are made and newsletters are produced, etc.
SOURCE: Example from Ritzwoller et al. (2009), reprinted with permission.

method for valuing the resource is to use a **shadow price** (Commonwealth of Australia, 2006; European Commission, 2008; Gray et al., 2010; Joint United Nations Programme on HIV/AIDS, 2000; The World Bank, 2010; Treasury Board of Canada Secretariat, 2007; Walter and Zehetmayr, 2006; World Health Organization, 2006, 2012). Examples of the use of shadow prices are the shadow wage rate for adjusting labor prices to account for distortions in the labor market and the shadow price of capital, which is used to adjust the valuation of costs for the effects of government projects on resource allocation in the private sector (European Commission, 2008; National Center for Environmental Economics, 2010; Office of Management and Budget, 1992; World Health Organization, 2006). Examples of the shadow price of wages include the value of the time friends or family spend providing unpaid care (Gray et al., 2010) and the value of volunteer time, which are based on the wage rate for someone carrying out similar work (World Health Organization, 2006). An example of the shadow price of capital is the use of the price of comparable private-sector land for the price of government-owned land (Commonwealth of Australia, 2006).

Sensitivity Analyses A recent and notable addition to the list of steps for conducting a cost evaluation (whether CA or some other method), from the Children's Bureau[10] and others (Haddix et al., 2003; Yates, 2009), is to conduct sensitivity analysis and examine cost variation (Corso et al., 2013; Crowley et al., 2012). The consensus in the literature is that sensitivity analysis should be performed whenever estimates, data, or outcomes are uncertain. It is accepted that providing the results of sensitivity analysis when reporting the results of cost analysis is best practice, both internationally and domestically (Benefit-Cost Analysis Center;[11] Hjelmgren et al., 2001; Levin and McEwan, 2001; Luce et al., 1996; Marshall and Hux, 2009; Messonnier and Meltzer, 2003; Office of Management and Budget, 1992; Pharmaceutical Benefits Board, 2003; Ramsey et al., 2005; Siegel et al., 1996; Walker, 2001; World Health Organization 2000). Recommendations on sensitivity analyses are usually generic and often are centered on the discussion of discount rates. In some instances, however, especially in international contexts, particular methods are specified (Hjelmgren et al., 2001; Marshall and Hux, 2009; Walker, 2001); Canada, for example, encourages the use of Monte Carlo simulations (Walker, 2001). Further discussion of sensitivity analysis is provided later in this chapter.

CONCLUSION: *According to best practices, after establishing the perspective, defining the intervention, and specifying the base year and time period over which the intervention will be assessed, cost analysis includes the following steps:*

- *inventorying the resources, in specific units (which may vary across different resources), required for all activities entailed in the intervention;*
- *calculating the real (adjusted for inflation) cost per unit of each resource used, including fringe benefits associated with wages (P);*
- *counting the number of units of each resource used (Q) in the specified time period for the number of children, youth, or families served;*

---

[10] For more information, see http://www.acf.hhs.gov/programs/cb/resource/cost-workgroup [March 2016].

[11] Available: http://evans.uw.edu/sites/default/files/public/Federal_Agency_BCA_PS_Social_Programs.pdf [March 2016].

- *calculating the total costs of the intervention by multiplying all resources used by their unit costs (sum of all P × Q);*
- *calculating the expected cost per child, youth, or family served— i.e., average costs—by dividing P × Q by the number served during the specified time period of the intervention;*
- *calculating the expected cost per one more child, youth, or family served—that is, marginal costs—by differentiating between fixed and variable costs; and*
- *conducting sensitivity analysis to test the uncertainty of assumptions made about quantity and price.*

Reporting the Results of Cost Analyses

Acknowledging the limitations of a CA requires transparency as to the methods used and the assumptions made. An overall goal is to achieve so much transparency that another community can implement the same intervention with complete understanding of all resources required (even if some resources are donated). As noted earlier, therefore, *all* resources need to be inventoried, even if all cannot be valued. For example, if one is conducting a cross-site evaluation of the costs to deliver a home visiting intervention and training costs are not available across all sites, these costs may be excluded for purposes of comparability across sites. However, the CA still needs to note that these costs are an important resource required to implement the intervention, even if they are not explicitly included in the CA results.

Because CAs generate such a wide array of estimates that the level of information can overwhelm even the most discerning reader and obscure useful information, reporting transparent and generalizable results is essential to ensure that the results of the analysis can be translated into effective policy. It is important in reporting, then, to balance detail with useful information. Also important is acknowledging that some unit cost estimates are more robust than others. Specifying where data are limited sets the stage for sensitivity analysis of cost estimates based on those variables and creates a research agenda for those implementing the intervention in the future.

DETERMINING INTERVENTION IMPACTS

Investors in interventions for children, youth, and families may want to know more than an intervention's cost; they may also desire economic analysis of the return on investment in the intervention, which can be measured in various ways. As described briefly in Chapter 2, CEA compares resource investments with intervention impacts measured in their natural units, while

BCA compares investments with impacts that have been monetized. Cost-utility analysis is a form of CEA that compares investments with impacts expressed in quality-adjusted life years (QALYs) or disability-adjusted life years (DALYs).[12] The common thread in these approaches is that they all rest on evidence that the intervention *caused* one or more favorable outcomes to occur. Evidence of impact may be drawn from a completed program evaluation, as in an ex post economic evaluation, or it may be presumed, as in the case of an ex ante economic evaluation, conducted, for example, for planning purposes.

Without valid evidence of causal impact, there is no reliable return on investment to capture in economic evaluation (Karoly, 2008; Washington State Institute for Public Policy, 2015). Causality, the main topic of this section, is one of several major impact-related issues that producers of economic evaluations need to consider in preparation for estimating cost-effectiveness or the return on intervention investment. Other issues common in economic evaluations of interventions serving children, youth, and families include how to combine evidence when multiple evaluations of a given intervention exist, which effects to include in a CEA or BCA, and how to handle uncertainty in intervention effect sizes—all addressed in subsequent sections of this chapter.

Research Designs and Evidence of Intervention Impact

An underlying premise of CEA and BCA is that the outcomes being subjected to economic evaluation were *caused* by the intervention.[13] Logic models can help articulate an intervention's putative causal mechanisms, but evidence that the intervention caused an outcome comes from certain research designs used in program evaluation. Some research designs can increase confidence that an observed difference was caused by an intervention, such as using many repeated measures over time and space; making comparisons with jurisdictions, population groups, or outcomes that should not be affected; replicating; and establishing that a

---

[12] A QALY is defined as a measure of quality of life where 1 is a year lived in perfect health and 0 is death. In some circumstances, values less than 0 (fates worse than death) are allowed. Absent equity weights, a QALY is 1 minus a DALY. Quality-of-life measurement is anchored in part in functional capacity, which gives it some objectivity (Wilson and Cleary, 1995).

[13] Causal inference is one of many factors that is relevant to the validity of a study or a set of studies for any given decision. It can be challenging to address certain factors beyond causal inference because they are often dependent upon concerns that the researcher cannot reasonably foresee or control (e.g., generalizability of study context).

dose-response relationship[14] existed (Shadish et al., 2002; Wagenaar and Komro, 2013).[15]

Many, if not most, methodologists believe that the clearest unbiased evidence of causal impact comes from well-conducted experimental designs or **randomized controlled trials** because these designs minimize threats to internal validity, or the chance that something other than the intervention caused the observed differences in outcomes between intervention participants and nonparticipants (Cook and Campbell, 1979; Fisher et al., 2002; Gottfredson et al., 2015; Jones and Rice, 2011). Although research has shown that "real-world" randomized controlled trials of complex programs and policies are more feasible than originally thought (Cook and Payne, 2002; Donaldson et al., 2008; Gerber et al., 2013), relevant concerns have been raised regarding their limitations. These potential limitations include issues related to external validity (e.g., artificial circumstances defined by eligibility criteria, participants failing to represent particular populations, trials by definition only including volunteers who agree to participate for treatment); issues related to the number of treatment and control groups used;[16] high costs; potential ethical concerns; and trade-offs with respect to generalizability and statistical power (Wagenaar and Komro, 2013).

Given the limitations of randomized controlled trials, certain methodologists have recommended the use of other research designs. For example, researchers have studied the extent to which **quasi-experimental designs** can provide unbiased causal evidence (Bloom et al., 2005; Cook et al., 2008; Shadish et al., 2008). These researchers present convincing examples in which well-designed prospective evaluations of laws and regulations using comparison **time series designs**—where randomization was not a possibility—provided strong causal evidence through careful attention to other design elements.

In addition, **regression discontinuity designs** (where individuals are compared with those who receive an intervention based on an arbitrary cut-off point) have also been shown to provide unbiased causal estimates (Gottfredson et al., 2015).[17] For instance, children who miss eligibility for

---

[14] The term "dose-response relationship" refers to the change in an outcome resulting from different degrees of exposure to an intervention.

[15] With increasing occurrence, these types of alternative designs are used in both implementation and effectiveness studies. The ways in which these designs impact CAs, CEAs, and BCAs, although noteworthy, are not a primary focus of this chapter.

[16] This limitation makes it difficult to ascertain what aspect(s) of the treatment are responsible for the observed effect. The ideal trial design would have multiple different treatment groups, with the potential for multiple control groups; however, these efforts are often a challenge to implement because of cost and logistical issues.

[17] As is noted throughout this report, describing the research design and sample on which an economic evaluation is based aids in accurate interpretation of the evaluation results. For regression discontinuity designs, this is particularly important as impacts apply to participants

preschool by 1 or 2 months (based on birthdate cut-offs) can be compared with children whose birthdays are 1 or 2 months on the other side of the cut-off. Nonrandomized controlled trial designs such as these have been used to evaluate the effectiveness of universal pre-K programs in Boston, Tulsa, and in the state of Georgia (Yoshikawa et al., in press). Additionally, two other nonrandomized controlled trial designs, difference-in-difference and fixed effects, also have been shown to be effective and have been used to examine the efficacy of preschool (e.g., Bassok et al., 2014; Magnuson et al., 2007).

Propensity matching, propensity scoring, and instrumental variable designs also are popular alternatives, but at times are misapplied (Austin, 2009; Basu et al., 2007) or yield questionable results. Too often, propensity matching studies match to an intervention serving nonequivalent people (e.g., those who declined the intervention), and the instrumental variables chosen violate essential independence requirements. Quasi-experimental studies are intended to serve a useful purpose; however, the literature has several examples of such studies that are poorly designed, and many grapple with the same issues as those encountered with randomized controlled trials.

Ultimately, analysts conducting economic evaluations need to assess and describe the overall quality of the impact evaluation evidence that forms the basis for the economic evaluation, whether that evidence comes from experimental or quasi-experimental designs or both. For some interventions, strong evidence will come from experimental designs. For others, a randomized control trial is not feasible, but other strong quasi-experimental designs can contribute credible evidence.[18] Often, there may be multiple evaluations and analysts can use the overall body of evidence as part of the economic evaluation. For example, researchers often pool data from a variety of interventions derived from randomized controlled trials as well as other useful research designs (see blueprintsprograms.com for examples). When multiple impact studies exist, systematic reviews and/or meta-analyses may be necessary to draw valid conclusions about impacts. For a discussion of major issues involved in systematic reviews and meta-

---

who are at or near the eligibility threshold, or cut-off score, for receiving an intervention. Reporting of information about the entire group served by the intervention, the cut-off value, and the portion of the group to which the impact estimates apply is encouraged to add transparency to economic evaluation findings that are based on impacts from these designs.

[18] As an example, the research examining the intended and unintended effects of the Earned Income Tax Credit (EITC) on employment and other outcomes has relied on several quasi-experimental methods because an experimental design for evaluating this federal program has not been an option. Analysts have used natural experiments, such as the expanded eligibility for the program in the 1990s, the adoption of state EITC add-ons, and the calendar timing of receipt of the lump sum tax credit (Bitler and Karoly, 2015).

analyses of interventions for children, youth, and families, see the paper by Valentine and Konstantopoulos (2015) commissioned for this study.

Issues in Practice

As research on quasi-experimental designs suggests, standards for evidence evolve over time. Best research design practices and methods also may differ across disciplines, for which different concerns may apply. In the real world, moreover, the only available evidence of intervention impact may be from research designs that are not optimal, and impact estimates may indeed be biased. In such cases, should the economic evaluation go forward? Sometimes the answer is no. For example, if the evidence was produced with no comparison group, if measurement was very weak, or if the evaluation is judged to be of poor quality for other reasons, proceeding with a BCA or CEA is probably unwise. In other situations, such as when several quasi-experimental designs consistently suggest positive impact, it may make sense to proceed.[19] In such cases, however, conducting sensitivity analyses with varying effect sizes to test the robustness of conclusions about impact is important. Another approach that can be taken in the absence of causal or unbiased evidence is to estimate how strong intervention impacts would have to be to produce economically favorable results and then judge whether such effect sizes appear feasible. If only a small effect size is required, it may be relatively easy to conclude that the investments in the intervention are economically sound.

Placing the goal of using only the highest-quality, unbiased impact estimates in BCA and CEA in the context of real-world realities and imperfections leads to several practical suggestions for economic analysts. First, seek impact evaluations conducted in accordance with the strongest research designs and best practices within a given field or discipline. Second, critically evaluate all design elements and methods used to estimate impact. Third, when available evidence is based on nonoptimal designs or impact estimates are likely to be biased, it may be possible to proceed with caution, including acknowledging possible bias and conducting sensitivity analyses on economic findings. Finally, if economic evaluations appear too speculative to be valid, the next best step may be to attempt a higher-quality efficacy analysis that produces higher-quality evidence of impact.

---

[19] See the paper by Valentine and Konstantopoulos (2015) commissioned for this study, which emphasizes the importance of identifying all evidence about an intervention's impact (published and not; positive, negative, and null) before conducting an economic evaluation to avoid publication bias.

CONCLUSION: *The credibility of cost-effectiveness analyses, benefit-cost analyses, and related methods is enhanced when estimates of intervention impact are based on research designs shown to produce unbiased causal estimates. Meta-analysis may be used when impact estimates are available from multiple studies of the same or similar interventions. When evidence of impact comes from designs that may be biased because of selectivity or other methodological weaknesses, it is important for researchers to conduct sensitivity analyses to test the robustness of their findings to variation in effect size and to acknowledge the limitations of the underlying evidence base in their reports.*

VALUING OUTCOMES

To assess return on investment in an intervention, producers of economic evidence may choose CEA, BCA, or the related methods outlined in Chapter 2. In CEA, results are expressed as the cost per unit of a single outcome, such as dollars per life saved, dollars per incarceration prevented, or dollars per additional college graduate. Costs come from a CA and outcomes from an impact evaluation. As discussed above, the ideal is for outcomes to be linked causally to the intervention being subjected to CEA; when this is not the case, it is important to disclose the fact and to interpret results of the analysis with caution.

In contrast to CEA, BCA compares the economic value of an intervention's outcomes, expressed in the selected monetary unit, with the costs of the intervention as determined by a CA. When the value of the outcomes exceeds the intervention costs (after both have been adjusted as necessary for inflation and discounting), an intervention can be said to be "cost-beneficial." For example, a BCA of an obesity prevention intervention would involve estimating the economic gains, or benefits, from reducing obesity and determining whether they exceeded intervention investments (after both had been adjusted for inflation and discounting). As discussed earlier, comprehensive BCAs take a societal perspective, but some BCAs are conducted from a more narrow perspective, such as that of the government or an agency. These more narrow BCAs may under- or overstate both costs and benefits, a limitation that needs to be disclosed when results are communicated.

BCA is an attractive method for interventions impacting multiple outcomes, as is common in interventions for children, youth, and families, because the dollar benefits of each outcome can be summed to produce an estimated total economic impact. Yet while BCA is a powerful tool that increasingly has become part of evidence-based decision making (White and VanLandingham, 2015), monetizing outcomes can be a complex and time-consuming process. Many organizations lack the capacity to undertake these analyses without consulting experts in the method. Moreover, the valuation of some outcomes—for example, a human life—can be controversial and lead to skepticism regarding the findings and conclusions of the analysis. Haddix and colleagues (2003) suggest this is why CEA became the dominant analytic method for economic evaluation in health care after the 1980s. In other fields concerned with positive development for children and youth, however, interest in BCA is growing.

Consistent with the overall goal of this chapter, this section addresses issues related to valuing intervention outcomes as part of a high-quality BCA (Boardman et al., 2011; Crowley et al., 2014; Karoly, 2012; Vining and Weimer, 2010). As the discussion proceeds, the economic value of the outcomes from an intervention is referred to as the resulting "benefits." In practice, however, an intervention may generate some favorable outcomes that result in higher costs (e.g., an intervention that increases educational attainment adds education costs as an outcome), or an intervention may generate some unanticipated unfavorable outcomes that translate into higher costs (e.g., an increased use of special education rather than the expected decrease).

Typically, benefit streams are estimated over time and then discounted back to the present to reflect monetary time preferences according to the following formula:

$$\text{Present Value Benefit} = \sum_{y=start}^{N} \left((Q_y \times P_y) / (1+d)^y \right) \qquad (3.1)$$

The size of economic impact in each year (Q_y) and the price per unit of economic impact in each year (P_y) both need to be estimated and a discount rate (d) selected. The total present-value benefit is the sum of all intervention-related discounted benefits streams. Producing high-quality estimates requires careful attention to each component: quantity, price, changes in each over time, and discount rate. It also involves assessing the implications of uncertainty for the estimates and summary measures derived from the evaluation. This section describes issues involved in estimating economic impacts and their prices over time. The basic rationale for discounting was addressed earlier in the chapter, while uncertainty and summary measures are discussed in subsequent sections.

Quantifying Outcomes for BCA

Undertaking a BCA requires several decisions with respect to the outcomes that result from the intervention being analyzed. As discussed below, these decisions include which outcomes to include in the analysis; whether the outcomes can be valued directly or linked to other outcomes with economic value; and what the appropriate time horizon for the analysis is, including whether outcomes can be projected beyond the point of last observation to capture expected future outcomes.

Which Impacts to Include in the Analysis

In conducting a BCA, the analysis needs to identify all outcomes impacted by the intervention and determine which ones to include in the analysis. BCAs typically incorporate a subset of outcomes because not all outcomes can be monetized. For example, interventions may impact the quality of parent-child relationships, but the economic consequences of these gains have not been studied. Other reasons for exclusion of outcomes relate to methodological shortcomings, as there may not be a satisfactory approach to or precedent for monetizing them.[20] For instance, social and emotional learning outcomes, which may be instrumental in healthy development, generally are not included in BCAs, although research in this area is progressing (Belfield et al., 2015). There may be too much uncertainty in how the outcomes are estimated, such as effects on populations not directly targeted by the intervention (Institute of Medicine and National Research Council, 2014; Karoly, 2012; Vining and Weimer, 2009c). Finally, another common factor in the choice of outcomes is convenience: analysts may focus on the outcomes that are easiest to work with or on those that are more relevant to their field of study or to the intended audience for the analysis (Institute of Medicine, 2006). An important consequence of the exclusion of outcomes for any of these reasons is potential underestimation of the economic benefits of an intervention (or overestimation, if excluded outcomes indicated harms from the intervention). BCA reports need to include information about which intervention outcomes were not included and why.[21]

Once monetizable outcomes have been identified, an additional consideration is which ones to include in the BCA. Some argue that all measured impacts, both significant and nonsignificant, should be included in the BCA, provided they can be monetized. Monte Carlo methods that account for standard errors associated with estimates can be used to evaluate the implications of uncertainty in the estimates (Farrow and Zerbe, 2013; Vining and Weimer, 2009b). This approach avoids the selection of impacts based on a somewhat arbitrary level of statistical significance. The drawback is that it may mean including impacts that are theoretically plausible but not well supported by evidence. Haddix and colleagues (2003) recommend

---

[20] See, for example, Vining and Weimer (2009a), who provide a list of shadow prices that need to be estimated (or improved) and are important to the economic evaluation of social programs.

[21] Double counting also becomes an issue if some outcomes are inputs for other outcomes. For example, it would be tricky to include both education and earnings as outcomes for an intervention.

that studies include all benefits and harms that have a meaningful impact on the results of the analysis. In its recent report on standards of evidence for efficacy, effectiveness, and scale-up in prevention science, the Society for Prevention Research concludes that prevention programs can be deemed efficacious only with respect to impacts with a "consistent pattern of non-chance findings in the desired direction" (Gottfredson et al., 2015, p. 908). These studies would suggest a more narrowly constructed BCA.

A related concern is that randomized controlled trials of interventions by the interventions' developers often collect longitudinal data on scores of outcomes indicated by program logic models, test significance by time period and subgroup, and then produce confidence intervals by time period-subgroup combination. Statistical test results may or may not be corrected for multiple comparisons and the possibility of chance findings. The first Nurse-Family Partnership trial, for example, has tracked many child outcomes through age 19. Publications report multiple outcomes across time and for relevant subgroups. Additional outcomes are reported in interim or final grant reports (Miller, 2015). In such cases, some filtering of outcomes is necessary before a BCA is conducted.

Absent agreement within the field about whether to include all or a subset of measured impacts, a way forward is to adopt an explicit rationale for which impacts to include, employ the rationale in a consistent manner, and disclose the rationale when reporting on methods and results. It is important for each included impact to follow from the intervention's theory of change. Additional criteria might include the statistical significance of the impact, as well as the power to detect effects given the research design and sample size. If conventional levels of significance ($p < .05$ or $p < .10$) appear to be too restrictive (Institute of Medicine and National Research Council, 2014), analysts can explain why additional impacts were included. If the outcome change is large and preferably supported by significant changes in intermediate outcomes (e.g., significant gains in math and reading achievement scores could justify including a rise in high school graduation rate with a significance of $p = .18$), and the BCA includes a probabilistic sensitivity analysis, one might want to include this impact.[22] The variance of the overall benefit-cost estimate will account for its large variance. Further sensitivity analysis with and without the nonsignificant impacts also will aid in understanding the implications for the BCA's bottom line.[23]

---

[22] The power to detect an impact of a given size could be quite high even if significance levels were moderate, for example, $p < .15$.

[23] It is important that evaluators not cherry pick results but rather formulate an approach that is applied consistently to all impacts. This means that the same rules apply to intervention impacts that are in the expected direction and those that are counter to what was expected, or iatrogenic impacts.

Types of Impacts

Intervention impacts may have direct economic implications or may be linked to other impacts that have economic value. Comprehensive estimates consider both. *Direct economic impacts* are measured in the impact evaluation and reflect changes in the outcomes targeted by the intervention. For example, a job training program may lead to an increase in employment among its participants, which has economic consequences in the form of higher wages for participants, increased taxes to government, and the like.

Linked economic impacts are not measured directly in the impact evaluation but are caused by other, direct intervention impacts.[24] If a truancy prevention program causes lower absenteeism and higher graduation rates, for example, its linked impacts may be increased college enrollment, better-paying jobs, etc. As another example, expanding Medicaid and the State Children's Health Insurance Program is associated with increased tax receipts (Brown et al., 2015) and greater rates of high school and college completion (Cohodes et al., 2014). Linked impacts can be numerous, vary in magnitude, and cover a wide range of domains (e.g., employment, health, crime). They also can be intangible, such as improved quality of life from obtaining employment or reductions in pain and suffering from lower rates of crime or child abuse. To include linked impacts in their analysis, researchers conducting BCAs typically rely on evidence established by other research (e.g., meta-analysis, databases linking smoking or alcohol use to illness rates and/or death) that makes it possible to estimate the size of the linked relationship. As with evidence of intervention impact, evidence of causal linkage is desirable but not always feasible. Evidence from correlational studies or other noncausal designs needs to be used with appropriate caution, and conducting sensitivity analyses incorporating different effect sizes is important. Table 3-2 provides several examples of BCA studies including direct impacts, linked impacts, or a combination of the two.

Time Horizon for Estimated Impacts

The goal of many interventions for children, youth, and families is to improve lives not just in the present but over time. In conducting a BCA, it is important to describe the time horizon over which intervention impacts are being estimated. Strong theory linking present to future behavior, supported by empirical data, can help justify these choices (Crowley et al., 2014; Institute of Medicine and National Research Council, 2014). Some outcomes, such as the effect of increasing educational attainment on wages,

---

[24] If a study is long enough, researchers may be able to gather evidence on linked outcomes directly. Often this is not the case, so producers need to rely on evidence from the research literature.

TABLE 3-2 Examples of Direct and Linked Economic Impacts in Three Benefit-Cost Analysis Studies

	Benefits and Costs of Intensive Foster Care Services: The Casey Family Programs Compared with State Services (Kessler et al., 2008; Zerbe et al., 2009)	The High/Scope Perry Preschool Program Cost-Benefit Analysis Using Data from the Age 40 Follow-up (Belfield et al., 2006)	Benefit-Cost Analysis of Communities That Care Outcomes at Grade 12 (Kuklinski et al., 2015)
Description	Comparison of adult educational, health, and social outcomes among children who received private intensive foster care services compared with children who received public foster care services	Comparison of adult outcomes at age 40 among children who participated in the Perry Preschool Program compared with children who did not	Comparison of sustained effects of the Communities That Care (CTC) prevention system on grade 12 outcomes observed in a panel of youth involved in a community-randomized trial of CTC efficacy
Treatment, Control, or Comparison Group	Quasi-experimental design: • Treatment—Children placed in Casey Family Programs intensive foster care services • Control—Children placed in public program (matched using propensity scoring methods)	Randomized controlled trial: • Treatment—Children received 1-2 years of intensive preschool (center-based program, home visits, parent groups) • Control—Children did not receive intensive preschool	Community-randomized trial: • Treatment—Panel of youth from 12 communities trained to implement CTC prevention system • Control—Panel of youth from 12 communities matched in pairs within state based on sociodemographic characteristics
Measured Program Outcomes	• Adult impacts (age 24)—significant differences favoring treatment group: – Greater educational attainment – Higher rate of employment – Fewer physical disorders – Fewer mental health disorders – Higher rate of marriage—not monetized	• Adult impacts (age 40)—comparison of economic outcomes at age 40 in treatment versus control participants: – Education costs – Earnings and taxes – Crime – Welfare	• Grade 12 impacts—significant differences favoring panel exposed to CTC: – Lower onset of delinquency – Lower onset of alcohol use – Lower onset of cigarette smoking

		– More positive relationships with relatives—not monetized	
Program Outcomes with Direct Economic Impacts	• Physical disorders • Mental health disorders	• Education • Earnings and taxes • Crime • Welfare	• Delinquency
Linked Economic Impacts	• Lifetime earnings and taxes—from higher educational attainment	• Lifetime earnings and taxes—from higher educational attainment	• Lifetime alcohol disorder, heavy regular smoking—from lower onset of alcohol use, cigarette smoking • Educational attainment—from lower onset of delinquency
Actual or Estimated Economic Impacts	Estimated	Combination	Estimated

may last over an individual's working life; others, such as the association between early test scores and educational attainment, may fade over time (Washington State Institute for Public Policy, 2015). Even when the empirical literature indicates long-term economic impact, the analyst may be pressed to consider economic consequences over shorter time periods. This pressure may reflect decision makers' values and priorities, but it also can reflect that uncertainty increases over time because the world changes in unpredictable ways.

Some argue that the best way to understand the long-term effects of interventions is to collect real data by following participants over time and learning what happened to them (National Research Council and Institute of Medicine, 2009). Studies that used administrative or other data for long-term follow-up have demonstrated important long-term economic impact from investments made in childhood. The age 40 follow-up of the Perry Preschool Program documented persistent economic impacts including higher earnings for participants, higher tax revenues, lower criminal justice system expenditures, and lower welfare payments (Belfield et al., 2006). Several studies examining the implications of expanded childhood Medicaid coverage also showed long-term improvements to a range of health-related outcomes (Miller and Wherry, 2014; Wherry and Meyer, 2015; Wherry et al., 2015). However, interventions rarely produce these data because resource constraints prevent long-term follow-up, and measurement typically is limited to outcomes closely related to the intervention's goals (Karoly, 2012). Because unmeasured linked impacts can represent a significant portion of an intervention's benefits—for example, 70 percent of the Perry Preschool Program's estimated benefits were due to long-term reductions in criminal activity among males (Belfield et al., 2006)—ignoring them is likely to bias BCA estimates. Constant follow-up evaluations would help in acknowledging long-term benefits, as well as changes in needs, interests, or contexts.

The alternative is to estimate or project impacts over time. In some cases, developing projections is relatively straightforward. For example, the long-term impact of adolescent smoking consists mainly of poorer health in adulthood. Good estimates of this effect are readily available from epidemiologic studies; thus, results from a short-term evaluation of an adolescent smoking prevention intervention can be combined with estimates from the literature on the long-term effects of smoking to project the intervention's long-term impact. In other cases, projections are more complex. For example, the Washington State Institute for Public Policy has developed a sophisticated model for estimating the impact of reducing delinquency and crime that involves the marginal and operating costs for different types of crime, recidivism rates and related costs, victimization costs related to different types of crimes, and other elements (Washington State Institute for Public Policy, 2015)

At present there are no standards or widely accepted guidelines on how to generate projections. More straightforward approaches involve combining estimates found in the literature with results estimated from program data; for example, the analysis of an intervention that increases academic achievement may project impact on lifetime earnings based on published studies of how academic achievement causally affects earnings (Heckman et al., 2014). More complex approaches may involve the development of large microsimulation models using parameters derived from program evaluations, administrative and survey data, and the literature (Thomas, 2012). Variation also exists in how researchers decide which outcomes to project. If the focus is on outcomes that are easier to project, benefits are likely to be under- or conservatively estimated. If the focus is on including outcomes that are more difficult to project, estimates may be imprecise and have wide confidence intervals. Relatedly, projecting outcomes adds uncertainty to a study's results, especially over longer time periods or when empirical evidence of causal relationships is not well developed (e.g., intervention impacts on peers or siblings [Institute of Medicine and National Research Council, 2014; Karoly, 2012]).

CONCLUSION: *Preparation for a high-quality benefit-cost analysis requires consideration of which impacts to value in the analysis, including whether to include outcomes that are not statistically significant. It is also necessary to determine which outcomes may justifiably be linked to other outcomes that can be valued and that may be projected into the future. In each of these areas, standards or widely accepted guidelines for best practice are lacking. At a minimum, best practice requires transparency in reporting the approach taken. Consideration may also be given to conducting sensitivity analyses to determine whether results are robust to alternative approaches.*

Valuing Outcomes for Economic Evaluation

To estimate the economic benefits of an intervention (e.g., avoided costs, increased income, increased tax revenues), the analyst must assign prices to its impacts, a process that includes consideration of price changes over time. Some outcomes have **market prices** that reflect their economic value; that is, the prices reflect an individual's or society's willingness to pay them. Examples include wages paid for different types of jobs, health insurance costs, and home prices.

However, some outcomes of interest to children, youth, and families (e.g., lower student absenteeism, greater self-respect, reduced loss of freedom) do not have market prices, or their market prices are distorted (e.g., prices do not reflect the outcomes' actual economic value). An example of the latter is health care utilization as measured by hospital charges, which often are poor indicators of costs or even of what hospitals actually are paid for their services. In these cases, researchers can estimate the outcomes' economic value by turning to shadow prices, which, as discussed earlier, are indirect estimates of how much individuals or society would be willing to pay for the outcomes. At times, assignment of shadow prices is relatively straightforward. For example, although there is not a direct market for educational attainment, its shadow price is routinely captured in BCAs through higher wages associated with higher levels of attainment (Oreopoulos and Petronijevic, 2013; Washington State Institute for Public Policy, 2015).

Other approaches for estimating shadow prices, such as **revealed preferences** and **stated preferences**, are more complex.[25] The revealed preferences approach looks at what people pay for products with the attributes that need to be valued but are not priced directly. For example, regression analyses of how home prices vary with water quality or neighborhood safety can reveal how much homebuyers value drinkable water or safety (Bickel and Rainer, 2005; Gayer et al., 2002; Nelson, 1978; World Health Organization, 2012), outcomes with import for children, youth, and families. Other revealed preference studies have valued family safety by examining how demand for home smoke alarms grew as their price dropped (Miller, 1990) and estimated how parents value children by analyzing the market for child bicycle helmets (Jenkins et al., 2001).

The stated preferences approach uses survey data to estimate prices where markets do not exist or are distorted. Survey questions ask respondents what they are willing to pay for the attribute that needs to be valued. Alternatively, respondents are asked to choose their preference among scenarios that differ in the attribute. The attribute may be tangible, such as high-quality childcare for children, or intangible, such as honesty. Because surveys allow for detailed descriptions of what is being valued, preferences can be elicited for very specific features of interest (Ryan et al., 2008).

The two most common stated preferences methods are (1) **contingent valuation,** where individuals are asked directly how much they would be willing to pay (or be paid) for a certain outcome (e.g., a reduction in the risk of death), contingent on a hypothetical scenario; and (2) **discrete choice** experiments, in which respondents' preferences are assessed from a sequence of hypothetical scenarios that vary along several attributes, which can include the price of the nonmarket commodity of interest. Widely ac-

---

[25] A more complete discussion of pricing and monetization methods used in BCAs can be found in Vining and Weimer (2009b).

cepted guidelines exist for contingent valuation survey design and proce-dures (Arrow et al., 1993; Bateman et al., 2002). Examples of how these methods have been used include estimations of the value of environmental policies, food safety, injury prevention, and various health-related outcomes (Boxall et al., 1996; Hanemann, 1994; Lindhjem et al., 2011; Loureiro and Umberger, 2007; Olsen and Smith, 2001; Schwab-Christe and Soguel, 1995).

A major challenge in applying contingent valuation methods is that respondents have difficulty putting a price on intangibles reliably and repro-ducibly (Mitchell and Carson, 1989). Often, the methods yield overstated values (Hausman, 2012). Hausman (2012, p. 43) concludes the method has intractable "problems of embedding and scope. . . . [r]espondents to contingent valuation surveys are often not responding out of stable or well-defined preferences, but are essentially inventing their answers on the fly, in a way which makes the resulting data useless for serious analysis." Dis-crete choice models address these problems by asking individuals to choose among alternatives with different sets of tangible and intangible attributes (Bridges et al., 2011). Among stated preference methods, the discrete choice approach has "become the most frequently applied approach in healthcare" (Johnson et al., 2013). Consensus panels also have developed guidelines for discrete choice survey design and procedures (Bridges et al., 2011; Johnson et al., 2013).

Despite having strong theoretical foundations and being viewed favor-ably by such agencies as the U.S. Office of Management and Budget (2003), revealed and stated preference methods only recently became used more widely in health care economics, primarily in international health, and they remain rare in studies of social interventions. Examples of such work relevant to investments in children, youth, and families include analyses of parents' willingness to pay for preschool programs for their children (Escobar et al., 1988) or for protecting their children against house fires, road crashes, human papillomavirus, the common cold, asthma, and fatal diseases (Alberini and Šcasný, 2011; Blomquist et al., 1996; Brandt et al., 2012; Brown et al., 2010; Hammitt and Haninger, 2010; Jarahi et al., 2011; Liu et al., 2000; Miller, 1990; Takeuchi et al., 2008). Studies with valuations not limited to respondents' own families have examined the value of crime reduction; employer-sponsored childcare; library services; community cultural, sports, and leisure activities; arts performances; pre-venting a child's death due to maltreatment; and publicly funded health interventions (Bosworth et al., 2010, 2015; Cohen et al., 2004; Connelly et al., 2004; Corso et al., 2011, 2013; Hendrie, 2013; Ludwig and Cook, 2001; Thompson et al., 2002).

Revealed and stated preference methods can facilitate the inclusion of important **intangible benefits**, such as increased motivation or self-confidence (Belfield, 2014), in BCAs of interventions for children, youth, and families. Failing to monetize intangible benefits may lead to underestimating the value of outcomes considered in a BCA, particularly for interventions that have few or difficult-to-measure tangible effects. Examples of such outcomes include those related to behavioral/emotional problems, marriage and divorce, mental health, and reproductive health (Karoly, 2008).

Several recent studies have incorporated intangibles in the valuation of intervention outcomes. A recent study using willingness-to-pay methods, for example, estimated a value of $18.3 million for preventing a child's death due to maltreatment, in contrast to earlier estimates of $1 million calculated from future productivity losses and $7.7 million based on juries' willingness to award (Corso et al., 2007, 2011; Miller et al., 2001, 2006). In BCAs of health care interventions, including intangibles, allow researchers to go beyond valuing health outcomes simply by aggregating future health care cost savings and increases in productivity; rather, the intangible value of improved health status to patients and their families (e.g., Gentilello et al., 2005; Nichol, 2001; Takenaga et al., 1985) becomes part of the equation, resulting in dramatic increases in estimated intervention benefits (Dickie and Gerking, 2002; Miller and Hendrie, 2012).

Valuing children's lives directly using willingness to pay would be problematic (Office of Management and Budget, 2003). Young children have limited ability to perceive risk (Barton and Schwebel, 2007), much less value it. The brain's prefrontal cortex, which regulates emotions and promotes sound decision making, is still developing in late adolescence to early adulthood (Gogtay et al., 2004; Nelson et al., 2006). Adolescents consequently take irrational risks, with both their revealed and stated preferences for risk being skewed downward from their preferences at maturity. Using those immature values in societal decision making seems unwise, and many countries have strong traditions of safety legislation to constrain adolescent risk decision making.

A better option is to use the values parents or the broader society place on children (Alberini et al., 2010). The literature provides more than a dozen U.S. value estimates (Alberini et al., 2010; Scapecchi, 2006; Williams, 2013), as well as results of and stated preference surveys for a variety of risks in the Czech Republic and Italy (Alberini et al., 2010), cold protection in Taiwan (Liu et al., 2000), vaccination in Bangladesh (Islam et al., 2008) and the Philippines (Palanca-Tan, 2014), and arsenic-free water in Bangladesh (Aziz, 2007). Although not unanimous, these studies generally find that parents place a greater value on the safety of their children than on themselves (Alberini et al., 2010). OECD (2012) and Williams (2013) recommend valuing children's lives at 1.5 to 2.0 times adult values.

CONCLUSION: *In support of high-quality benefit-cost analysis, valuing intervention outcomes requires measuring society's willingness to pay for each outcome. In some cases, market prices may provide the required economic values, but many outcomes affected by interventions for children, youth, and families do not have market prices. Indirect economic values, or shadow prices, are used to capture economic values using various methods, such as linking the outcome of interest to another outcome that can be valued. Revealed and stated preference methods can be used to estimate willingness to pay, potentially enabling both tangible and intangible outcomes to be valued. Using valuation methods that fail to account for the value of intangible outcomes may result in biased estimates (typically undervaluation) of intervention benefits.*

Estimating shadow prices can be costly. It also can yield values with wide variance and even means that differ considerably among high-quality studies. Consider, for example, the published estimates of willingness to pay to avoid a homicide, in 2014 dollars, in Table 3-3. The means range from $6.3 million to $47.5 million, with the 95 percent confidence intervals from three studies not even overlapping. The value chosen obviously could make a major difference in the BCA outcome for a crime reduction intervention. One way to facilitate quality analyses, encourage sensitivity analysis around uncertain values, reduce expenditures on shadow pricing, and encourage consistent value choices that support benefit-cost comparisons across studies is to catalog quality values in a clearinghouse. The Tufts Cost-Effectiveness Registry (Thorat et al., 2012) has taken this approach with QALY estimates for health conditions, with the result that studies increasingly are using established values instead of developing their own.

TABLE 3-3 Means and 95 Percent Confidence Intervals of Values of Willingness to Pay to Prevent a Homicide, by Study (in millions of 2014 dollars)

Data Sources	Mean	Lower Confidence Limit	Upper Confidence Limit
Cohen et al. (2004)	14.2	12.5	16.2
Corso et al. (2013) (child maltreatment death)	18.3	16.1	20.8
Kochi and Taylor (2011)	6.3	1.7	10.9
Scotton and Taylor (2011)	11.6	0.0	64.3
Scotton and Taylor (2011)	47.5	7.4	87.7

Similarly, meta-analyses of outcomes developed by the Cochrane Collaborative (The Cochrane Public Health Group, 2011), the Community Guides to Preventive Services, the U.S. Substance Abuse and Mental Health Services Administration's National Registry of Evidence-based Programs and Practices, and the U.S. Office of Justice Programs' CrimeSolutions.gov increase the quality and completeness of effectiveness evidence readily available for use in economic analysis.

CONCLUSION: *Registries can increase uniformity of practice, reduce the costs and time required for shadow pricing, and increase the accessibility and comparability of cost-outcome estimates for interventions targeting children, youth, and families. To support these functions, registries could be established to evaluate the quality of and archive (1) values for common nonmarket outcomes such as those related to crime and special education, and (2) cost-outcome estimates for interventions for children, youth, and families.*

Valuing Quality of Life

Quality of life is a particularly important intangible that is likely to be relevant in valuing outcomes for interventions for children, youth, and families. Indeed, virtually all such interventions affect quality of life to some degree. Moreover, quality-of-life impacts may constitute a large share of the benefits of such interventions (see, e.g., the benefit-cost estimates for various interventions shown in Table 36.6 in Miller and Hendrie [2012]). Consequently, an economic evaluation that excludes these impacts may fail to capture the full economic value of the intervention being analyzed, typically underestimating its benefits. In addition, if the value of quality-of-life impacts is omitted, it is difficult to compare the economic returns on investments in different sectors, such as health interventions versus prevention or other social interventions. Nonetheless, the difficulty of measuring and valuing quality-of-life impacts is a long-standing concern regarding economic evaluations of interventions serving children, youth, and families.

In the case of health interventions, quality of life accounts for a large portion of the benefits. For this reason, according to the first Panel on Cost-Effectiveness in Health and Medicine (Gold et al., 1996, p. 84), "In order to capture health outcomes beyond simple survival it is necessary to obtain information on the health-related quality-of-life associated with different interventions." Health and environmental analysts generally have taken two approaches to measuring quality-of-life gains. The first examines what people are willing to pay—and actually do pay—for goods that represent the effects on quality of life (e.g., a reduced risk of death or criminal victimization) (Dréze, 1964; Schelling, 1968). The second measures impact on

BOX 3-1
Assessing Approaches to Measuring Quality-of-Life Gains

An advantage of quality-adjusted life years (QALYs) or disability-adjusted life years (DALYs) is that one can apply a single quality-of-life measure to track changes across a range of interventions instead of collecting willingness-to-pay data on multiple outcomes. This advantage is especially important in valuing such things as reductions in drunk driving crashes versus distracted driving crashes, which produce different profiles of injuries (Blincoe et al., 2015). It would be difficult to describe those injury mixes to survey respondents in a way that would enable them to provide well-informed willingness-to-pay estimates, and much easier to use a standardized instrument to collect objective data on the functional capacity lost to the injuries and convert that loss into QALYs. QALYs also are not constrained by what respondents can afford or their difficulty in accurately pricing something that cannot be purchased.

On the other hand, an advantage of willingness to pay is that the valuation is in dollars. It is difficult to interpret a cost-utility estimate of, say, $75,000 per QALY saved. Often the value choice is left to decision makers, with country-specific yet arbitrary maximum acceptable value ranges emerging over time (Harris et al., 2008; World Health Organization, 2001). To better inform those choices, more than a third of recent cost-utility studies conducted a sensitivity analysis using a **cost-effectiveness acceptability curve** (**CEAC**), which displayed the probability that an intervention yielded a positive return at different monetary values of a QALY (Meckley et al., 2010). Another alternative is to place a dollar value on a QALY. Popular approaches to QALY valuation are to use a willingness-to-pay survey (e.g., Gyrd-Hanson, 2003) or simply to divide the value of statistical life by the number of QALYs left in an average life (discounted to present value) (e.g., Cutler and Richardson, 1998; Miller et al., 1989). Both valuation approaches ignore economic theory and supporting empirical evidence, which suggest that the value of a QALY is situational (Hammitt, 2007; Hammitt and Haninger, 2010, Haninger and Hammitt, 2011; Johannesson and Johansson, 1997; Mortimer and Segal, 2008; von Stackelberg and Hammitt, 2009).

The Committee to Evaluate Measures of Health Benefits for Environmental, Health, and Safety Regulation (Institute of Medicine, 2006) concluded that although DALY/QALY "measures are based on surveys reflecting individual choices, these choices may not fully reflect individual preferences and are not entirely consistent with the tenets of utility theory that underlie welfare economics" (p. 36). The committee concluded that since these measures were not homogeneous across ages or permanency of the impairment, the dollar value of a QALY/DALY was not fixed. Ironically, those same concerns arise with willingness to pay for a statistical life, a year of life expectancy, or avoidance of functional capacity loss, but the patterns of variation differ, which Hammitt (2007) concludes means using willingness to pay for a QALY violates social welfare theory. An alternative view is that a QALY is not a homogeneous good, and its value thus is specific to the details of the QALY. That conclusion is equally valid for a statistical life or many other intangible goods. Policy analysts sometimes handle this issue by using an average value but warning of its imprecision.

continued

BOX 3-1 Continued

While interest in the use of happiness or well-being measures has grown, such measures have been found to be subjective, framed by a person's disposition, expectations, adaptation, and coping strategies (Andrews and Withey, 1976; Diener et al., 1999). Indeed, Richardson and colleagues (2013) found that across six countries, a well-being scale explained only 7 percent of the variation in QALY scores among 8,022 respondents stratified to oversample people with chronic health problems. Happiness correlates poorly with income (Andrews and Withey, 1976; Argyle, 2001) but tends to be strongly influenced by personal disposition, and in the short to medium term by family events. In addition, people tend to have happiness set-points. Over time, adaptation causes happiness changes resulting from most major life events to fade, although unemployment tends to have a lasting effect (Diener and Oishi, 2005; Lucas et al., 2004; Robinson et al., 2012). Thus, well-being measures appear better suited for use as mediators and moderators than as outcome measures. Lacking an objective component to keep them in balance, they are better at predicting how people will react to change than at measuring change.

---

health-related quality of life directly using nonmonetary measures—either DALYs reduced (Murray and Lopez, 1996) or QALYs saved (Fanshel and Bush, 1970; Torrance et al., 1972; Weinstein et al., 2009). Researchers also have experimented with happiness or well-being measures, but their subjective nature can make their use in program evaluation challenging (Andrews and Withey, 1976; Diener et al., 1999). The considerations associated with each of these approaches are described more fully in Box 3-1.

Several generic QALY or DALY scales are commonly used in economic evaluation of health services (McDowell, 2006; Miller, 2000). Both systematic reviews (Spicer et al., 2011) and surveys that collected data using multiple scales (Richardson et al., 2015) provide insight into consistency and equivalences across scales and even support translation between some scales (Gray et al., 2006). The committee reviewed the major scales to see whether any of them accounted for aspects of well-being that extend beyond health. One widely used set of QALY scales did: the World Health Organization's (WHO) 100-item quality-of-life instrument (WHOQOL) (World Health Organization Quality of Life Group, 1998) and a reduced 26-question WHOQOL-BREF (Skevington et al., 2004) that usually can be administered in less than 5 minutes. The WHOQOL-BREF instrument encompasses four domains—physical, psychological, social, and environmental—and includes questions about shelter and educational opportunities. It has been administered in more than 40 languages, and more than 11,000 respondents worldwide were polled to test its validity, reliability, and discriminant ability. WHOQOL development and refinement extended from 1991 to 2004 and was a joint effort of 24 WHO collaborating centers.

The WHOQOL instruments originally were designed for adult respondents. However, they have been used successfully with adolescents in a range of countries, validated for adolescent use, and shown to be concordant with parent proxy reports (with a question about satisfaction with one's sex life often being omitted or modified to be age- and culture-appropriate) (Agnihotri et al., 2010a, 2010b; Al-Fayez and Ohaeri, 2011; Chau et al., 2012; Cruz et al., 2014; Izutsu et al., 2005; Jirojanakul and Skevington, 2000).

Given this evidence, the WHOQOL-BREF appears to be a promising tool for estimating QALY gains from interventions for children, youth, and families that are not targeted to health. It provides proof of concept that aspects of well-being beyond health can be captured in a valid and reliable way. Indeed, it may be the forerunner of a family of quality-of-life measurement tools that are sensitive to gains in outcomes extending well beyond health to include educational, employment, social welfare, and other domains of well-being. Especially in the United States, such tools have been applied too rarely in impact evaluations and related economic evaluations of interventions for children, youth, and families to judge whether their promise can become a reality.

CONCLUSION: *Quality-of-life impacts may be an important outcome of interventions for children, youth, and families, yet they are rarely accounted for in economic evaluations of such interventions, largely because of the difficulty of measuring and valuing them. Approaches for this purpose have been developed for use in economic evaluations in other policy areas, such as health and the environment, which may provide promising strategies for use in economic evaluations of social programs. A quality-of-life measure embedded in a willingness-to-pay estimate or one that can be compared with the quality-adjusted life years/disability-adjusted life years measures used in economic evaluations of health interventions would facilitate the ability to compare across sectors.*

Aggregating Economic Values

As this discussion suggests, estimating direct and linked impacts and assigning prices to them, including choosing an appropriate time period for the analysis, is often a challenging, time-consuming endeavor that involves many decisions and assumptions on the part of the analyst. Once the process has been completed, however (at least for monetized benefits), valuing interventions for purposes of a BCA is relatively straightforward.[26] After ensuring that impact quantities and prices are in comparable units, flows over time can be calculated, summed, and discounted according to equation (3.1) presented earlier in this chapter to determine the present value of intervention benefits. Issues involved in comparing intervention benefits with costs to determine whether an intervention investment is cost-beneficial are described next.

GETTING TO RESULTS: THE DEVELOPMENT AND REPORTING OF SUMMARY MEASURES

The final step in producing economic evidence related to investments in interventions for children, youth, and families is the development of summary measures appropriate to the audience, perspective, and scope of the analysis. In CA, summary measures may include **total costs, average costs,** and **marginal costs.** In CEA, summary measures may include the **cost-effectiveness ratio,** the measure of net health benefits or net monetary benefits, or the cost-effectiveness acceptability curve. In BCA, summary measures may include a measure of **net benefits,** a **benefit-cost, ratio, the internal rate of return,** or **return on investment.** Different summary measures convey different information, and they have different strengths and limitations. In each type of analysis, the type of summary measure that is developed needs to be informed by the study question, the scope of the analysis, and the audience. Further, discussing these measures a priori is critical for successful utilization by policy makers.

Summary Measures: Cost Analysis

Total costs of an intervention are its aggregate costs, calculated by multiplying all resources used by their unit costs and then summing these totals. As noted earlier, if costs are incurred over time, decisions about inflation and discounting are applied. Total costs can be disaggregated by typical cost categories, such as personnel versus nonpersonnel, or by activity category, such as direct client services versus administrative costs. It also may be helpful to aggregate according to intervention startup, implementation, and sustainability phases (Crowley et al., 2014). A measure of total costs is useful for summarizing costs over time, across intervention sites, and across funders, and is helpful in providing key feedback to intervention administrators. However, a measure of total costs may not explain why an intervention in one site costs more than that in another because differences in aggregate costs often are due to differences in the number of children,

---

[26] See the later discussion of nonmonetized benefits.

youth, or families served. To understand difference in intervention costs across sites, one needs to examine the average costs of an intervention.

Average costs of an intervention express the expected cost per child, youth, or family served and are calculated by dividing total costs by the number served during the specified time period. This measure can be used to compare resource needs and costs across sites. Differences in average per participant costs by site suggest that factors other than the numbers served are driving cost differentials. Costs may vary as a result of differences in the individual characteristics of those served (e.g., non-English-speaking versus native-English-speaking, having a disability versus able-bodied), the intensity of services (e.g., part-day or full-day programming), the characteristics of the providers (e.g., nurses versus social workers), the characteristics of the intervention (e.g., startup versus ongoing, enhanced versus standard), or the characteristics of the community (e.g., urban versus rural).

Another important summary measure in CA is marginal costs, which are derived by calculating the expected cost per additional child, youth, or family served. As noted earlier, calculating marginal costs requires differentiating between fixed and variable costs in the CA. Marginal cost summary measures are helpful when budget planning is possible or necessary because they can be used to determine how many more individuals could be served, for example, if the budget were to increase or decrease by a certain percentage. Some resources—such as the building where the intervention is being delivered if not operating at capacity (a fixed cost)—would not need to be considered in an expansion of the intervention scale, while other resources—such as reading materials provided to a child in a reading-ready intervention—would need to be considered.

Summary Measures: Cost-Effectiveness Analysis

The main summary measure in a CEA is the **cost-effectiveness (CE) ratio**, derived by dividing the intervention **costs** (discounted and adjusted for inflation, as appropriate) **net of monetized outcomes** by the change in a focal outcome measured in its natural unit (e.g., cases prevented, percent reduction in crime, percent increase in high school completion rate, QALYs saved). An incremental CE analysis compares a set of two or more interventions arrayed in order of increasing effectiveness (with "no intervention" or "usual standards of care" often being the least effective). The set of comparative ratios is called *incremental CE ratios (ICERs)*. The Panel on Cost-Effectiveness in Health and Medicine (Gold et al., 1996) and others (Drummond et al., 2005; Haddix et al., 2003; Levin and McEwan, 2001) provide detailed, cogent guidance on how to calculate ICERs.

Cost-effectiveness analysis is increasingly used to guide resource allocation decisions in high- as well as low- and middle-income countries.

These decisions typically concern allocations to social-sector interventions in the larger context of other government expenditures. For development interventions, decisions are made by national governments, as well as by global funding organizations and aid agencies. To support decision making, it is necessary to know the extent of additional resources a payer should be prepared to devote to incremental gains in the desired outcome areas. The *cost-effectiveness threshold* is the standard means for assessing the acceptability or affordability of an estimated incremental cost-effectiveness ratio. Box 3-1, presented earlier, includes discussion of the lack of theoretical justification for any threshold for a maximum acceptable cost per QALY or DALY and the ad hoc approaches used to handle the question.

Summary Measures: Benefit-Cost Analysis

The preferred summary measure for BCA is **net present-value (NPV) benefits**, which reflects the present value of all benefits attributable to an intervention less the present value of the costs required to conduct the intervention (after adjusting for inflation). When the NPV is positive, it provides an economic argument for investing in the intervention because it implies that the benefits of the intervention outweigh the costs after discounting. An attractive feature of this measure is that it is not sensitive to how costs and benefits are labeled (e.g., if negative benefits are treated as costs). It also provides information about the magnitude of benefits expected. Both total NPV and NPV per unit (e.g., child, youth, family) are informative.

The results of a BCA also are commonly expressed in terms of the **benefit-cost ratio** (BCR), which is calculated by dividing total benefits by total intervention costs after relevant discounting and inflationary adjustments have been performed. If the resulting ratio is greater than 1, benefits exceed costs, and an economic case can be made for the investment. The BCR also is popular with stakeholders because it allows for concise statements about the "dollar return per dollar invested," making it possible to focus on where the next dollar should be spent or the last dollar shifted among comparable interventions. However, the BCR can be misleading for several reasons. First, as a ratio, it fails to capture the magnitude of benefits or costs. For example, a 3:1 BCR could result from an intervention that cost $100 per child and returned $300 or one that cost $10,000 but returned $30,000. Decision makers facing limited budgets, pressures to reach certain numbers of children, and other constraints benefit from more information than is captured by a BCR alone. Further, the ability to treat some costs as "negative benefits" or benefits as "negative costs" means that the ratio can be manipulated.[27]

---

[27]This may not be a relevant issue for certain subfields.

Another summary measure in BCA is **return on investment (ROI)**, which captures the percentage of return for every dollar invested. It is calculated by dividing intervention benefits net of intervention costs (as opposed to total benefits as in the BCR) by intervention costs. Common in the business sector, ROI summary measures often are narrowly constructed, focusing on financial gain to the intervention provider or funder over a short time horizon rather than overall benefits for society over a short or long time period. At times it also is used as a first-approximation measure of what might be gained from further investments of a similar type, although see the discussion above about issues surrounding projections. More recently, the concept of ROI has increasingly been used to describe investments in health and education (Psacharopoulos and Patrinos, 2004; Robert Wood Johnson Foundation, 2013). In reality, many of the interventions that target children, youth, and families may not necessarily save money in the short term.

Somewhat similar to ROI, the **internal rate of return (IRR)**, calculated as the discount rate that makes the NPV equal to 0, is yet another summary measure used in BCAs—typically in BCAs of business investments. An intervention with an IRR above some predetermined threshold (the social discount rate or the rate of return required by the business or organization providing the intervention) is deemed acceptable. The IRR provides valuable information as to the sensitivity of the NPV or BCR to the choice of the discount rate. For a given discount rate (say, 3%), if the estimated net benefits are positive, the IRR shows how high the discount rate could go before the NPV was zero. Conversely, if the estimated net benefits are negative, the IRR indicates how low the discount rate would have to be for the NPV to become positive. As a summary measure, however, IRR can be problematic because interventions can have multiple IRRs, depending on the timing of costs and benefits, and the IRR will not necessarily rank interventions in the same order as the NPV (Zerbe and Dively, 1974).[28] Further, unlike net benefits as a summary measure but like the BCR, the IRR does not provide information on the scale of the intervention—that is, the scale of costs required to implement the intervention.

Economic evaluations producing summary measures based on nonlocal samples and prices may not inform local decisions. Understanding how investments yield benefits depends critically on preintervention problem levels as well as an intervention's reach; that is, context matters (see Chapter 4). The local context may be very different from the context that produced a favorable NPV or BCR. As a specific example, if a community has a base-

---

[28] To address this issue, Zerbe (2010) proposes a reliable IRR (IRRr). Zerbe and Dively (1974) also discuss an approach for adjusting for projects with different costs because the BCR can provide different rankings.

line rate of youth substance misuse that is much lower than the national average, a school-based substance misuse intervention in that community is likely to have a lower BCR than the same intervention in a community with a higher baseline rate. Similarly, if a community implements the same intervention but in a different setting (e.g., family-centered rather than school-based), the intervention may have a different cost structure relative to that in other communities; population characteristics may differ as well, including different baseline levels of the problem behavior. Data needed to fully inform local decision making typically are not available.

Reporting Summary Measures

Regardless of the method of economic evaluation employed, all the methods involve CA, so it is important to, at a minimum, report results framed in the context of the unit cost of the investment. Specifically, a CA would report the average and marginal cost for each participant unit. In addition, a CEA would report the average and incremental cost-effectiveness per unit of outcome achieved (e.g., cost per emergency department visit prevented), while a BCA would report the NPV per participant along with the BCR. Together, such estimates can prevent consumers of the evidence derived from BCAs, in particular, from assuming that the intervention with the lowest cost or highest total savings is inherently the better choice.

CONCLUSION: *The literature supports a number of summary measures for economic evaluation:*

- *Cost analysis—In addition to total cost, informative summary measures include the unit cost of the investment (e.g., cost per participant or average cost) and marginal cost.*
- *Cost-effectiveness analysis (CEA)—The preferred summary measures for a CEA are the average and incremental cost-effectiveness per unit of outcome achieved (CE ratio). Cost-effectiveness thresholds may also inform the analysis, although clearer guidance is needed on the valid thresholds to apply based on the outcomes and the setting.*
- *Benefit-cost analysis (BCA)—The preferred primary summary measure for a BCA is net-present value benefits. The benefit-cost ratio, return on investment, and the internal rate of return also can be valuable and may be required in many decision-making contexts, including projections of returns on further investments.*

HANDLING UNCERTAINTY IN ECONOMIC EVALUATION

Uncertainty is intrinsic to evaluation in general and economic evaluation in particular. Vining and Weimer (2010, p. 17) explain, as follows:

> The application of BCA to social policies typically involves producing predictions of net benefits based on imprecise predictions of numerous effects and their monetization with relatively uncertain shadow prices. Effectively, net benefits are the sums of products of random variables.

Even if the research design used to evaluate an intervention provided causal evidence of impact, uncertainty in the magnitude of that impact would remain an issue. A wide range of factors—for example, sampling error; **selection bias**; sample **attrition**, particularly differential attrition; measurement error due to imprecision or weak instrumentation; failure to control adequately for covariates—all may contribute to uncertainty about the true magnitude of intervention impact (Trochim and Donnelly, 2006).

Crowley and colleagues (2014) identify three different sources of uncertainty: (1) *model uncertainty*, related to decisions on which costs and outcomes are included in the analysis and assumptions regarding the relationships between them; (2) *measurement uncertainty*, which originates from imprecision in the measurement of analysis inputs and from sampling practices; and (3) *parameter uncertainty*, related to such assumptions as the discount rate or the probabilities used in state-transition models. Yet despite the ubiquity of uncertainty in economic evaluation, studies often fail to acknowledge uncertainty in their main results. In a summary of methodological choices made in 14 BCAs published between 1996 and 2010, Karoly (2012) found that only 4 of them reported the standard errors of their results.

Sensitivity analysis, as alluded to earlier, is used to address uncertainty in an economic evaluation. Although different methods can be used to conduct sensitivity analysis, in general they all are designed to test the robustness of results to variability in the study's assumptions. Probabilistic methods (more formally, a Monte Carlo simulation analysis) that address multiple sources of uncertainty simultaneously provide a comprehensive assessment of the implications of uncertainty for economic estimates (Vining and Weimar, 2009a). In contrast, one-way (or multiway) sensitivity analysis varies values of a single parameter (or multiple parameters) over a range the analyst considers plausible (e.g., the magnitude of the effect size for a given outcome, the magnitude of the relationship between an observed and linked or projected outcome, the discount rate), leaving all other parameters and assumptions unchanged, and recalculates results for each new value. Repeating this exercise for all major parameters allows the analyst to understand how robust baseline results are to uncertainty in each parameter or combination of parameters. This method, however, provides a less complete picture of the implications of uncertainty than that obtained with a Monte Carlo simulation (Boardman et al., 2011; Weinstein et al., 1997), a limitation that needs to be acknowledged when this method is used.

Monte Carlo simulation is becoming standard practice for analyzing measurement uncertainty, as reflected in its being recommended by the U.S. Office of Management and Budget (2003) and the Canadian government (Treasury Board of Canada Secretariat, 2007). It is also standard practice in BCAs conducted by the Washington State Institute for Public Policy (Aos et al., 2004). The method entails repeated sampling, often thousands of times, of the probability distributions for each parameter in the cost or cost-outcome equation to estimate the variance around the economic estimate. Typically, a Monte Carlo analysis uses standard deviations of outcomes drawn from the intervention evaluation, although other probability distributions are possible. For unit costs, standard deviations often come from administrative data sets that are not program-specific (e.g., on school cost per pupil day) or even may simply assume a normal distribution with a standard deviation of 10 percent of the mean. A more complex example is a sensitivity analysis involving the value of preventing a homicide, in which the mean and standard deviation of each of three conflicting stated preference surveys is assumed to have an equal probability of being the correct distribution.

A limitation of the use of Monte Carlo methods for estimating the standard deviation of a complex cost-outcome equation involving multiple outcomes is that the procedure typically samples the probability distribution for each outcome independently. In reality, intervention performance often will be good or bad based on multiple outcomes simultaneously. If Monte Carlo methods do not take this covariance into account, they may underestimate the standard deviation.

Analysts may choose to supplement Monte Carlo analysis with one-way or multiway sensitivity analyses of key parameters. Such analyses, for example, can demonstrate the effects on economic evaluation results of smaller outcomes expected in intervention replication, a shorter time horizon for benefits, omission of an outcome with weak evidence, or an alternative discount rate. One-way sensitivity analyses also can provide information that facilitates comparisons across analyses. Notably, the first Panel on Cost-Effectiveness in Health and Medicine (Gold et al., 1996) recommended that all CEAs provide an estimate at a 3 percent discount rate either as the base case or in a sensitivity analysis. Because of that recommendation, the Tufts Cost-Effectiveness Registry has been able to catalog thousands of CEA estimates from around the world that can be compared without distortion by differing discount rates. Thus, the comparison case at a 3 percent discount rate has served the CEA community well. Of course at different discount rates, interventions could end up being ranked differently in terms of such criteria as net benefits, but this qualification does not mitigate the need to use a common discount rate to compare interventions. Decision makers employing economic evaluations of interventions serving children, youth, and families would also be expected to benefit from having a 3 percent standard discount rate, either in a base case or as part of a sensitivity analysis.

A final important consideration in the analysis of uncertainty is the communication of results. A thorough sensitivity analysis may require that the analyst expend a great deal of effort on summarizing the implications of the analysis for decision makers, who may have a low tolerance for complex technical discussions (Robinson and Hammitt, 2011). In the case of BCA, Vining and Weimer (2010) recommend communicating a simple indicator of uncertainty to decision makers: the proportion of Monte Carlo trials yielding a positive net benefit. They argue that if the central concern in a BCA is whether an intervention produces positive net benefits, decision makers can be confident about the likelihood of making a favorable investment if the proportion of trials with zero or negative benefits is small. The Washington State Institute for Public Policy has adopted this practice in its BCA reports (Washington State Institute for Public Policy, 2015).

CONCLUSION: *For all economic evaluation methods, one or more types of uncertainty usually are associated with the evaluation findings. The literature supports the following practices for addressing uncertainty in high-quality economic evaluations:*

- *An emerging best practice for providing a comprehensive assessment of the implications of multiple sources of uncertainty is the use of Monte Carlo methods—either alone or in combination with one-way sensitivity analyses.*
- *In the case of benefit-cost analyses, a recommended summary measure from Monte Carlo simulations is the proportion of trials with positive net benefits.*
- *Conducting economic evaluations of interventions for children, youth, and families using a 3 percent discount rate as a base case or in a sensitivity analysis will facilitate the ability to make more and consistent comparisons across studies.*

ADDRESSING EQUITY CONSIDERATIONS

In Chapter 2, equity is identified as an important concern in resource allocation targeting children, youth, and families. Equity considerations range from progressivity (vertical equity), to equal treatment of equals (horizontal equity or equal justice), to individual equity (the right to returns from one's efforts and labor). Yet, as acknowledged in Chapter 2 and in the paper by Cookson (2015) commissioned for this study, the economic evaluation methods discussed in this chapter typically do not take distributional issues into account. Results are reported in the aggregate for society or the stakeholder whose perspective is adopted. To some extent, the distributional consequences of an intervention can be discerned by disaggregating the total results by different stakeholder groups, such as intervention participants, the rest of society, and the government sector. There may be interest, however, in taking into account the distribution of costs and benefits according to particular characteristics of the participants, such as their income level, race-ethnicity, geographic location, or other defining features that are valued by the decision maker.

Accordingly, some economic evaluations assign differential weights to the costs and benefits accruing to different subgroups affected by an intervention based on the differential means or needs of the subgroups or variation in other socially relevant characteristics. The challenge in defining and applying such weights is to ascertain the appropriate weights to use, as they may vary across different members of the target audience for an economic evaluation. To address this issue, the weights may be determined through formal mechanisms or formulas. The commissioned paper by Cookson (2015) provides much greater detail on how some of these formal mechanisms have evolved to date. Usually they involve some weighting of outcomes according to the initial well-being of the child, youth, or family being served. For instance, a particular dollar of expenditure may be given greater weight if spent on a child in a low-income family rather than a child in a high-income family. Likewise, if the World Bank seeks to allocate some efficient health expenditure on the basis of the capability of recipient countries, it may rank countries along some scale, such as per capita income. Yet even that scalar requires determining how differently to treat desperately poor countries and those with income somewhat below the median.

Of course, income is not the only measure of progressivity. Consider educational attainment. It is not uncommon for an educational intervention to rate its success by the percentage of those below some educational standard who are brought above that standard. A BCA examining such an intervention, however, needs somehow to count the gains to those already above the standard, or losses to the extent that resources were shifted from them.

Often more informal methods will be applied that may or may not involve some amount of quantitative assessment. For instance, a decision may be made to allocate spending to interventions with a wide range of progressivity but not to regressive interventions. Even here, care needs to be exercised in reporting whether an intervention is progressive. A regressive intervention making use of progressive taxation may still be progressive overall. By some measures, for example, Social Security survivor benefits provided to children might generate higher benefits for children from higher-income families, but through the intervention's tax structure, still redistribute benefits from those who are better off to those who are worse off (Steuerle and Bakija, 1994).

Ultimately, both formal and informal approaches to incorporating equity weights can be controversial. Yet it is known that decision makers often bring such equity considerations to the table in making decisions about resource allocation. Explicit attempts to incorporate equity considerations, especially as part of sensitivity analyses, can help illuminate the distributional consequences of a given intervention while still acknowledging that the weights any given decision maker would use may differ from those applied in the analysis (Karoly, 2012).

> CONCLUSION: *Acknowledging equity concerns can enhance the quality and usefulness of economic evaluations. Presenting results disaggregated by key stakeholder groups provides one way of demonstrating the distributional consequences of an intervention (e.g., the costs and benefits for intervention participants versus the rest of society or for relevant subgroups of intervention participants). Applying distributional weights is a more controversial approach but one that can be informative, especially in the context of sensitivity analyses.*

RECOMMENDATIONS FOR BEST PRACTICES FOR PRODUCING AND REPORTING HIGH-QUALITY ECONOMIC EVIDENCE

"Regarding comparability, if you have a system where the studies are put in looking at everything in a comparable way, it is several orders of magnitude easier to do those kinds of comparisons."

—Dan Rosenbaum, senior economist, Economic Policy
Division, Office of Management and Budget,
in the committee's open session on March 23, 2015.

"One of the things that generates the most angst among ReadyNation members is that the estimates are all over the ballpark. One of the issues that we work on is early childhood education. What is the benefit for preschool: $7.00 for every $1.00; $14.00; $100.00? When members hear that, it makes them very suspicious. Having some standards around that is really important."

—Sandra Bishop-Josef, deputy director of
research, ReadyNation, in the committee's
open session on March 23, 2015.

"There is a need for some type of standardization when it comes to displaying information about the evidence, the costs, and the benefits, and then ultimately the economic evidence. We have seen that there are very limited standards for the documentation of evidence."
—Danielle Berfond, consultant, The Bridgespan Group,
in the committee's open session on June 1, 2015.

The purpose of this chapter has been to address issues involved in producing high-quality evidence from three major economic evaluation methods: CA, CEA, and BCA. The committee determined this focus was warranted because to truly inform and be useful for decisions about investing in interventions for children, youth, and families, evidence needs to be derived using the best available methods and practices for the question(s) at hand. The evidence also needs to be communicated in a way that supports its credibility and fosters its appropriate use by decision makers. Achieving each of these goals can be a challenge given the complexity of the methods and the multiple decisions entailed in carrying them out, as well as the inevitable uncertainty in the estimates produced. This section presents the committee's recommended best practices for producing high-quality economic evidence, drawing on the material presented in previous sections. It also offers recommended best practices for reporting the results of economic evaluations so as to achieve transparency, consistency, and usefulness to decision makers. Although this discussion is geared toward those producing economic evidence, it also should be helpful to consumers of the evidence, particularly with respect to assessing the quality and completeness of the evidence presented to them.

Recommended Best Practices for Producing High-Quality Economic Evidence

As the prior sections of this chapter should make clear, conducting an economic evaluation requires careful consideration of a number of assumptions, decisions, and possible practices to produce economic evidence that is of high quality. In broad terms, attention is needed to several different aspects of the evaluation, each of which was discussed earlier in this chapter: requirements for conducting and defining the scope of the evaluation; issues specific to evaluating intervention costs (relevant to CA, CEA, and BCA), determining intervention impacts (relevant to CEA and BCA), and valuing outcomes (relevant particularly to BCA); choices among several possible summary measures, depending on the method and the evaluation question(s); methods for handling uncertainty; and, where relevant, equity considerations.

The best practices identified by the committee are based on the material presented previously in this chapter and reflect a review of the existing literature, as well as the expert consensus views of the committee members. In many areas, the literature and committee members' consensus provide clear guidance on best practices. These practices are identified as "best practices for all economic evaluation methods" and as "core practices" for specific evaluation methods. Adopting these practices will help ensure the production of sound economic evidence, facilitate comparisons across different evaluations, and provide information that can help decision makers evaluate alternative investment options. However, the core practices will not fully resolve limits on study comparability because of the many possible sources of difference among interventions and economic evaluation methods and assumptions.

In other areas, the literature and committee members' views were not as clear-cut. Nonetheless, the committee concluded that several "advancing practices" could be identified for each method. Although not essential or even possible in every evaluation, these practices have the potential to improve the quality and utility of the evidence produced for some evaluation questions and investment decisions. Producers of economic evidence are encouraged to adopt these methods when possible.

Finally, it should be noted that the practices identified by the committee reflect the current state of economic evaluation methods. As the field moves forward, some of the advancing practices listed are likely to become core practices, and additional best practices will undoubtedly be identified.

RECOMMENDATION 1: In support of high-quality economic evaluations, producers[29] of economic evidence should follow the best practices delineated in the checklist below for conducting cost analyses (CAs), cost-effectiveness analyses (CEAs), benefit-cost analyses (BCAs), and related methods. Producers should follow the core practices listed and, where feasible and applicable, the advancing practices as well. Consumers of economic evidence should use these recommended best practices to assess the quality of the economic evidence available to inform the investment decisions they are seeking to make.

---

[29] Chapter 2 identifies in detail the producers of economic evidence.

Checklist of
Best Practices for Producing High-Quality Economic Evidence

For All Economic Evaluation Methods, Report the Following:

— Specify the intervention for the economic evaluation, including a description of the intervention's purpose, its intended recipients, the intensity and duration of services provided, the approach to implementation, the causal mechanisms, and the intended impact(s).

— Specify the context in which the intervention was or will be implemented, such as characteristics of the population served; the time, place, and scale of implementation; and other relevant contextual factors.

— Specify the counterfactual condition, including whether the alternative is no intervention, an alternative intervention, or business as usual. In the case of cost-effectiveness analysis (CEA) and benefit-cost analysis (BCA), ensure that the same counterfactual applies to the cost analysis (CA) and the impacts used for the CEA or BCA.

— Determine the scope of the economic evaluation, including the type of method to be used and the perspective (and any subperspectives) for the analysis; if the societal perspective is not adopted, discuss limitations of the evidence and/or generate results from the societal perspective in a sensitivity analysis.

— Determine the currency and reference year for all monetary values.

— If new taxes will be used to fund the intervention, determine the assumed deadweight loss parameter. If a 0 percent rate is selected (i.e., no deadweight loss), generate results in a sensitivity analysis using loss parameters greater than 0 when accounting for new revenue required to pay for an intervention or for impacts on taxes paid or transfer payments.

— Determine the time horizon for the analysis, and when costs or outcomes accrue over multiple years, the base case discount rate and age or point in time to which to discount (e.g., start of the intervention or a standardized child age). If a 3 percent discount rate is not selected, generate results using a 3 percent discount rate in a sensitivity analysis.

— Determine the method for addressing uncertainty, and apply it to generate standard errors and confidence intervals for all summary measures, such as estimates of total (present-discounted-value [PDV]) costs, total (PDV) benefits, net (PDV) benefits, cost-effectiveness and benefit-cost ratios, and internal rate of return.

— Employ sensitivity analyses to test the robustness of estimates under a variety of assumptions, including alternative discount rates, deadweight loss parameters, and estimates of the societal perspective if not the main perspective.
— Determine whether equity issues need to be addressed.
— Follow the reporting guidelines on the checklist for best practices for reporting economic evidence below.

For CA

Core Practices:
— Value all resources needed to implement the intervention, including infrastructure needs.
— Use shadow prices to derive an accurate estimate of the value of a resource when a market price is not available.
— Allocate overhead costs based on use.
— Annuitize capital investments.
— Calculate total costs and cost components: fixed, variable, and marginal costs.
— Calculate unit costs (e.g., cost per participant) to facilitate implementation and replication.

Advancing Practices (all core practices plus the following):
— Prospectively plan for cost analyses to be integrated into program evaluation.
— Use micro costing procedures whenever possible to improve the quality of intervention cost estimates and facilitate implementation and replication.
— Define major intervention activities and identify costs associated with each, including who bears those costs.
— Estimate costs for intervention planning, development, and adoption separately from those for intervention implementation.
— Use Monte Carlo methods to evaluate simultaneously the implications of multiple sources of uncertainty.
— Develop or modify budgetary and other management information systems to include relevant cost categories.

For CEA and Related Methods (in addition to best practices for CA)

Core Practices:
— Determine an explicit rationale for including intervention impacts

in the CEA and selecting the focal impact that will not be valued in the monetary unit. All included impacts should be attributable to the intervention's theory of change. When available and relevant to the evaluation question(s), use information from well-conducted systematic reviews and/or meta-analyses to inform intervention impact estimates.

— Determine whether the CEA will use a quality-of-life measure (e.g., quality-adjusted life years [QALYs], disability-adjusted life years [DALYs]) as the focal impact and what method will be used for scoring that measure.

— Determine whether the CEA will be limited to direct, observable economic impacts, or linked or projected impacts also will be included.

— For impacts valued in the monetary unit (if any), use willingness-to-pay methods to calculate their prices. This may mean using a combination of market prices and shadow prices.

— Calculate the average cost-effectiveness ratio and, where feasible, the incremental cost-effectiveness ratio.

Advancing Practices (all core practices plus the following):

— Conduct CEA only when an intervention has been evaluated using research designs that can produce unbiased causal estimates of impact.

— Conduct CEA from a societal perspective to produce the most comprehensive economic estimates.

— Link or project observed outcomes only when strong causal evidence of the assumed relationship exists.

— Estimate costs and benefits separately by perspective (e.g., participant, agency, government, other beneficiary) and by category (e.g., income, crime, health care).

— Use Monte Carlo methods to evaluate simultaneously the implications of multiple sources of uncertainty.

For BCA and Related Methods (in addition to best practices for CA)

Core Practices:

— Determine an explicit rationale for including intervention impacts in the BCA. All included impacts should be attributable to the intervention's theory of change. When available and relevant to the evaluation question(s), use information from well-conducted systematic reviews and/or meta-analyses to inform intervention impact estimates.

— Determine whether the BCA will be limited to direct, observable economic impacts, or linked or projected impacts also will be included.
— Determine whether the BCA will include intangible as well as tangible economic impacts.
— Use willingness-to-pay methods to calculate prices for impacts. This may mean using a combination of market and shadow prices.
— Estimate linked or projected economic impacts using the strongest available theoretical and empirical literature. When available, use information from well-conducted systematic reviews and/or meta-analyses to inform estimates used for linking and projections.
— Calculate PDV costs, benefits, and net benefits (total and unit). Where relevant, also calculate benefit-cost ratio, return on investment, and internal rate of return.
— When there is concern that impact estimates may be biased (e.g., nonexperimental design, quasi-experimental design), test the robustness of findings to variation in effect size.

Advancing Practices (all core practices plus the following):
— Conduct BCA only when an intervention has been evaluated using research designs that can produce unbiased causal estimates of impact.
— Conduct BCA from a societal perspective to produce the most comprehensive economic estimates.
— Link or project observed outcomes only when strong causal evidence of the assumed relationship exists.
— Generate tangible and intangible values separately.
— Estimate costs and benefits separately by perspective (e.g., participant, agency, government, other beneficiary) and by category (e.g., income, crime, health care).
— Use Monte Carlo methods to evaluate simultaneously the implications of multiple sources of uncertainty.

Recommended Best Practices for Reporting Economic Evidence

How the results of an economic evaluation are reported can greatly influence the credibility of the findings and the usefulness of the evidence for the target audience. Throughout this chapter, in the discussion of methods for producing high-quality economic evidence, it has been noted that best practice also dictates reporting the evidence in a comprehensive and transparent manner. Recommendation 2 includes best practices for reporting the results of economic evaluations. As in the best practices under Recommendation 1, those practices listed first are appropriate regardless of the economic evaluation method employed, while those listed subsequently are specific to CA, CEA, and BCA.

Adopting these reporting practices will ensure that information about the methods and findings of an economic evaluation is made available in a thorough and consistent manner, and that issues pertinent to assessing the internal and external validity of the findings, as well as the comparability of findings across different studies, are conveyed. To avoid overwhelming users with analytic details that could obscure the bottom line, it may be helpful to prepare a brief summary report along with a separate technical appendix detailing assumptions and methods. Producing clear and comprehensive reports will strengthen the credibility of the evidence derived from economic evaluation for users and facilitate its appropriate use by decision makers.

RECOMMENDATION 2: In support of high-quality and useful economic evaluations of interventions for children, youth, and families, producers of economic evidence should follow the best practices delineated in the checklist below for reporting the results of cost analyses, cost-effectiveness analyses, and benefit-cost analyses, and related methods.

Checklist of
Best Practices for Reporting Economic Evidence

For All Economic Evaluation Methods, Report the Following:

— The features of the intervention analyzed (e.g., logic model, intended recipients, intensity and duration of services, implementation, and other intervention features)
— The context in which the intervention was or will be implemented (e.g., population served; time, place, and scale of operation)
— The counterfactual (baseline or status quo) with which the intervention is compared
— The perspective for the analysis and any subperspectives examined, with associated results
— The currency and reference year for all monetary values
— The assumed deadweight loss parameter, if one was used
— The horizon for measuring economic values and, when discounting is used, the discount rate and time (or age) to which discounted
— Summary measures of the economic evaluation results (see below for each specific method)
— When relevant, results disaggregated by stakeholder
— The approach for addressing uncertainty, details on how the method was implemented, and the associated standard errors or confidence intervals for all summary measures
— Sensitivity analyses performed and associated results*
— When relevant, any equity considerations

For CEA, BCA, and Related Methods That Employ Impact Estimates Also Report:

— The evaluation method, the intervention impacts* and their statistical significance,* potential biases in estimates of causal effects, and any adjustments to estimated intervention impacts
— All limitations resulting from the strength of the evidence of causal intervention impacts

In Addition to the Elements for All Methods, for CA and the CA Component of a CEA or BCA Also Report:

— The costing method (e.g., micro costing)
— The inventory of resources used and those that are valued versus not valued in the CA

— The method for obtaining information on how much of each resource is used, any related assumptions made, and how much of each resource is used
— The method for obtaining unit costs, prices, or shadow prices for each type of resource; any related assumptions made; and the resulting values*

CA Results
— Total costs and unit cost (e.g., cost per participant)
— Fixed, variable, and marginal costs
— The implications of methods (e.g., omission of resources, prices applied) for under- or overestimating intervention costs

In Addition to the Elements for All Methods and for CA, for a CEA Also Report:

— Which impacts measured in the evaluation are valued in the CEA and which are not*
— Which impacts are observed versus linked or projected, for whom they are linked or projected, and the linking or projection method
— For the impacts valued in the monetary unit (if any), the prices used,* their derivation, and the geographic or jurisdictional boundary to which the valuations apply*
— If the focal impact is a quality-of-life measure (e.g., QALYs, DALYs), how that measure was scored

CEA Results
— The average cost-effectiveness ratio and, where feasible, the incremental cost-effectiveness ratio
— The implications of methods (e.g., omission of resources in CA, prices applied in CA, causal evidence on outcomes, linkages or projections of outcomes, valuation for outcomes) for under- or overestimating cost-effectiveness

In Addition to the Elements for All Methods and for CA, for a BCA Also Report:

— Which impacts measured in the evaluation are valued in the BCA and which are not*
— Which impacts are observed versus linked or projected, for whom they are linked or projected, and the linking or projection method

— For each impact valued, the price or shadow price used,* its derivation, and the geographic or jurisdictional boundary to which the valuation applies*

BCA Results
— PDV societal costs, benefits, and net benefits
— Benefit-cost ratio, return on investment, and/or internal rate of return
— The PDV benefits (or costs) of each outcome valued,* with disaggregation by outcomes observed versus projected and, where possible and relevant, by tangible versus intangible benefits (e.g., for crime or child abuse and neglect)
— The implications of methods (e.g., omission of resources in CA, prices applied in CA, causal evidence on outcomes, exclusion of outcomes, linkages or projections of outcomes, valuation for outcomes) for under- or overestimating intervention net benefits

NOTE: An asterisk denotes reporting that may be suitable for a table.

REFERENCES

Academy of Managed Care Pharmacy. (2012). *A Format for Submission of Clinical and Economic Evidence of Pharmaceuticals in Support of Formulary Consideration.* Alexandria, VA: Academy of Managed Care Pharmacy.

Agnihotri, K., Awasthi, S., Singh, U., Chandra, H., and Thakur, S. (2010a). A study of concordance between adolescent self-report and parent-proxy report of health-related quality of life in school-going adolescents. *Journal of Psychosomatic Research, 69*(6), 525-532.

Agnihotri, K., Awasthi, S., Chandra, H., Singh, U., and Thakur, S. (2010b). Validation of WHO QOL-BREF instrument in Indian adolescents. *The Indian Journal of Pediatrics, 77*(4), 381-386.

Alberini, A., and Ščasný, M. (2011). Context and the VSL: Evidence from a stated preference study in Italy and the Czech Republic. *Environmental and Resource Economics, 49*(4), 511-538.

Alberini, A., Loomes, G., Ščasný, M., and Bateman, I. (2010). *Valuation of Environment-Related Health Risks for Children.* Paris, France: OECD.

Al-Fayez, G.A., and Ohaeri, J.U. (2011). Profile of subjective quality of life and its correlates in a nationwide sample of high school students in an Arab setting using the WHOQOL-Bref. *BMC Psychiatry, 11*(71).

American Humane Association. (2009). Replicating the Family Connections Program: Lessons learned. *Protecting Children, 24*(3), 1-88.

Andrews, F.M., and Withey, S.B. (1976). *Social Indicators of Well-Being.* New York: Plenum Press.

Aos, S., Lieb, R., Mayfield, J., Miller, M., and Pennucci, A. (2004). *Benefits and Costs of Prevention and Early Intervention Programs for Youth.* Olympia: Washington State Institute for Public Policy.

Argyle, M. (2001). *The Psychology of Happiness.* New York: Taylor & Francis.

Arrow, K., Solow, R., Portney, P.R., Leamer, E.E., Radner, R., and Schuman, H. (1993). Report of the NOAA Panel on Contingent Valuation. *Federal Register, 58*(10), 4601-4614.

Austin, P.C. (2009). The relative ability of different propensity score methods to balance measured covariates between treated and untreated subjects in observational studies. *Medical Decision Making. 29(6),* 661-677.

Aziz, S.N., Boyle, K.J., and Crocker, T.D. (2007). *Valuation of Avoiding Arsenic in Drinking Water in Rural Bangladesh: An Averting Behavior Analysis* (Doctoral dissertation, Doctoral thesis, The University of Maine). Available: http://www.ncbi.nlm.nih.gov/pmc/articles/PMC4058837/pdf/fpubh-02-00057.pdf [March 2016].

Barnett, P.G. (2009). An improved set of standards for finding cost for cost-effectiveness analysis. *Medical Care, 47*(7, Suppl. 1), S82-S88.

Barton, B.K., and Schwebel, D.C. (2007). The roles of age, gender, inhibitory control, and parental supervision in children's pedestrian safety. *Journal of Pediatric Psychology, 32*(5), 517-526.

Bassok, D., Fitzpatrick, M., and Loeb, S. (2014). Does state preschool crowd-out private provision? The impact of universal preschool on the childcare sector in Oklahoma and Georgia. *Journal of Urban Economics, 83,* 18-33.

Basu, A., Heckman, J.J., Navarro-Lozano, S., and Urzua, S. (2007). Use of instrumental variables in the presence of heterogeneity and self-selection: An application to treatments of breast cancer patients. *Health Economics, 16(1),* 1133-1157.

Bateman, I.J., Carson, R.T., Day, B., Hanemann, M., Hanley, N., Hett, Jones-Lee, M., Loomes, G., Mourato, S., Ozedemiroglu, E., Pearce D.W., Sugden, R., and Swanson, J. (2002). *Economic Valuation with Stated Preference Techniques: A Manual.* Cheltenham, UK: Edward Elgar.

Belfield, C.R. (2014). Cost-benefit analysis and cost-effectiveness analysis. In H.F. Ladd and M.E. Goertz (Eds.), *Handbook of Research in Education Finance and Policy* (pp. 141-156). New York: Routledge.

Belfield, C.R., Nores, M., Barnett, S., and Schweinhart, L. (2006). The High/Scope Perry Preschool Program. *Journal of Human Resources, XLI*(1), 162-190.

Belfield, C.R., Bowden, B., Klapp, A., Levin, H., Shand, R., and Zander, S. (2015). *The Economic Value of Social and Emotional Learning.* Available: http://blogs.edweek.org/edweek/rulesforengagement/SEL-Revised.pdf [March 2016].

Benefit-Cost Analysis Center. (2012). *Federal Agency Benefit-Cost Analysis Principles and Standards for Social Programs.* Available: http://evans.uw.edu/sites/default/files/public/Federal_Agency_BCA_PS_Social_Programs.pdf [March 2016].

Bickel, P., and Rainer, F. (2005). *ExternE Externalities of Energy: Methodology 2005 Update.* Available: https://ec.europa.eu/research /energy/pdf/kina_en.pdf [February 2016].

Bitler, M.P. and Karoly L.A. (2015). Intended and unintended effects of the war on poverty: What research tells us and implications for policy. *Journal of Policy Analysis and Management, 34*(3), 639-696.

Blincoe, L.J., Miller T.R, Zaloshnja, E., and Lawrence, B.A. (2015). *The Economic Impact of Motor Vehicle Crashes, 2010.* Washington, DC: National Highway Traffic Safety Administration.

Blomquist, G.C. (2004). Self-protection and averting behavior, values of statistical lives, and benefit-cost analysis of environmental policy. *Review of Economics of the Household, 2(1),* 89-110.

Blomquist, G.C., Miller, T.R., and Levy, D.T. (1996). Values of risk reduction implied by motorist use of protection equipment: New evidence from different populations. *Journal of Transport Economics and Policy,* 55-66.

Blomquist, G.C., Dickie, M., and O'Conor, R.M. (2011). Willingness to pay for improving fatality risks and asthma symptoms: Values for children and adults of all ages. *Resource and Energy Economics 33(2)*, 410-435.

Bloom, H.S., Michalopoulos, C., and Hill, C.J. (2005). Using experiments to assess nonexperimental comparison-group methods for measuring program effects. In H.S. Bloom (Ed.), *Learning More from Social Experiments* (pp. 173-235). New York: Russell Sage Foundation.

Boardman, A.E., and Greenberg, D.H. (1998). Discounting and the social discount rate. In F. Thompson and M.T. Green (Eds.), *Handbook of Public Finance* (pp. 269-318). New York: Marcel Dekker.

Boardman, A.E., Greenberg, D.H., and Vining, A.R. (2011). *Cost-Benefit Analysis: Concepts and Practice*. Upper Saddle River, NJ: Prentice Hall.

Bosworth, R., Cameron, T.A., and DeShazo, J.R. (2010). Is an ounce of prevention worth a pound of cure? Comparing demand for public prevention and treatment policies. *Medical Decision Making, 30(4)*, E40-E56.

Bosworth, R., Cameron, T.A., and DeShazo, J.R. (2015). Willingness to pay for public health policies to treat illnesses. *Journal of Health Economics, 39*, 74-88.

Boxall, P.C., Adamowicz, W.L., Swait, J., Williams, M., and Louviere, J. (1996). A comparison of stated preference methods for environmental valuation. *Ecological Economics, 18(3)*, 243-253.

Brandt, S., Vásquez Lavín, F., and Hanemann, M. (2012). Contingent valuation scenarios for chronic illnesses: The case of childhood asthma. *Value in Health, 15(8)*, 1077-1083.

Bridges, J.F.P., Hauber, A.B., Marshall, D., Lloyd, A., Prosser, L.A., Regier, D.A., Johnson, F.R., and Mauskopf, J. (2011). Conjoint analysis applications in health—a checklist: A report of the ISPOR Good Research Practices for Conjoint Analysis Task Force. *Value in Health, 14(4)*, 403-413.

Brodowski, M.L., and Filene, J.H. (2009). Engaging program staff in economic evaluation: Lessons learned and recommendations for practice. *Protecting Children, 24(3)*, 70-77.

Brown, D.S., Johnson, F.R., Poulos, C., and Messonnier, M.L. (2010). Mothers' preferences and willingness to pay for vaccinating daughters against human papillomavirus. *Vaccine, 28(7)*, 1702-1708.

Brown, D.W., Kowalski, A.E., and Lurie, I.Z. (2015). *Medicaid as an investment in children: what is the long-term impact on tax receipts?* NBER Working Paper 20835. Cambridge, MA: National Bureau of Economic Research.

Calculating the Costs of Child Welfare Services Workgroup. (2013). *Cost Analysis in Program Evaluation: A Guide for Child Welfare Researchers and Service Providers*. Washington, DC: Children's Bureau, Administration for Children and Families, U.S. Department of Health and Human Services. Available: http://www.acf.hhs.gov/sites/default/files/cb/cost_analysis_guide.pdf [March 2016].

Capri, S., Ceci, A., Terranova, L., Merlo, F., and Mantovani, L. (2001). Guidelines for economic evaluations in Italy: Recommendations from the Italian Group of Pharmacoeconomic Studies. *Therapeutic Innovation & Regulatory Science, 35(1)*, 189-201.

Centers for Disease Control and Prevention. (2010). *Healthier Worksite Initiative: Logic Model*. Available: http://www.cdc.gov/nccdphp/dnpao/hwi/programdesign/logic_model.htm [July 2015].

Chatterji, P., Caffray, C.M., Jones, A.S., Lillie-Blanton, M., and Werthamer, L. (2001). Applying cost analysis methods to school-based prevention programs. *Prevention Science, 2(1)*, 45-55.

Chau, K., Baumann, M., Kabuth, B., and Chau, N. (2012). School difficulties in immigrant adolescent students and roles of socioeconomic factors, unhealthy behaviours, and physical and mental health. *BMC Public Health, 12(453)*.

Cisler, R., Holder, H.D., Longabaugh, R., Stout, R.L., and Zweben, A. (1998). Actual and estimated replication costs for alcohol treatment modalities: Case study from Project MATCH. *Journal of Studies on Alcohol and Drugs, 59*(5), 503-512.

Cohen, M.A., Rust, R.T., Steen, S., and Tidd, S.T. (2004). Willingness-to-pay for crime control programs. *Criminology, 42*(1), 89-110.

Cohodes, S., Grossman, D., Kleiner, S., and Lovenheim, M.F. (2014). *Effect of Child Health Insurance Access on Schooling.* Working Paper 20178. Cambridge, MA: National Bureau of Economic Research.

Commonwealth of Australia. (2006). *Handbook of Cost-Benefit Analysis.* Australia: Commonwealth of Australia Department of Finance and Administration, Financial Management Group. Available: http://www.finance.gov.au/sites/default/files/Handbook_of_CB_analysis.pdf [March 2016].

Connelly, R., Degraff, D.S., and Willis, R.A. (2004). The value of employer-sponsored child care to employees. *Industrial Relations, 43*(4), 759-792.

Cook, T.D., and Campbell, D.T. (1979). *Quasi-Experimentation: Design and Analysis Issues for Field Settings.* Boston, MA: Houghton Mifflin.

Cook, T.D., and Payne, M.R. (2002). Objecting to the objections to using random assignment in educational research. *Evidence Matters: Randomized Trials in Education Research,* 150-178.

Cook, T.D., Shadish, W.R., and Wong, V.C. (2008). Three conditions under which experiments and observational studies produce comparable causal estimates: New findings from within-study comparisons. *Journal of Policy Analysis and Management, 27*(4), 724-750.

Cookson, R. (2015). *Methods for Incorporating Equity into Economic Evaluation of Social Investments.* Commissioned paper for the Committee on the Use of Economic Evidence to Inform Investments in Children, Youth, and Families. Available: http://sites.nationalacademies.org/cs/groups/dbassesite/documents/webpage/dbasse_171854.pdf [June 2016].

Corso, P.S., Mercy, J., Simon, T., Finkelstein, E., and Miller, T. (2007). Medical costs and productivity losses due to interpersonal and self-directed violence in the United States. *American Journal of Preventive Medicine, 32*(6), 474-482.

Corso, P.S., Fang, X., and Mercy, J.A. (2011). Benefits of preventing a death associated with child maltreatment: Evidence from willingness-to-pay survey data. *American Journal of Public Health, 101*(3), 487-490.

Corso, P.S., Ingels, J., and Roldos, M. (2013). A comparison of willingness to pay to prevent child maltreatment deaths in Ecuador and the United States. *International Journal of Environmental Research and Public Health, 10*(4), 1342-1355.

Cowen, T., and Parfit, D. (1992). Against the social discount rate. In P. Laslett and J. Fishkin (Eds.), *Philosophy, Politics, and Society* (pp. 144-161). New Haven, CT: Yale University Press.

Crowley, D.M., Jones, D.E., Greenberg, M.T., Feinberg, M.E., and Spoth, R.L. (2012). Resource consumption of a diffusion model for prevention programs: The PROSPER delivery system. *Journal of Adolescent Health, 50*(3), 256-263.

Crowley, D.M., Hill, L. G., Kuklinski, M.R., and Jones, D.E. (2014). Research priorities for economic analyses of prevention: Current issues and future directions. *Prevention Science, 15*(6), 789-798.

Cruz, M.L.S., Cardoso, C.A.A., Darmont, M.Q., Souza, E., Andrade, S.D., D'al Fabbro, M.M., Fonseca, R., Bellido, J.G., Monteiro, S.S., and Bastos, F.I. (2014). Viral suppression and adherence among HIV-infected children and adolescents on antiretroviral therapy: Results of a multicenter study. *Jornal de Pediatria, 90*(6), 563-571.

Cutler, D.M., and Richardson, E. (1998). The value of health: 1970-1990. *American Economic Review, 88*(2), 97-100.

Derzon, J.H., Miller, T., and Zaloshnja, E. (2005). *Recommended Cost Bands for Substance Abuse Prevention*. Calverton, MD: Pacific Institute for Research and Evaluation.

Detsky, A.S., and Naglie, I.G. (1990). A clinician's guide to cost-effectiveness analysis. *Annals of Internal Medicine, 113*(2), 147-154.

Dickie, M., and Gerking, S. (2002). *Willingness to Pay for Reduced Morbidity*. Presentation at the workshop Economic Valuation of Health for Environmental Policy: Assessing Alternative Approaches, March, 18-19, Orlando, FL.

Dickie, M., and Gerking, S. (2009). Family behavior: Implications for health benefits transfer from adults to children. *Environmental and Resource Economics, 43(1)*, 31-43.

Dickie, M., and Messman, V.L. (2004) Parental altruism and the value of avoiding acute illness: are kids worth more than parents? *Journal of Environmental Economics and Management, 48(3)*, 1146-1174.

Dickie, M., and Ulery, V.L. (2001, June). Valuing health in the household: Are kids worth more than parents? *Association of Environmental and Resource Economists 2001 Workshop: Assessing and Managing Environmental and Public Health Risks*, 13-15.

Diener, E., and Oishi, S. (2005). The nonobvious social psychology of happiness. *Psychological Inquiry, 16*(4), 162-167.

Diener, E., Suh, E.M., Lucas, R.E., Smith, H.E. (1999). Subjective well-being: Three decades of progress. *Psychological Bulletin, 125*(2), 276-302.

Donaldson, S.I., Christie, C.A., and Mark, M.M. (2008). *What Counts as Credible Evidence in Applied Research and Evaluation?* London: Sage. Available: http://cgu.edu/PDFFiles/sbos/Donaldson_Credible_Evidence_Epilogue.pdf [March 2016].

Dréze, J.H. (1964). Some postwar contributions of French economists to theory and public policy: With special emphasis on problems of resource allocation. *Amercian Economic Review, 54*(4), 2-64.

Drummond, M.F., and Jefferson, T.O. (1996). Guidelines for authors and peer reviewers of economic submissions to the BMJ. *British Medical Journal, 313*(7052), 275-283.

Drummond, M.F., and Sculpher, M. (2005). Common methodological flaws in economic evaluations. *Medical Care, 43*(Suppl. 7), II-5-II-14.

Drummond, M.F., Sculpher, M.J., Torrance, G.W., O'Brien, B.J., and Stoddart, G.L. (2005). *Methods for the Economic Evaluation of Health Care Programmes*. New York: Oxford University Press.

Escobar, C.M., Barnett, W.S., and Keith, J.E. (1988). A contingent valuation approach to measuring the benefits of preschool education. *Educational Evaluation and Policy Analysis, 10*(1), 13-22.

European Commission. (2008). *Guide to Cost-Benefit Analysis of Investment Projects: Structural Funds, Cohesion Fund and Instrument for Pre-Accession*. Available: http://ec.europa.eu/regional_policy/sources/docgener/guides/cost/guide2008_en.pdf [February 2016].

European Regional Development Fund. (2013). *Guidance Manual for Cost Benefit Analysis Appraisal in Malta*. Malta: Parliamentary Secretariat for the EU Presidency 2017.

Fanshel, S., and Bush, J.W. (1970). A health-status index and its application to health-services outcomes. *Operations Research, 18*(6), 1021-1066.

Farrow, S., and Zerbe, R.O. (Eds.). (2013). *Principles and Standards for Benefit-Cost Analysis*. Cheltenham, UK: Edward Elgar.

Federal Accounting Standards Advisory Board. (2014). *FASAB Handbook of Federal Accounting Standards and Other Pronouncements, as Amended*. Washington, DC: Federal Accounting Standards Advisory Board.

Fisher, C.B., Hoagwood, K., Boyce, C., Duster, T., Frank, D.A., Grisso, T., Levine, R.J., Macklin, R., Spencer, M.B., Takanishi, R., Trimble, J.E., and Zayas, L.H. (2002). Research ethics for mental health science involving ethnic minority children and youths. *American Psychologist, 57*(12), 1024-1040.

Foster, E.M., Dodge, K.A., and Jones, D. (2003). Issues in the economic evaluation of prevention programs. *Applied Developmental Science, 7*(2), 76-86.

Foster, E.M., Porter, M.M., Ayers, T.S., Kaplan, D.L., and Sandler, I. (2007). Estimating the costs of preventive interventions. *Evaluation Review, 31*(3), 261-286.

Gayer, T., Hamilton, J.T., and Viscusi, W.K. (2002). The market value of reducing cancer risk: Hedonic housing prices with changing information. *Southern Economic Journal, 69*(2), 266-289.

Gentilello, L.M., Ebel, B.E., Wickizer, T.M., Salkever, D.S., and Rivara, F.P. (2005). Alcohol interventions for trauma patients treated in emergency departments and hospitals: A cost-benefit analysis. *Annals of Surgery, 241*(4), 541-550.

Gerber, A.S., Greena, D.P., and Carnegie, A.J. (2013). Evaluating public health law using randomized experiments. In A.C. Wagenaar and S.C. Burris (Eds.), *Public Health Law Research: Theory and Methods* (pp. 283-305). Somerset, NJ: Wiley.

Gill, A.M., Dishion, T.J., and Shaw, D.S. (2014). The family check-up. In *Wellbeing: A Complete Reference Guide* (pp. 1-21). Hoboken, NJ: Wiley-Blackwell.

Gold, M.R., Siegel, J.E., Russell, L.B., and Weinstein, M.C. (Eds.). (1996). *Cost-Effectiveness in Health and Medicine.* New York: Oxford University Press.

Gogtay, N., Giedd, J.N., Lusk, L., Hayashi, K.M., Greenstein, D., Vaituzis, A.C., Nugent, T.F., Herman, D.H., Clase, L.S., Toga, A.W., and Rapoport, J.L. (2004). Dynamic mapping of human cortical development during childhood through early adulthood. *Proceedings of the National Academy of Sciences, 101*(21), 8174-8179.

Gottfredson, D.C., Cook, T.D., Gardner, F.E.M., Gorman-Smith, D., Howe, G.W., Sandler, I.N., and Zafft, K.M. (2015). Standards of evidence for efficacy, effectiveness, and scale-up research in prevention science: Next generation. *Prevention Science, 16*(7), 893-926.

Graf von der Schulenburg, J.M., and Hoffmann, C. (2000). Review of European guidelines for economic evaluation of medical technologies and pharmaceuticals. *Health Economics in Prevention and Care, 1*(1), 2-8.

Gray, A.M., Rivero-Arias, O., and Clarke, P. (2006). Estimating the association between SF-12 responses and EQ-5D utility values by response mapping. *Medical Decision Making, 26*(1), 18-29.

Gray, A.M., Clarke, P.M., Wolstenholme, J.L., and Wordsworth, S. (2010). *Applied Methods of Cost-Effectiveness Analysis in Healthcare.* New York: Oxford University Press.

Greenberg, D.H., and Appenzeller, U. (1998). *Cost Analysis Step by Step: A How-to Guide for Planners and Providers of Welfare-to-Work and Other Employment and Training Programs.* New York: Manpower Demonstration Research Corporation.

Gyrd-Hanson, D. (2003). Willingness to pay for a QALY. *Health Economics, 12*(12), 1049-1060.

Haddix, A.C., Teutsch, S.M., and Corso, P.S. (2003). *Prevention Effectiveness: A Guide to Decision Analysis and Economic Evaluation.* New York: Oxford University Press.

Hammitt, J.K. (2007). Valuing changes in mortality risk: Lives saved versus life years saved. *Review of Environmental Economics and Policy, 1*(2), 228-240.

Hammitt, J.K., and Haninger, K. (2010). Valuing fatal risks to children and adults: Effects of disease, latency, and risk aversion. *Journal of Risk and Uncertainty, 40*(1), 57-83.

Hanemann, W.M. (1994). Valuing the environment through contingent valuation. *Journal of Economic Perspectives*, 19-43.

Haninger, K., and Hammitt, J.K. (2011). Diminishing willingness to pay per quality-adjusted life year: Valuing acute foodborne illness. *Risk Analysis, 31*(9), 1363-1380.

Harris, A.H., Hill, S.R., Chin, G., Li, J.J., and Walkom, E. (2008). The role of value for money in public insurance coverage decisions for drugs in Australia: A retrospective analysis 1994-2004. *Medical Decision Making, 28*(5), 713-722.

Hausman, J. (2012). Contingent valuation: From dubious to hopeless. *Journal of Economic Perspectives, 26*(4), 43-56.

Haute Autorité de Santé. (2012). *Choices in Methods for Economic Evaluation.* Saint-Denis La Plaine, France: Department of Economics and Public Health Assessment, Haute Autorité de Santé.

Hawkins, J.D., Catalano, R.F., and Kuklinski, M.R. (2014). Communities that care. *Encyclopedia of Criminology and Criminal Justice,* 393-408.

Heckman, J.J., Moon, S.H., Pinto, R., Savelyev, P., and Yavitz, A. (2010). *A New Cost-Benefit and Rate of Return Analysis for the Perry Preschool Program: A Summary.* NBER Working Paper 16180. Cambridge, MA: National Bureau of Economic Research.

Heckman, J.J., Humphries, J.E., Veramendi, G., and Urzua, S. (2014). *Education, Health and Wages.* Cambridge, MA: National Bureau of Economic Research.

Hendrie, D. (2013). *Economic Analysis of Health Sponsorship in Australia.* Unpublished Doctoral Thesis.

Her Majesty's Treasury. (2003). *The Green Book: Appraisal and Evaluation in Central Government: Treasury Guidance.* London, UK: Stationery Office.

Hibbs, E.D., Clarke, G., Hechtman, L., and Abikoff, H.B. (1997). Manual development for the treatment of child and adolescent disorders. *Psychopharmacology Bulletin, 33*(4), 619.

Hjelmgren, J., Berggren, F., and Andersson, F. (2001). Health economic guidelines—similarities, differences and some implications. *Value in Health, 4*(3), 225-250.

Honeycutt, A., Clayton, L., Khavjou, O., Finkelstein, E., Prabhu, M., Blitstein, J., Evans, W., and Renaud, J. (2006). *Guide to Analyzing the Cost-Effectiveness of Community Public Health Prevention Approaches.* Available: http://aspe.hhs.gov/pdf-report/guide-analyzing-cost-effectiveness-community-public-health-prevention-approaches [June 2016].

Hunink, M.G.M., Glasziou, P.P., Siegel, J.E., Weeks, J.C., Pliskin, J.S., Elstein, A.S., and Weinstein, M.C. (2001). *Decision Making in Health and Medicine.* Cambridge, UK: Cambridge University Press.

Institute for Quality and Efficiency in Health Care. (2009). *General Methods for the Assessment of the Relation of Benefits to Costs.* Cologne, Italy: Institute for Quality and Efficiency in Health Care.

Institute of Medicine. (2006). *Valuing Health for Regulatory Cost-Effectiveness Analysis.* W. Miller, L.A. Robinson, and R.S. Lawrence (Eds.). Committee to Evaluate Measures of Health Benefits for Environmental, Health, and Safety Regulation; Board on Health Care Services. Washington, DC: The National Academies Press.

Institute of Medicine and National Research Council. (2014). *Considerations in Applying Benefit-Cost Analysis to Preventive Interventions for Children, Youth, and Families.* S. Olson and K. Bogard (Rapporteurs). Board on Children, Youth, and Families. Washington, DC: The National Academies Press.

Islam, Z., Maskery, B., Nyamete, A., Horowitz, M.S., Yunus, M., and Whittington, D. (2008). Private demand for cholera vaccines in rural Matlab, Bangladesh. *Health Policy, 85*(2), 184-195.

Izutsu, T., Tsutsumi, A., Islam, M., Matsuo, Y., Yamada, H., Kurita, H., and Wakai, S. (2005). Validity and reliability of the Bangla version of WHOQOL-BREF on an adolescent population in Bangladesh. *Quality of Life Research, 14*(7), 1783-1789.

Jamison, D.T., Breman, J.G., Measham, A.R., Alleyne, G., Claeson, M., Evans, D.B., Jha, P., Mills, A., and Musgrove, P. (2006). *Priorities in Health.* Washington, DC: The International Bank for Reconstruction and Development/The World Bank Group.

Jarahi, L., Karbakhsh, M., and Rashidian, A. (2011). Parental willingness to pay for child safety seats in Mashad, Iran. *BMC Public Health, 11*(1), 281.

Jenkins, N.R., Owens, N., and Wiggins, E. (2001). Valuing reduced risks to children: The case of bicycle safety helmets. *Contemporary Economic Issues, 19*(4), 397-408.

Jirojanakul, P., and Skevington, S. (2000). Developing a quality-of-life measure for children aged 5-8 years. *British Journal of Health Psychology, 5*(3), 299-321.

Johannesson, M., and Johansson P.-O. (1997). Is the valuation of a QALY gained independent of age? Some empirical evidence. *Journal of Health Economics, 16*(5), 589-599.

Johnson, F.R., Lancsar, E., Marshall, D., Kilambi, V., Mühlbacher, A., Regier, D.A., Bresnahan, B.W., Kanninen, B., and Bridges, J.F.P. (2013). Constructing experimental designs for discrete-choice experiments: Report of the ISPOR Conjoint Analysis Experimental Design Good Research Practices Task Force. *Value in Health, 16*(1), 3-13.

Joint United Nations Programme on HIV/AIDS. (2000). *Costing Guidelines for HIV Prevention Strategies.* Available: http://data.unaids.org/Publications/IRC-pub05/jc412-cost guidel_en.pdf [March 2016].

Jones, A.M., and Rice, N. (2011). Econometric evaluation of health policies. In S. Glied and P.C. Smith (Eds.), *The Oxford Handbooks of Health Economics.* Oxford, UK: Oxford University Press.

Karoly, L.A. (2008). *Valuing Benefits in Benefit-Cost Studies of Social Programs.* Technical Report. Santa Monica, CA: RAND.

Karoly, L.A. (2012). Toward standardization of benefit-cost analysis of early childhood interventions. *Journal of Benefit-Cost Analysis, 3*(1).

Keeler, E.B., and Cretin, S. (1983). Discounting of life-saving and other nonmonetary effects. *Management Science, 29*(3), 300-306.

Kessler, R.C., Pecora, P.J., Williams, J., Hiripi, E., O'Brien, K., English, D., White, J., Zerbe, R., Downs, A.C., Plotnick, R., Hwang, I., and Sampson, N.A. (2008). Effects of enhanced foster care on the long-term physical and mental health of foster care alumni. *Archives of General Psychiatry, 65*(6), 625.

Kochi, I., and Taylor, L. (2011). Risk heterogeneity and the value of reducing fatal risks: Further market-based evidence. *Journal of Benefit-Cost Analysis, 2*(3), Article 1.

Kuklinski, M.R., Fagan, A.A., Hawkins, J.D., Briney, J.S., and Catalano, R.F. (2015). Benefit-cost analysis of a randomized evaluation of communities that care: Monetizing intervention effects on the initiation of delinquency and substance use through grade 12. *Journal of Experimental Criminology, 11*(2), 165-192.

Laupacis, A., Feeny, D., Detsky, A.S., and Tugwell, P.X. (1992). How attractive does a new technology have to be to warrant adoption and utilization? Tentative guidelines for using clinical and economic evaluations. *Canadian Medical Association Journal, 146*(4), 473-481.

Lee, S., and Aos, S. (2011). Using cost-benefit analysis to understand the value of social interventions. *Research on Social Work Practice, 21*(6), 682-688.

Leonard, B. (2009). *GAO Cost Estimating and Assessment Guide: Best Practices for Developing and Managing Capital Program Costs.* Collingdale, PA: Diane.

Leung, J., and Guria, J. (2006). Value of statistical life: Adults versus children. *Accident Analysis and Prevention, 38*(6), 1208-1217.

Levin, H.M., and Belfield, C. (2013). *Guiding the Development and Use of Cost-Effectiveness Analysis in Education.* New York: Center for Benefit-Cost Studies of Education, Columbia University. Available: http://cbcse.org/wordpress/wp-content/uploads/2013/08/Guiding-the-Development-And-Use-of-Cost-effectiveness-Analysis-in-Education.pdf [February 2016].

Levin, H.M., and McEwan, P.J. (2001). *Cost-Effectiveness Analysis* (2nd Edition). Thousand Oaks, CA: Sage.

Lindhjem, H., Navrud, S., Braathen, N.A., and Biausque, V. (2011). Valuing mortality risk reductions from environmental, transport, and health policies: A global meta-analysis of stated preference studies. *Risk Analysis, 31*(9), 1381-1407.

Liu, J.-T., Hammitt, J.K., Wang, J.-D., and Liu, J.-L. (2000). Mother's willingness to pay for her own and her child's health: A contingent valuation study in Taiwan. *Health Economics, 9*(4), 319-326.

Loureiro, M.L., and Umberger, W.J. (2007). A choice experiment model for beef: What U.S. consumer responses tell us about relative preferences for food safety, country-of-origin labeling, and traceability. *Food Policy, 32*(4), 496-514.

Lucas, R.E., Clark, A.E., Georgellis. Y., and Diener, E. (2004). Unemployment alters the set point for life satisfaction. *Psychologial Science, 15*(1), 8-13.

Luce, B.R., Manning, W.G., Siegel, J.E., and Lipscomb, J. (1996). Estimating costs in cost-effectiveness analysis. In M. Gold, M. Weinstein, J. Siegel, M. Kamlet, and L. Russell (Eds.), *Cost-Effectiveness in Health and Medicine* (pp. 176-213). New York: Oxford University Press.

Ludwig, J., and Cook, P.J. (2001). The benefits of reducing gun violence: Evidence from contingent-valuation survey data. *Journal of Risk and Uncertainty, 22*(3), 207-226.

Magnuson, K.A., Ruhm, C., and Waldfogel, J. (2007). The persistence of preschool effects: Do subsequent classroom experiences matter? *Early Childhood Research Quarterly, 22(1)*, 18-38.

Mansley, E.C., Duñet, D.O., May, D.S., Chattopadhyay, S.K., and McKenna, M.T. (2002). Variation in average costs among federally sponsored state-organized cancer detection programs: Economies of scale? *Medical Decision Making, 22*(5), S67-S79.

Marshall, D.A., and Hux, M. (2009). Design and analysis issues for economic analysis alongside clinical trials. *Medical Care, 47*(7, Suppl. 1), S14-S20.

Maynard, R.A., and Hoffman, S.D. (2008) The costs of adolescent childbearing. In R.A. Maynard and S.D. Hoffman (Eds.) *Kids Having Kids: Economic Costs and Social Consequences of Teen Pregnancy* (2nd Edition). Washington, DC: Urban Institute Press.

McDowell, I. (2006). *Measuring Health* (3rd Edition). New York: Oxford University Press.

Meckley, L.M., Greenberg, D., Cohen, J.T., and Neumann, P.J. (2010). The adoption of cost-effectiveness acceptability curves in cost-utility analyses. *Medical Decision Making, 30*(3), 314-319.

Messonnier, M., and Meltzer, M. (2003). Cost-benefit analysis. In A.C. Haddix, S.M. Teutsch, and P.S. Corso (Eds.), *Prevention Effectiveness: A Guide to Decision Analysis and Economic Evaluation* (2nd Edition). New York: Oxford University Press.

Miller, S., and Wherry, L. (2014). *The Long-Term Health Effects of Early Life Medicaid Coverage*. Working paper. Available: http://www-personal.umich.edu/~mille/millerwherry_prenatal2014.pdf [March 2016].

Miller, T.R. (1990). The plausible range for the value of life—Red herrings among the mackerel. *Journal of Forensic Economics, 3*(3), 17-39.

Miller, T.R. (2000). Valuing non-fatal quality of life losses with quality-adjusted life years: The health economist's meow. *Journal of Forensic Economics, 13*(2), 145-168.

Miller, T.R. (2015). Projected outcomes of Nurse-Family Partnership home visitation during 1996-2013, USA. *Prevention Science, 16*(6), 765-777.

Miller, T.R., and Hendrie, D.V. (2012). *Economic Evaluation of Public Health Laws and Their Enforcement*. Available: http://publichealthlawresearch.org/sites/default/files/downloads/resource/EconomicEvaluationPHL-Monograph-MillerHendrie2012.pdf [February 2016].

Miller, T.R., and Hendrie, D. (2013). Economic evaluation of public health laws and their enforcement. In A.C. Wagenaar and S.C. Burris (Eds.), *Public Health Law Research: Theory and Methods* (pp. 347-378). San Francisco, CA: Jossey-Bass.

Miller, T.R., and Hendrie, D.V. (2015). Nurse family partnership: Comparing costs per family in randomized trials versus scale-up. *The Journal of Primary Prevention, 36*(6), 419-425.

Miller, T.R., Calhoun, C., and Arthur, W.B. (1989). Utility-adjusted impairment years: A low-cost approach to morbidity valuation. In *Estimating and Valuing Morbidity in a Policy Context: Proceedings of June 1989 AERE Workshop*. EPA-230-08-89-065. Washington, DC: U.S. Environmental Protection Agency.

Miller, T.R., Fisher, D.A., and Cohen, M.A. (2001). Costs of juvenile violence: Policy implications. *Pediatrics, 107*(1), E3.

Miller, T.R., Levy, D.T., Cohen, M.A., and Cox, K.L. (2006). The costs of alcohol and drug-involved crime. *Prevention Science, 7*(4), 333-342.

Mitchell, R.C., and Carson, R.T. (1989). *Using Surveys to Value Public Goods: The Contingent Valuation Method*. Washington, DC: Resources for the Future.

Mortimer, D., and Segal L. (2008). Is the value of a life or life-year saved context specific? Further evidence from a discrete choice experiment. *Cost Effectiveness and Resource Allocation, 6*(8).

Mount, T., Weng, W., Schulze, W., and Chestnut, L. (2001, June). Automobile safety and the value of statistical life in the family: Valuing reduced risk for children, adults and the elderly. *Association of Environmental and Resource Economists Workshop*, Bar Harbor, Maine (Vol. 1315). Available: https://www.researchgate.net/publication/237278864_AUTOMOBILE_SAFETY_AND_THE_VALUE_OF_STATISTICAL_LIFE_IN_THE_FAMILY_VALUING_REDUCED_RISK_FOR_CHILDREN_ADULTS_AND_THE_ELDERLY [June 2016].

Muennig, P., and Khan, K. (2002). *Designing and Conducting Cost Effectiveness Analyses in Medicine and Health Care*. San Francisco, CA: Jossey-Bass.

Murray, C.J.L., and Lopez, A.D. (Eds.). (1996). *The Global Burden of Disease: A Comprehensive Assessment of Mortality and Disability from Diseases, Injuries and Risk Factors in 1990 and Projected to 2020*. Cambridge, MA: Harvard University Press.

National Center for Environmental Economics. (2010). *Guidelines for Preparing Economic Analyses*. Washington, DC: U.S. Environmental Protection Agency.

National Institute for Health and Care Excellence. (2013). *Guide to the Methods of Technology Appraisal 2013*. London, UK: National Institute for Health and Care Excellence.

National Research Council and Institute of Medicine. (2009). *Strengthening Benefit-Cost Analysis for Early Childhood Interventions*. A. Beatty (Rapporteur). Committee on Strengthening Benefit-Cost Methodology for the Evaluation of Early Childhood Interventions. Board on Children, Youth, and Families. Division of Behavioral and Social Sciences and Education. Washington, DC: The National Academies Press.

Nelson, C.A., de Haan, M., and Thomas, K.M. (2006). *Neuroscience and Cognitive Development: The Role of Experience and the Developing Brain*. New York: Wiley.

Nelson, J.P. (1978). Residential choice, hedonic prices, and the demand for urban air quality. *Journal of Urban Economics, 5*(3), 357-369.

Nichol, K.L. (2001). Cost-benefit analysis of a strategy to vaccinate healthy working adults against influenza. *Archives of Internal Medicine, 161*(5), 749-759.

OECD. (2012). *Mortality Risk Valuation in Environment, Health and Transport Policies*. Paris, France: OECD.

Office of Management and Budget. (1992). *Circular A-94: Guidelines and Discount Rates for Benefit-Cost Analysis of Federal Programs*. Washington, DC: Office of Management and Budget.

Office of Management and Budget. (2003). *Circular A-4: Regulatory Analysis*. Washington, DC: Office of Budget and Management.

Office of Management and Budget. (2004a). *Circular A-21: Cost Principles for Educational Institutions*. Available: https://www.whitehouse.gov/omb/circulars_a021_2004 [November 2015].

Office of Management and Budget. (2004b). *Circular A-122: Cost Principles for Non-Profit Organizations*. Available: https://www.whitehouse.gov/omb/circulars_a122_2004 [November 2015].

Oliver, K., Innvar, S., Lorenc, T., Woodman, J., and Thomas, J. (2014). A systematic review of barriers to and facilitators of the use of evidence by policymakers. *BMC Health Services Research, 14*(1), 2.

Olsen, J.A., and Smith, R.D. (2001). Theory versus practice: A review of willingness-to-pay in health and health care. *Health Economics, 10*(1), 39-52.

Ontario Ministry of Health and Long-Term Care. (1994). *Ontario Guidelines for Economic Analysis of Pharmaceutical Products*. Toronto, ON: Ontario Ministry of Health and Long-Term Care.

Oreopoulos, P., and Petronijevic, U. (2013). Making college worth it: A review of the returns to higher education. *The Future of Children, 23*(1), 41-65.

Palanca-Tan, R. (2014). Estimating the value of statistical life for children in Manila. In S. Barrett, K.-G., Mäler, and E. S. Maskin (Eds.), *Environment and Development Economics*. Oxford University Press. Available: https://idl-bnc.idrc.ca/dspace/bitstream/10625/46114/1/132605.pdf [March 2016].

Pew-MacArthur Results First Initiative. (2013). *States' Use of Cost-Benefit Analysis: Improving Results for Taxpayers*. Washington, DC: Pew-MacArthur Results First Initiative.

Pharmaceutical Benefits Board. (2003). *General Guidelines for Economic Evaluations from the Pharmaceutical Benefits Board*. Available: http://www.tlv.se/Upload/English/Guidelines-for-economic-evaluations-LFNAR-2003-2.pdf [March 2016].

Pritchard, C., and Sculpher, M. (2000). *Productivity Costs: Principles and Practice in Economic Evaluation*. London, UK: Office of Health Economics.

Psacharopoulos, G., and Patrinos, H.A. (2004). Returns to investment in education: A further update. *Education Economics, 12*(2), 111-134.

Ramsey, S., Willke, R., Briggs, A., Brown, R., Buxton, M., Chawla, A., Cook, J., Glick, H., Liljas, B., Petitti, D., and Reed, S. (2005). Good research practices for cost-effectiveness analysis alongside clinical trials: The ISPOR RCT-CEA Task Force report. *Value in Health, 8*(5), 521-533.

Richardson, J., Iezzi, A., Khan, M., and Maxwell, A. (2013). *Subjective Wellbeing, Utility and Quality of Life: Results from the Multi Instrument Comparison (MIC) Project*. Melbourne, Australia: Centre for Health Economics, Monash University.

Richardson, J., Iezzi, A., and Khan, M.A. (2015). Why do multi-attribute utility instruments produce different utilities: The relative importance of the descriptive systems, scale and 'micro-utility' effects. *Quality of Life Research, 24*(8), 2045-2053.

Ritzwoller, D.P., Sukhanova, A., Gaglio, B., and Glasgow, R.E. (2009). Costing behavioral interventions: A practical guide to enhance translation. *Annals of Behavioral Medicine, 37*(2), 218-227.

Robert Wood Johnson Foundation. (2013). *Return on Investments in Public Health: Saving Lives and Money*. Available: http://www.rwjf.org/en/library/research/2013/12/return-on-investments-in-public-health.html [February 2016].

Robinson, K., Kennedy, N., and Harmon, D. (2012). Happiness: A review of evidence relevant to occupational science. *Journal of Occupational Science, 19*(2), 150-164.

Robinson, L.A., and Hammitt, J.K. (2011). Behavioral economics and regulatory analysis. *Risk Analysis, 31*(9), 1408-1422.

Ryan, M., Gerard, K., and Amaya-Amaya, M. (Eds.). (2008). *Using Discrete Choice Experiments to Value Health and Health Care*. Dordrecht, The Netherlands: Springer.

Scapecchi, P. (2006). *Economic Valuation of Environmental Health Risks to Children*. Paris, France: OECD.

Schelling, T. (1968). The life you save may be your own. In S.B. Chase (Ed.), *Problems in Public Expenditure Analysis* (pp. 127-162). Washington, DC: Brookings Institution.

Schelling, T.C. (1995). Intergenerational discounting. *Energy Policy, 23*(4-5), 395-401.

Schulz, K.F., Altman, D.G., and Moher, D. (2010). CONSORT 2010 statement: Updated guidelines for reporting parallel group randomised trials. *BMC Medicine, 8*(1), 18.

Schwab-Christe, N.G., and Soguel, N.C. (Eds.). (1995). *Contingent Valuation, Transport Safety and the Value of Life*. Boston, MA: Kluwer Academic.

Scotton, C.R., and Taylor, L.O. (2011). Valuing risk reductions: Incorporating risk heterogeneity into a revealed preference framework. *Resource and Energy Economics, 33*(2), 381-397.

Shadish W.R., Cook, T.D., and Campbell, D.T. (2002). *Experimental and Quasi-Experimental Designs for Generalized Causal Inference*. Boston, MA: Wadsworth Cengage Learning.

Shadish, W.R., Clark, M.H., and Steiner, P.M. (2008). Can nonrandomized experiments yield accurate answers? A randomized experiment comparing random and nonrandom assignments. *Journal of the American Statistical Association, 103*(484), 1334-1344.

Siegel, J.E., Weinstein, M.C., Russell, L.B., and Gold M.R. (1996). Recommendations for reporting cost-effectiveness analyses. Panel on Cost-Effectiveness in Health and Medicine. *Journal of the American Medical Association, 276*(16), 1339-1341.

Skevington, S.M., Lotfy, M., and O'Connell, K.A. (2004). The World Health Organization's WHOQOL-BREF quality-of-life assessment: Psychometric properties and results of the international field trial. *Quality of Life Research, 13*(2), 299-310.

Smith, T., Scahill, L., Dawson, G., Guthrie, D., Lord, C., Odom, S., Rogers, S., and Wagner, A. (2006). Designing research studies on psychosocial interventions in autism. *Journal of Autism and Developmental Disorders, 37*(2), 354-366.

Spicer, R.S., Miller, T.R., Hendrie, D., and Blincoe, L (2011). Quality-adjusted life years lost to road crash injury: Updating the Injury Impairment Index. *Annals of Advances in Automotive Medicine, 55*, 365-377.

Steuerle, C.E., and Bakija, J.M. (1994). *Retooling Social Security for the 21st Century: Right and Wrong Approaches to Reform*. Washington, DC: Urban Institute.

Suter, C.R. (2010). *Economic Evaluation of a Community-Based, Family-Skills Prevention Program*. Pullman: Washington State University.

Takenaga, N., Kai, I., and Ohi, G. (1985). Evaluation of three cervical cancer detection programs in Japan with special reference to cost-benefit analysis. *Cancer, 55*(10), 2514-2519.

Takeuchi, K., Kishimoto, A., and Tsuge, T. (2008). *Altruism and Willingness to Pay for Reducing Child Mortality*. Kobe, Japan: Graduate School of Economics, Kobe University.

Task Force on Community Preventive Services. (2005). *The Guide to Community Preventive Services: What Works to Promote Health?* New York: Oxford University Press.

The Cochrane Public Health Group. (2011). *Guide for Developing a Cochrane Protocol*. London, UK: The Cochrane Public Health Group.

Thomas, A. (2012). Three strategies to prevent unintended pregnancy. *Journal of Policy Analysis and Management, 31*(2), 280-311.

Thompson, E., Berger, M., Blomquist, G., and Allen, S. (2002). Valuing the arts: A contingent valuation approach. *Journal of Cultural Economics, 26*(2), 87-113.

Thorat, T., Cangelosi, M., and Neumann, P.J. (2012). Skills of the trade: The Tufts Cost-Effectiveness Analysis Registry. *Journal of Benefit-Cost Analysis, 3*(1), 1-9.

Torrance, G.W., Thomas, W.H., and Sackett, D.L. (1972). A utility maximization model for evaluation of health care programs. *Health Services Research, 7*(2), 118-133.

Treasury Board of Canada Secretariat. (2007). *Canadian Cost-Benefit Analysis Guide: Regulatory Proposals.* Available: https://www.tbs-sct.gc.ca/rtrap-parfa/analys/analys-eng.pdf [March 2016].

Trochim, W.M.K., and Donnelly, J.P. (2006). *Research Methods Knowledge Base* (3rd Edition). Boston, MA: Cengage Learning.

Valentine, J.C., and Konstantopoulos, S. (2015). *Using Systematic Reviews and Meta-Analyses to Inform Public Policy Decisions.* Commissioned paper for the Committee on the Use of Economic Evidence to Inform Investments in Children, Youth, and Families. Available: http://sites.nationalacademies.org/cs/groups/dbassesite/documents/webpage/dbasse_171853.pdf [June 2016].

Vincent, D., Oakley, D., Pohl, J., and Walker, D.S. (2000). Cost effectiveness analysis: An essential tool for practice management. *The Nurse Practitioner, 25*(9), 95-96.

Vining, A.R., and Weimer, D.L. (2009a). An agenda for promoting and improving the use of CBA in social policy. In D.L. Weimer and A.R. Vining (Eds.), *Investing in the Disadvantaged: Assessing the Costs and Benefits of Social Policies* (pp. 249-271). Washington, DC: Georgetown University Press.

Vining, A.R., and Weimer, D.L. (2009b). Assessing the costs and benefits of social policies. In D.L. Weimer and A.R. Vining (Eds.), *Investing in the Disadvantaged: Assessing the Costs and Benefits of Social Policies* (pp. 1-16). Washington, DC: Georgetown University Press.

Vining, A.R., and Weimer, D.L. (2009c). Overview of the state-of-the-art CBA in social policy. In D.L. Weimer and A.R. Vining (Eds.), *Investing in the Disadvantaged: Assessing the Costs and Benefits of Social Policies* (pp. 219-248). Washington, DC: Georgetown University Press.

Vining, A.R., and Weimer, D.L. (2010). An assessment of important issues concerning the application of benefit-cost analysis to social policy. *Journal of Benefit-Cost Analysis, 1*(1), 1-40.

von Stackelberg, K., and Hammitt, J. (2009). Use of contingent valuation to elicit willingness-to-pay for the benefits of developmental health risk reductions. *Environmental and Resource Economics, 43*(1), 45-61.

Wagenaar, A.C., and Komro, K.A. (2013). Natural experiments: Research design elements for optimal causal inference without randomization. In A.C. Wagenaar and S.C. Burris (Eds.), *Public Health Law Research: Theory and Methods* (Ch. 14, pp. 307-324). San Francisco, CA: Jossey-Bass.

Walker, D. (2001). Cost and cost-effectiveness guidelines: Which ones to use? *Health Policy and Planning, 16*(1), 113-121.

Walter, E., and Zehetmayr, S. (2006). *Guidelines on Health Economic Evaluation.* Consensus Paper. Vienna, Austria: Institut für Pharmaökonomische Forschung. Available: http://www.ispor.org/peguidelines/source/Guidelines_Austria.pdf [March 2016].

Washington State Institute for Public Policy. (2015). *Benefit-Cost Technical Documentation.* Olympia: Washington State Institute for Public Policy.

Weinstein, M.C., and Stason, W.B. (1977). Foundations of cost-effectiveness analysis for health and medical practices. *New England Journal of Medicine, 296*(13), 716-721.

Weinstein, M.C., Siegel, J.E., Gold, M.R., Kamlet, M.S., and Russell, L.B. (1997). Recommendations of the panel on cost-effectiveness in health and medicine. *Survey of Anesthesiology, 41*(6), 331-332.

Weinstein, M.C., Torrance, G., and McGuire, A. (2009). QALYs: The basics. *Value Health, 12*(Suppl. 1), S5-S9.

Wherry, L.R., and Meyer, B.D. (2015). Saving teens: Using a policy discontinuity to estimate the effects of Medicaid eligibility. *The Journal of Human Resources.* doi:10.3368/jhr.51.3.0913-5918R1.

Wherry, L.R., Miller, S., Kaestner, R., and Meyer, B.D. (2015). *Childhood Medicaid Coverage and Later Life Health Care Utilization*. NBER Working Paper 20929. Cambridge, MA: National Bureau of Economic Research.

White, D., and VanLandingham, G. (2015). Benefit-cost analysis in the states: Status, impact, and challenges. *Journal of Benefit-Cost Analysis, 6*(2), 369-399.

Williams, S. (2013). Statistical children. *Yale Journal on Regulation, 30*(1), 63-124.

Wilson, I.B., and Cleary, P.D. (1995). Linking clinical variables with health-related quality of life. A conceptual model of patient outcomes. *Journal of the American Medical Association, 273*(1), 59-65.

W.K. Kellogg Foundation. (2004). *Logic Model Development Guide*. Battle Creek, MI: W.K. Kellogg Foundation.

The World Bank. (2010). *Cost-Benefit Analysis in World Bank Projects*. Washington, DC: The World Bank.

World Health Organization. (2000). *Workbook 8: Economic Evaluations*. Geneva, Switzerland: World Health Organization.

World Health Organization. (2001). *Macroeconomics and Health: Investing in Health for Economic Development*. Report of the Commission on Macroeconomics and Health. Geneva, Switzerland: World Health Organization.

World Health Organization. (2006). *Guidelines for Conducting Cost-Benefit Analysis of Household Energy and Health Interventions*. G. Hutton and E. Rehfuess (Eds.). Geneva, Switzerland: World Health Organization. Available: http://www.who.int/indoorair/publications/guideline_household_energy_health_intervention.pdf [March 2016].

World Health Organization. (2012). *WHO Guide to Cost-Effectiveness Analysis*. T.T.-T. Edejer, R. Baltussen, T. Adam, R. Hutubessy, A. Acharya, D. Evans, and C. Murray (Eds.). Geneva, Switzerland: World Health Organization.

World Health Organization Quality of Life Group. (1998). The World Health Organization Quality of Life (WHOQOL) assessment: Development and general psychometric properties. *Social Science & Medicine, 46*(12), 1569-1585.

Yates, B.T. (1996). *Analyzing Costs, Procedures, Processes, and Outcomes in Human Services: An Introduction* (Vol. 42). Thousands Oak, CA: Sage.

Yates, B.T. (2009). Cost-inclusive evaluation: A banquet of approaches for including costs, benefits, and cost-effectiveness and cost-benefit analyses in your next evaluation. *Evaluation and Program Planning, 32*(1), 54-56.

Yoshikawa, H., Weiland, C., and Brooks-Gunn, J. (in press). When does preschool matter? Submitted to *The Future of Children*.

Zerbe, R.O., Jr. (2010). *A Reliable Internal Rate of Return*. Unpublished manuscript.

Zerbe, R.O., Jr. , and Dively, D.D. (1974). *Benefit-Cost Analysis in Theory and Practice*. New York: Harper and Row.

Zerbe, R.O., Plotnick, R.D., Kessler, R.C., Pecora, P.J., Hiripi, E.V.A., O'Brien, K., Williams, J., English, D., and White, J. (2009). Benefits and costs of intensive foster care services: The Casey Family Programs compared to state services. *Contemporary Economic Policy, 27*(3), 308-320.

4

Context Matters

The production of high-quality economic evidence is necessary—but not sufficient—to improve the usefulness and use of this type of evidence in investment decisions related to children, youth, and families. Equally important is attention before, during, and after economic evaluations are performed to the context in which decisions are made. Consumers of the economic evidence produced by these evaluations will inevitably consider such factors as whether the evidence is relevant and accessible and whether meaningful guidance is provided on how to apply the evidence within existing organizational structures, as well as personnel and budget constraints. Consumers also will consider the influence on investment decisions of broader factors such as political pressures and value-based priorities. As discussed in Chapter 2, moreover, whether evidence (including economic evidence) is used varies significantly depending on the type of investment decision being made and the decision maker's incentives, or lack thereof, for its use (Eddama and Coast, 2008; Elliott and Popay, 2000; Innvaer et al., 2002; National Research Council, 2012). In addition, a decision maker may be faced with the pressing need to act in the absence of available or relevant evidence (Anderson et al., 2005; Simoens, 2010).

Apart from economic evaluations, decision makers rely on many other sources to inform their decisions, including expert opinion, community preferences, and personal testimonies (Armstrong et al., 2014; Bowen and Zwi, 2005; Orton et al., 2011). Reliance on these sources rises when the empirical evidence does not clearly point the decision maker in one direction or when there are conflicting views on the topic at hand (Atkins et al., 2005). The influence of a given type of evidence also may differ by the stage of the decision making process (i.e., policy agenda setting, policy formulation, policy implementation) or its objective (e.g., effectiveness, appropriateness, implementation) (Bowen and Zwi, 2005; Dobrow et al., 2004, 2006; Hanney et al., 2003; National Research Council, 2012).

With some noteworthy exceptions, efforts to improve the use of evidence have focused on the use of research evidence in general rather than on the use of economic evidence in particular. Even with this broader focus, however, the research base on the factors that guide decisions and on reliable strategies for increasing the use of evidence is scant in the United States (Brownson et al., 2009; Jennings and Hall, 2011; National Research Council, 2012). The committee therefore based its conclusions and recommendations in this area on multiple sources: the emerging literature on processes for improving evidence-based decision making, relevant literature on the use of economic evidence from other countries, the expertise of the committee members, and two public information-gathering sessions (Appendix A contains agendas for both of these sessions). Many lessons learned from broader efforts to understand and improve the use of research evidence apply to the use of economic evidence in decision making.

This chapter organizes the committee's review of contextual factors that influence the usefulness and use of evidence under three, sometimes overlapping, headings: (1) alignment of the evidence with the decision context, which includes the relevance of the evidence, organizational capacity to make use of the evidence, and the accessibility of reporting formats; (2) other factors in the use of evidence, which include the role of politics and values in the decision making process, budgetary considerations, and data availability; and (3) factors that facilitate the use of evidence, which include organizational culture, management practices, and collaborative relationships. The chapter then provides examples of efforts to improve the use of evidence, illustrating the role of the various factors discussed throughout the chapter. The final section presents the committee's recommendations for improving the usefulness and use of evidence.

ALIGNMENT OF EVIDENCE WITH THE DECISION CONTEXT

Optimal use of evidence currently is not realized in part because the evidence is commonly generated independently of the investment decision it may inform (National Research Council, 2012). Economic evaluations are undertaken in highly controlled environments with resources and supports that are not available in most real-world settings. The results, therefore, may not be perceived as relevant to a particular decision context or feasible to implement in a setting different from that in which the evidence was derived. In addition, findings from economic evaluations may be reported in formats that are not accessible to consumers of the evidence.

Relevance of Evidence to the Decision Context

"Often there is not an evaluation that addresses the specific questions that are important at a given time. Usually what is used are evaluations that have already been done, internally or externally, that may or may not have answered the current questions."

—Dan Rosenbaum, senior economist, Economic Policy
Division, Office of Management and Budget,
at the committee's open session on March 23, 2015.

"We think a lot about the question of scalability. You may have something with strong evidence that works really well in New York City. That same approach may not work as well in a small border town in Texas where your work is shaped by a very different set of local factors."

—Nadya Dabby, assistant deputy secretary for innovation
and improvement, U.S. Department of Education,
at the committee's open session on March 23, 2015.

The perceived relevance of an evaluation to a specific decision influences whether the evidence is used or cast aside (Asen et al., 2013; Lorenc et al., 2014). Yet producers and consumers of evidence generally operate in distinct environments with differing terminology, incentives, norms, and professional affiliations. The two communities also differ in the outcomes they value (Elliott and Popay, 2000; Kemm, 2006; National Research Council, 2012; Oliver et al., 2014a; Tseng, 2012). As a result, the evidence produced and the evidence perceived to be relevant to a specific decision often differ as well.

Evidence is most likely to be used when the evaluation that produces it is conducted in the locale where the decision will be made and includes attention to contextual factors (Asen et al., 2013; Hanney et al., 2003; Hoyle et al., 2008; Merlo et al., 2015; Oliver et al., 2014a). Decision makers want to know whether a given intervention will work for their population, implementing body, and personnel. Each of these factors, however, often differs from the conditions under which the evaluation was conducted. Even methodologically strong studies that demonstrate positive effects under prescribed conditions can be and often are discounted in the absence of research indicating that these outcomes can be achieved under alternative conditions (DuMont, 2015; Nelson et al., 2009; Palinkas et al., 2014).

One way to enhance the relevance—and thus the use—of evidence is to gain a more thorough understanding of the decision chain, the specific decision to be made, when it will be made, where responsibility for making it lies, and what factors will influence that person or organization (National Research Council, 2012). It is also useful for producers of economic evidence and intermediaries (discussed later in this chapter in the section on collaborative relationships) to consider the intended purpose of an existing intervention; the details of its implementation and administration; the culture and history of the decision making organization, particularly with respect to its use of various types of evidence; and the community in which the intervention is set (Armstrong et al., 2014; Eddama and Coast, 2008; van Dongen et al., 2013).

Ideally, economic evaluation goes beyond rigorous impact studies and associated cost studies to examine impact variability, particularly whether there are impacts for different settings, contexts, and populations, and whether and what adaptations can be effective; systems-level supports required for effective implementation; and the cost of implementation at the level of implementation fidelity required. Policy makers and practitioners attend not only to impacts but also to how to achieve them and the extent to which externally generated evidence applies within their own context (Goldhaber-Fiebert et al., 2011).

CONCLUSION: *Evidence often is produced without the end-user in mind. Therefore, the evidence available does not always align with the evidence needed.*

CONCLUSION: *Evidence is more likely to be used if it is perceived as relevant to the context in which the investment decision is being made.*

Capacity to Acquire and Make Use of Evidence

A key factor in promoting the use of economic evidence is ensuring that end-users have the capacity to acquire, interpret, and act upon the evidence. That capacity falls into two categories: the capacity to engage with and understand the research, and the capacity to implement the practices, models, or programs that the research supports. In both cases, that capacity can be developed internally in an agency or implementing organization or it can be supported through intermediaries who help translate evidence for decision makers or offer support to those implementing interventions with an evidence base.

Organizational Capacity to Acquire and Interpret Evidence

"We hire consultants more often than not [to access and analyze evidence] because we don't always have the capacity to do so, which means we have to also find a funding source to make that possible."
—Uma Ahluwalia, director, Montgomery County,
Maryland Department of Health and Human Services,
at the committee's open session on March 23, 2015.

"We've heard from some program administrators who would like to be able to have cost-benefit information, but lack the capacity to [access the necessary data]. In addition, agencies do not always have the expertise needed to conduct these kinds of data analyses."

—Carlise King, executive director, Early
Childhood Data Collaborative, Child Trends, at
the committee's open session of June 1, 2015.

As public pressure for accountability and efficiency grows, leaders in both public and nonprofit settings are increasingly called upon to collect, analyze, and interpret data on their agency's effectiveness. Similarly, policy makers and funders are expected to make use of economic data in making decisions. Yet many of these stakeholders lack the capacity, time, or expertise to perform these tasks (Armstrong et al., 2013; Merlo et al., 2015). For example, Chaikledkaew and colleagues (2009) found that 50 percent of government researchers and 70 percent of policy makers in Thailand were unfamiliar with economic concepts such as discounting and sensitivity analysis.

Within public and private or nonprofit agencies across multiple sectors, decision makers may have had little training in research and evaluation methodology, which limits their ability to understand and assess the research base and use it to inform policy or practice (Brownson et al., 2009; Lessard et al., 2010). One of the only studies of its kind on the training needs of the public health workforce in the United States identified large gaps in these decision makers' competence in the use of economic evaluation to improve their evidence-based decision making, as well as their ability to communicate research findings to policy makers (Jacob et al., 2014). Their ability to review the entire research base in the area of interest also may be limited by constraints of time and access. As a result, decision makers are vulnerable to presentations of evidence from vested interest groups that offer a limited view of what the evidence does and does not show.

Clearinghouses of evidence-based practices, discussed in the section below on reporting, can make existing knowledge accessible to many users on a common platform. However, decision makers would have difficulty summarizing all the evidence relevant to a particular decision at hand. Thus, organizations developing and implementing interventions need to have the internal or external capacity to interpret the evidence and determine how it applies to their specific context and circumstances.

One approach to building greater capacity for the analysis and use of research evidence, including economic evidence, is to incorporate stronger training on those topics into undergraduate and graduate curricula, as well as into other learning opportunities, including on-the-job or work-based learning and fellowships for future leaders and those seeking to inform decision making (Jacob et al., 2014; National Research Council, 2012). Senior executive service training in the federal government, for example, could include training in the use of economic evidence for federal executive leaders. Fellowship programs sponsored by philanthropies, government organizations, or other institutions could include training or practicums focused on the use of economic evidence. Graduate programs for those pursuing careers in government or service organizations or those seeking to influence decision makers—such as programs leading to a master's degree in public policy, public administration, public health, social work, law, journalism, or communications—could include coursework related to the acquisition, translation, and use of evidence of all types, including economic evidence. Finally, human resources agencies serving employees who work on interventions for children, youth, and families could provide training and opportunities for applied learning in the use of research evidence, including how to access and acquire the evidence, how to judge its quality, and how to apply it in decision making. An example of such capacity is provided in Box 4-1.

CONCLUSION: *Capacity to access and analyze existing economic evidence is lacking. Leadership training needs to build the knowledge and skills to use such evidence effectively in organizational operations and decision making. Such competencies include being able to locate economic evidence, assess its quality, interpret it, understand its relevance, and apply it to the decision context at hand.*

Capacity to Implement Evidence-Based Interventions

"The issue of implementation is huge. Our own research suggests that the quality and extent of implementation of any given program is at least as important in determining effects, or in many cases more important, than the actual variety of the program implemented locally. The question of whether or not one can reasonably expect the kinds of effects that the background evidence suggests is very much an open question and has a great deal to do with the quality of the monitoring systems, implementation fidelity, local resources, and a huge number of contextual factors that have to do with what is actually put on the ground under the label of one of these programs."

—Mark W. Lipsey, director, Peabody Research
Institute, Vanderbilt University, at the
committee's open session on June 1, 2015.

"The evidence conversation is tilted entirely toward the evidence of effectiveness and efficacy, and we need a better understanding of the use of evidence in implementation. There are good examples of those kinds of

---

BOX 4-1
Building Capacity to Seek and Use Evidence: An Example

Kaufman and colleagues (2006) provided training and technical assistance in support of a community awarded a federal Safe Start demonstration grant for an integrated system of care designed to reduce young children's exposure to violence. Their efforts represent an example of a university-community partnership that successfully improved the community's capacity to seek and use scientific evidence in its local decision making. Although the objective was to increase the community's acceptance of program evaluation data, the lessons learned could inform similar efforts to build stakeholders' capacity to use economic evaluations as an additional tool to guide investment decisions.

The academic evaluators effectively educated policy makers, community leaders, and providers on the benefits of scientific evidence by engaging in a number of efforts, including (1) spending time outside of the university setting and participating actively in community meetings and forums to build relationships and trust, (2) delivering on research that the community identified as critical to its operations, (3) providing continual feedback on research findings to selected target audiences using strategies and mechanisms that reflected how those audiences consumed information, (4) embedding training and technical assistance in the use of evidence in all aspects of the initiative to promote the evidence's broad utility, and (5) participating in project leadership meetings to ensure that the evidence was informing management decision making in real time. The investment of time and resources by the researchers led to an observable, sustained shift in the community's capacity to incorporate evidence at multiple levels of program management and policy making.

---

systems. As others have pointed out, they depend a lot upon the capacity of the people implementing."
—John Q. Easton, distinguished senior fellow,
Spencer Foundation, at the committee's
open session on June 1, 2015.

Even if an organization has the capacity to access and analyze evaluation evidence, it may not have the infrastructure and capacity to support effective implementation of evidence-based interventions (Jacob et al., 2014; LaRocca et al., 2012). For instance, if an evidence-based intervention requires a level of professional development that no one can afford, or a workforce that is unavailable in most communities, or much lower caseloads than are found in existing systems, it will not be well implemented.

Implementation fidelity is critical to ensuring that economic benefits are realized. Funding is essential not only for the cost of the intervention but also for the cost of the supports required to implement it. As discussed in Chapter 3, economic evaluators can break those costs out explicitly, since they may need to be funded from different sources. For instance, practitioners' time may be billable to Medicaid, but the cost of building a quality assurance system to monitor implementation may not be.

Incorporating economic evidence into conceptual frameworks and models of implementation may improve the dissemination and use of the evidence. These models have been developed to study some of the implementation issues discussed above, but little attention has been given to whether economic evidence should be incorporated into the models and if so, how. In the development of the Consolidated Framework for Implementation Research, for example, Damschroder and colleagues (2009) found that intervention costs were considered in only 5 of 19 implementation theories they reviewed. Although they decided to include costs in their framework as one of several intervention characteristics that affect implementation, they note that "in many contexts, costs are difficult to capture and available resources may have a more direct influence on implementation" (p. 7) without recommending increased attention to cost assessment in the development of new interventions. Similarly, a conceptual model developed by Aarons and colleagues (2011) includes funding as a factor affecting all phases of the implementation process but fails to consider that intervention costs could also play an important role in implementation, especially considering that funding must be commensurate with costs. In contrast, Ribisl and colleagues (2014) propose a much more prominent role for economic analysis in the design and implementation of new interventions. They argue that cost is an important barrier to the adoption of evidence-based practices and advocate for an approach in which intervention developers first assess what individuals and agencies are "willing to pay" for an intervention and then design interventions that are consistent with that cost range.

Two recent examples illustrate potential contributions of economic evaluation to implementation studies. Saldana and colleagues (2014) developed a tool for examining implementation activities and used it as a template for mapping implementation costs over and above the costs of the intervention; applying this tool to a foster care program, they found it valuable for comparing different implementation strategies. Holmes and colleagues (2014) describe the development of a unit costing estimation system (cost calculator) based on a conceptual model of core child welfare processes, and discuss how this tool can be used to determine optimal implementation approaches under different circumstances, as well as to estimate costs under hypothetical implementation scenarios.

These points were reinforced by a number of panelists who spoke at the committee's open sessions about their work in implementing evidence-based interventions at the federal, state, and local levels. Speakers noted that effective implementation depends on a number of factors, including data and monitoring systems, the workforce and its training, and resources that affect everything from provider compensation to the number of children or families seen by each provider. While knowledge of the effectiveness and cost-effectiveness of interventions is growing, there remains only limited information about what is required to support effective implementation of those interventions.

At the committee's June open session, panelist Mark Lipsey, director of the Peabody Research Institute at Vanderbilt University, commented that most cost-effectiveness research focuses on brand-name programs. However, the cost and infrastructure associated with implementing those programs are not feasible in most real-world settings. Communities generally lack the capacity and resources to implement the brand-name, model programs. Therefore, generic versions of the programs are implemented. Whether the effects suggested in research on brand-name programs can be expected in other settings is dependent upon the local resources available to implement the program, a large number of factors specific to the context where the program is implemented, and the quality of the implementation monitoring system. Lipsey suggested an alternative model to the traditional feed-forward approach in which highly controlled research on programs is conducted; synthesized, and placed in a clearinghouse, and efforts are then undertaken to implement those programs and replicate the findings in local settings. The context—population served, staff skills, resources, community, nature of the original problem—may differ from those of the programs in the original studies. Consequently, the results expected may not be realized in new settings. Alternatively, Lipsey suggested beginning with the monitoring and feedback systems currently in place in a particular setting and building incrementally toward evidence-based practice.

Gottfredson and colleagues (2015) also emphasize the importance of describing intervention implementation, although their focus is on prevention programs in health care. They note that the original research of economists and policy analysts "often generates conclusive answers to questions about what works under what conditions" (p. 895), but they give less attention to describing the intervention in subsequent trials in other settings and examining causes for variations in outcomes and costs. An example of the importance of implementation fidelity is described in Box 4-2.

In short, attention to the infrastructure and contextual aspects of effective implementation is often inadequate. Clearinghouses and registries have provided a systematic mechanism for synthesizing evidence of the effectiveness of interventions. Legislation has required the use of some of those evidence- or research-based models (Pew-MacArthur Results First Initiative, 2015) without necessarily addressing issues of fidelity or ensur-

---

BOX 4-2
The Importance of Implementation Fidelity: An Example

The experience of Washington State's implementation of Functional Family Therapy (FFT) illustrates the importance of implementation fidelity. In its 1997 Community Juvenile Accountability Act, the Washington State legislature required juvenile courts to implement "research-based" programs. To fulfill that mandate, the Washington State Institute for Public Policy (WSIPP) (which is described later in this chapter in the section on examples of efforts to improve the use of evaluation evidence) conducted a thorough review of the evidence base, and from that review, the state's Juvenile Rehabilitation Agency identified four model programs from which courts could choose. The evidence base for those programs was not specific to Washington State, so the legislature also required that WSIPP evaluate the models' effectiveness in Washington in "real-world" conditions. In its first evaluation of FFT, WSIPP estimated a $2,500 return on investment. However, that evaluation found that FFT was effective—and thus the returns were realized—only when therapists implemented the model with fidelity. In fact, WSIPP found that recidivism rates could actually increase relative to business as usual if delivered by therapists not appropriately trained. Thus, WSIPP recommended that the state work with FFT Inc. to develop a mechanism for training and monitoring therapists to ensure effective implementation of the program (Barnoski, 2002).

---

ing that resources are being devoted to effective implementation. Yet few model interventions have been demonstrated at scale, and it is not clear that those model interventions will produce the same or comparable outcomes when introduced into other settings and contexts with different resources available for implementation. Moving evidence-based practice and policy toward outcomes requires thinking in a holistic way about the range of evidence that is needed, its availability, and how the evidence aligns with existing systems and funding.

CONCLUSION: *Infrastructure for developing, accessing, analyzing, and disseminating research evidence often is lacking in public agencies and private organizations charged with developing and implementing interventions for children, youth, and families.*

CONCLUSION: *It is not sufficient to determine whether an investment is effective at achieving desired outcomes or provides a positive economic return. Absent investments in implementation in real-world settings, ongoing evaluation, and continuous quality improvement, the positive outcomes and economic returns expected may not be realized.*

CONCLUSION: *Conceptual frameworks developed in the field of implementation science may be relevant to improving the dissemination and use of economic evidence, but the implementation literature has not paid sufficient attention to the potential role of economic evidence in these models.*

Reporting

"Research often uses language and terms that require a PhD in economics to recall what the report is saying."
—Barry Anderson, deputy director, Office of the
Executive Director, National Governors Association,
at the committee's open session on March 23, 2015.

"We have to figure out a way to communicate this information in ways that resonate with different perspectives, so benefit-cost means something to people other than those who are in the field. During the times when policy has changed, it is because we found ways of communicating the power of change to different communities. It has to mean something to people in different parts of the political dynamic that we work with."
—Gary VanLandingham, director,
Pew-MacArthur Results First Initiative, at the
committee's open session on March 23, 2015.

"There has been increased attention to local data dashboards. This entails the presentation of relevant, timely information to the right people at the right time so they can use data for continuous quality improvement and decision making. What are needed are both a data system and organizational documents with embedded agreements and expectations for [leaders' and management teams'] timely use of local data on an ongoing basis. The administrative piece is just as important as the IT piece."
—Will Aldridge, implementation specialist and
investigator, FPG Child Development Institute,
University of North Carolina at Chapel Hill, at
the committee's open session on June 1, 2015.

The reporting of evidence derived from economic evaluation influences whether the evidence is used in decision making (National Research Council, 2012; O'Reilly, 1982; Orton et al., 2011; Tseng, 2012; Williams and Bryan, 2007). Relevant, credible evidence is more likely to be used if reported in a clear and concise format with actionable recommendations (Bogenschneider et al., 2013; DuMont, 2015). Reporting formats designed to suit the information needs and characteristics of target audiences also may increase the use of economic evidence.

The distinct communities of producers and consumers of economic evidence, discussed above in the section on relevance, influence how this evidence is typically reported. For example, economists tend to expect confidence limits, sensitivity analysis on key parameters such as discount rates, and other estimates of the range of a possible return. Sometimes they provide a range as their main finding. Legislators and top-level managers, however, like clear, crisp recommendations. Instead of estimates presented as ranges or by a table of estimates under different assumptions, they generally prefer a point estimate and a plain-English explanation without further numbers expressing the analysts' confidence in the results (Institute of Medicine and National Research Council, 2014; National Research Council, 2012). Policy makers also tend to want results given up front, with methods being described later and easy to skip without compromising comprehension. These preferences stand in marked contrast to the expectations of academic journals.

Similarly, when multiple economic analyses using different parameter choices are available for a single program, a plethora of inconsistent numbers can destroy the credibility of the results with decision makers. Instead, comparisons with prior estimates can be presented in a way that makes it clear at the outset which estimate is best, with why that estimate is better than prior ones then being explained.

Systematic reviews of evaluations and clearinghouses can be used to help decision makers sort through evidence to determine its relevance and practical implications. Yet many of these resources currently do not incorporate economic evidence. The work of the Washington State Institute for Public Policy (see Box 4-2 and the section below on examples of efforts to improve the use of evaluation evidence) is one exception, providing independent systematic reviews of evidence that include economic evidence. The Tufts University Cost-Effectiveness Analysis Registry is another tool that makes economic evidence accessible to users. Clearinghouses can help consumers acquire and assess the full range of evidence in a given area, but they are not a panacea since most present only evidence of effectiveness and typically only for the fairly circumscribed brand-name, model programs discussed in the previous section.

CONCLUSION: *Economic evidence is more likely to be used if it is reported in a form that is summarized and clear to target audiences and includes actionable recommendations.*

CONCLUSION: *Research summaries and publications often do not report contextual details that are relevant to whether positive impacts and economic returns should be expected in other settings.*

OTHER FACTORS IN THE USE OF EVIDENCE

The results of economic evaluation are one type of evidence on which decision makers may rely. Even when economic evaluations are of high quality (see Chapter 3), relevant to the decision setting, and feasible to implement, other factors—including political climate, values, budgetary considerations, and data availability—may influence whether the evidence they produce is used.

Political Climate and Values

"A project that has some prospects for success is subsidizing long-acting, reversible contraception. We received a grant from a philanthropist to do this on a volunteer basis with low-income girls and women. The results were amazing. There was a 40 percent drop in unwanted pregnancies. You can translate how much that would have cost the Medicaid Program. Here, we had a program with extremely compelling evidence and the potential to be duplicated within our state, but also touching this program were all of the politics around contraception, so there is a bit of an uphill climb on this one."

—Henry Sobanet and Erick Scheminske, director
and deputy director, Governor's Office of State
Planning and Budgeting, Colorado, at the
committee's open session on March 23, 2015.

"Over half of our county's budget is education costs. Education is a very important value in our county."

—Uma Ahluwalia, director, Montgomery County,
Maryland Department of Health and Human Services,
at the committee's open session on March 23, 2015.

"Data will never trump values by itself. But data that has a compelling [personal] story attached to it, and that also is linked to the ideology of the people we are trying to communicate with can trump an individual perspective."

—Gary VanLandingham, director,
Pew-MacArthur Results First Initiative, at the
committee's open session on March 23, 2015.

Economic evidence is but one of several factors that policy makers must weigh as they make decisions about choosing among competing priorities (Gordon, 2006). In a pluralistic society, diverse political views, cultural norms, and values help define the context within which individuals make investment decisions. Numerous external factors, such as stakeholder feedback, legal actions, and the media, affect the use of evidence in the policy-making process (Zardo and Collie, 2014). Existing political pressures and cultural belief systems influence not only decisions at the individual level, but also organizational practices and structures that may facilitate or hinder the use of scientific evidence in decision making (Armstrong et al., 2014; Flitcroft et al., 2011; Jennings and Hall, 2011; National Research Council, 2012; Nutbeam and Boxall, 2008).

Those working to increase the use of economic evidence will be more successful if they remain cognizant of the political environment within which an agency or institution is working. What are the external pressures? Are important external audiences open to diverse information, or are they only looking for confirmation for previously held views? Short-term budgetary concerns also may trump information about long-term efficiency. In addition, long-standing programs with little evidence of success often have strong, vocal allies in the form of providers and beneficiaries who exert pressure on agency leaders or local politicians who make resource allocation decisions.

Armstrong and colleagues (2014) state that "decision making is inherently political and even where research evidence is available, it needs to be tempered with a range of other sources of evidence including community views, financial constraints and policy priorities" (p. 14). In a study of the use of research by school boards, researchers found that school boards typically relied on a variety of information sources, including examples, experience, testimony, and local data (Asen et al., 2011, 2012). Research (defined as empirical findings, guided by a rigorous framework) was used infrequently compared with other types of evidence (Asen et al., 2013; Tseng, 2012). When research evidence was relied upon, it was cited in general rather than with reference to specific studies, and most commonly was used as a persuasive tool to support an existing position.

Studies of the use of economic evidence in local decision making across countries have found that political, cultural, and other contextual factors influence the application of such evidence, especially if it is found to contradict prevailing values or local priorities (Eddama and Coast, 2008). A European study found that the extent of knowledge about economic evaluation, the barriers to its use, the weight given to ethical considerations, and incentives promoting the integration of economic information into health care decision making varied by country. The authors suggest that if economic evidence is to have a stronger influence on policy making, the political and institutional settings within which decisions are made will require greater attention (Corbacho and Pinto-Prades, 2012; Hoffman and Von Der Schulenburg, 2000).

One area of contrast between the United States and some European countries is in the use of economic evidence in decisions on health policy (Eddama and Coast, 2008): the latter countries are more likely to rely on cost-effectiveness analysis (CEA) to shape their health policies (Neumann,

2004). In fact, language in the Patient Protection and Affordable Care Act (ACA) explicitly prohibits the application of CEA in the use of Patient-Centered Outcomes Research Institute (PCORI) funds that support the piloting of health care innovations (Neumann and Weinstein, 2010).

The use of economic evidence in policy making varies across U.S. policy-making enterprises. A number of federal agencies use benefit-cost analysis (BCA) or budgetary impact analysis to inform the legislative process (e.g., the Congressional Budget Office [CBO]) and in the approval of regulatory actions (e.g., the Office of Management and Budget [OMB]). In some fields methodological and ethical questions about the use of BCA—for example, to monetize certain outcomes, such as human life—can diminish the uptake of economic evidence (Bergin, 2013). The use of CEA to justify funding of preventive interventions but not treatment services under Medicare highlights the inconsistent and uneven use of economic evidence in policy making seen in the United States (Chambers et al., 2015).

Producers of economic evidence can consider contextual and organizational variables in their study design, analysis, and interpretation of findings so that research results better address the core issues decision makers face. Economic evaluations then are more likely to be seen as responsive, sensitive, and relevant to the local context and to increase the demand for and uptake of such work.

CONCLUSION: *Political pressures, values, long-standing practices, expert opinions, and local experience all influence whether decision makers use economic evidence.*

Budgetary Considerations

A budget process that takes into account only near-term costs and benefits—such as the 10-year window within which federal budget decisions are made, or the budget decisions of a foundation wishing to prove near-term success even with the use of economic evidence—will inherently entail a bias against investments in children, whose returns are long-term in nature. This observation creates an additional impetus for statistical entities such as the Census Bureau and the Internal Revenue Service (IRS) Statistics of Income program, as well as surveys supported by private foundations, to give significant budget weight to the development of longitudinal data on children.

Economic evaluation also tends to focus on the intervention, local community, or organization, comparing internal costs with internal benefits. Budget offices can mitigate the tendency to localize decision making by both providing information on gains (or costs) accruing outside of a local constituency or jurisdiction and suggesting policy options for maximizing all societal benefits in excess of costs. For instance, a federal program providing health care to children through states can account for net gains or losses nationwide, while budget analyses can inform policy makers of ways to design laws so as to avoid giving states incentives to discount gains outside their jurisdictions.

In formulating budgets, governments and private organizations ultimately decide how they will allocate their resources. Ideally, budget processes force governmental and private entities to make trade-offs at the broadest level, allocating monies to those interventions with the greatest benefits relative to costs. Under these ideal conditions, economic evaluations would be extensive and encourage decision making broadly across interventions while promoting negotiations among interventions, with multisector payoffs in mind. As has been made clear throughout this report, however, economic evaluations often are quite limited in both number and content. The total costs of an intervention frequently are excluded from the evaluations that are performed. Yet decisions will be made. The budget will be fully allocated one way or the other, even if the saving is deferred to another day or, in the case of government, returned to taxpayers. Bluntly, while one intervention's expansion may await further economic evaluation, the budget will, regardless, fully allocate 100 percent of funds.

In practice, in many if not most cases, government budgetary decisions and the delivery of services take place within silos. Different departments and legislative committees separately oversee education, food, housing, and health programs for children without fully taking into account the impact in other program areas. Similar silos often characterize foundations and other private organizations engaged in making investment decisions for children.

In the practical world of budgets, therefore, the ideal is never fully met, often because of limitations of time and resources. Even with the best of economic evidence available, the evidence is never fully informative at every margin of how the next dollar should be spent (or returned to taxpayers). Given these limitations, there are nonetheless three dimensions in which budget processes could be improved to take better advantage of the evidence derived from economic evaluations: (1) reporting on the availability *and absence* of economic evidence; (2) allocating budgetary resources to take fuller account of the time dimension that economic evaluation needs to encompass, particularly for children, whose outcomes often extend well into adulthood; and (3) accounting for net benefits and gains beyond any particular intervention, constituency, or organization.

Reporting on the Availability and Absence of Economic Evidence

While Chapter 3 emphasizes the gains possible from the production of high-quality economic evidence, the focus here is on what budget offices can do with the evidence that is and is not available. To the extent possible, decision makers need to be as informed as possible in their decision making. Thus they need to know what economic evaluations are available, not available, planned, and not planned for programs falling within their budget.

For example, OMB could list annually which programs do and do not have economic evaluations planned as part of their ongoing assessment, where the evaluations exist, and what has been evaluated. Such programs could include those implemented through tax subsidies or regulation, not just direct spending, as in the case of earned income tax credits, which accrue largely to households with children. Similarly, CBO regularly reports on options for reducing the federal budget deficit. In so doing, it could both report on the extent to which these options make use of economic evidence and recommend use of the availability of economic evidence as one criterion for decision making.

Allocation of Budgetary Resources to Account for Outcomes over Time

Returns on investments take place over time. No one would invest in a corporate stock based solely on the expected earnings of that corporation over 5 or even 10 years; the company's net value depends on its earnings over time. Similarly the returns on interventions for children often accrue over a lifetime, and, as indicated in Chapter 3, often take the form of longer-term noncognitive gains such as decreased dropout rates, lower unemployment upon leaving high school, or lower rates of teen pregnancy.

Unfortunately, it is often easier to negotiate support for interventions with near-term gains since those gains may be both more visible and more likely to accrue to the benefit of public and private officials running for office or being promoted on the basis of their near-term successes. Likewise, a school board may more easily gain support for an intervention aimed at children ages 3 to 5 if it will improve performance in second grade 3 years later than if it will improve graduation rates 14 years later. Even CBO reports on the budgetary effects of proposed changes in the law cover only 10 years, with some exceptions for programs such as Social Security.

Since this is not a report on budget process reform, only two basic points are important to make here. First, decision making will be improved when decision makers are fully informed of these limitations. This is a particular issue when, as noted, program allocations are being made with and without economic evidence at hand. Particularly when it comes to investments in children, a short-term horizon biases those budgetary decisions in favor of interventions with short- but not long-term benefits, such as higher consumption levels for beneficiaries within a budget window and returns to existing voters but not those younger or not yet born. Economic evaluations that similarly focus on the short term add to those budgetary biases.

Second, if returns on investments in children are long term, data are needed to follow those children over extended periods of time. Relatedly, the linkage of long-term data across systems and sectors is an important step toward improving their use. Although there are challenges to the systematic linkage of data (e.g., the outdated design of administrative structures and systems, data privacy, tracking of children and families),[1] there is still significant potential in these efforts (Brown et al., 2015; Chetty et al., 2015; Cohodes et al., 2014; Lens, 2015). Establishing personal relationships between the collectors and users of the data, shadowing successful project designs (e.g., the Project on Human Development in Chicago Neighborhoods,[2] the Three City Study[3]), or seeking guidance from other fields (e.g., criminal justice) could provide opportunities for continuing to address these challenges.[4] (See Chapter 5 for additional discussion of data linkage.)

On the other hand, one could depend on developing new and expensive data sets with each new experiment or program adoption or extension. But that approach likely would be cumbersome and expensive, even if worthwhile. Statistical entities, such as the Census Bureau and the IRS's Statistics of Income Program or those associated with state K-12 and early childhood education, could gain more from their limited budgets if they gave significant budget weight to the development of longitudinal data following individuals. Foundations interested in economic evaluation could also assess the relative importance of a new experiment requiring new data development and more investment in data that could inform multiple investments. Students and youth provide an ideal case in point. Educational and early childhood reform efforts consistently try new experiments, many of which are amenable to economic evaluation. Well-developed data following young children and students over extended periods of time could allow multiple evaluations to make use of a common set of data, such as progress along various outcome scales, even if the separate evaluations still required additional input of data, say, on cost differences related to different experimental designs.

---

[1] Observation made at the committee's open session on June 1, 2015, Panel 2; see Appendix A.

[2] For more information on this effort, see http://www.icpsr.umich.edu/icpsrweb/PHDCN/about.jsp# [June 2016].

[3] For more information on this effort, see http://web.jhu.edu/threecitystudy [June 2016].

[4] Observation made at the committee's open session on June 1, 2015, Panel 2; see Appendix A.

Accounting for Net Benefits and Costs Across Interventions,
Constituencies, and Organizations

Compartments, silos, and limited frameworks constantly affect budget decision making, and as a result, the economic savings from investing in effective strategies may not accrue to the intervention, constituency, or government entity making the investment. For instance, a community may invest in early childhood education, but given the mobility of families, the gains from that investment often will accrue to jurisdictions to which those families move. In technical BCA terms, when internal costs are compared with internal benefits, external costs and benefits are ignored. One study, for instance, found that the societal return needed to realize government savings on drug and crime prevention interventions varies widely among sectors, and even for government saving alone, depends on whether the calculation is made at the federal level or at the federal, state, and local levels combined (Miller and Hendrie, 2012).

How can budget offices make a difference here? For one, budget decisions frequently are made at high levels at which gains across boundaries can be combined. For instance, OMB often guides final budget decisions for the President when reviewing particular agency requests. Even a particular agency, as long as its goal is the well-being of constituents, can mitigate its own tendency to localize decision making by reporting economic evaluations across program areas, even those not under their jurisdiction.

Budget offices also can identify for policy makers and administrators incentives that might offset built-in tendencies to account only for local costs and benefits. For example, many federal programs in areas affecting children are implemented on the ground through state and local officials, and many state programs are implemented through local officials, thus resulting in transfers of benefits and costs across jurisdictions. Additional features can be added to programs so that offsetting transfers are made to compensate jurisdictions bearing costs for benefits they do not receive. Economic evaluations can account for gains and losses across all jurisdictions.

OMB, for example could list which programs do and do not have economic evaluations planned as part of their ongoing assessment. Such programs could include those implemented through tax subsidies or regulation, not just direct spending. In addition, in its annual review of options for reducing the deficit, CBO could recommend using the availability of economic evaluation as one criterion for decision making.

CONCLUSION: Budgets allocate resources one way or the other.
Those decisions will be made regardless of whether the results of
economic evaluation and other forms of evidence are at hand or the

research is planned for the future. It is desirable to have access to as much information as reasonably possible. Economic evaluation can be influential in a world where decision making is made with incomplete information.

CONCLUSION: *Budget choices often factor in only near-term cost avoidance and savings and, even when evidence from benefit-cost analysis is available, near-term benefits. Benefits from investments in children, youth, and families, however, often are measured most accurately over extended periods continuing into adulthood.*

CONCLUSION: *The economic savings that result from investing in effective strategies may accrue to constituencies or government entities other than those making the investments.*

Data Availability

"There aren't archives out there where researchers or administrators or anybody else can go to get linked administrative data at the local, state, or federal level to do what we need to do. It's the access issue that is the concern here."

> —Robert M. George, senior research fellow,
> Chapin Hall at University of Chicago, at the
> committee's open session of June 1, 2015.

"At times it can be difficult to get the federal government to share data across different agencies. It can be even harder to get state agencies to share data across its agencies or with the federal government."

> —Beth A. Virnig, director, Research Data
> Assistance Center, University of Minnesota, at the
> committee's open session of June 1, 2015.

Opportunities exist to use administrative data to help meet the data needs of different types of economic evaluation.[5] In particular, cost analysis (CA), CEA, cost-savings analysis, and BCA produce distinct types of evidence that can be used to answer different questions. They also use different types of administrative data and leverage those data in different ways. Figure 4-1 depicts the potential uses of administrative data in economic evaluations.

CA benefits from accessing administrative data that are qualitatively

---

[5] Big data, innovative data-sharing technologies, and the emerging field of data science are relevant to the discussion of the use of economic evidence; within this report, however, these topics are not explored in depth.

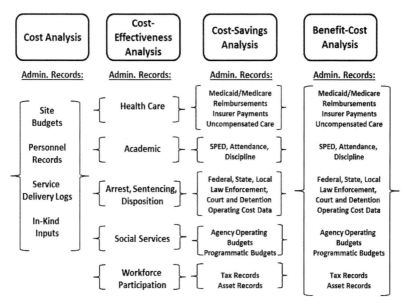

FIGURE 4-1 Opportunities for the use of administrative data in economic evaluations.
NOTE: SPED = special education.
SOURCE: Adapted from Crowley (2015).

different from those used for other types of economic evaluation. Particularly key is the use of site budgets, personnel records, and service delivery logs. Site budgets, often one of the main sources of administrative data used for CAs, help establish the quantity of resources used and provide the actual prices paid to operate an intervention. Personnel records are used to determine what labor resources were used for what intervention activities. And service delivery logs are used to determine the size of the population served. Programs that use coordinated data systems to track service delivery at the individual level produce administrative records that allow for individual cost estimates by apportioning total costs to specific individuals. This process can provide more precise estimates than average cost estimates with poorly understood variability. Finally, reports on in-kind contributions that may supplement parental grants or contracts also can be mined to estimate the total costs for an intervention. Ignoring such supplemental resources can result in underestimating the cost of infrastructure and jeopardize future replication of an intervention.

CEA uses many of the same records considered in an effectiveness analysis. Record domains including health care, education, criminal justice, social services, and workplace participation all are relevant. In a CEA, impacts captured by outcomes on administrative records can be considered in the context of an intervention's cost. Whether the intervention is considered cost-effective depends on the payer's willingness to pay for the achieved change in outcomes.

Cost savings analysis makes it possible to consider an intervention's impact and efficiency in more absolute terms. Cost savings analyses can leverage administrative data similar to those used in CEA, but often look to data that are linked to budgetary outlays. In health care these data include Medicaid and Medicare reimbursements, private insurer payments to providers, and uncompensated care costs at both the provider and government levels. In education, the focus is often on cost drivers such as special education and disciplinary costs, as well as areas linked to public spending, such as attendance. Criminal justice records for individuals often are combined with administrative data on law enforcement spending, as well as court and detention operating costs. Specifically, when criminal records indicate the quantity of criminal justice resources spent on individuals, data on local, state, and federal spending can be used to estimate the price of those resources. In a similar fashion, individual-level social services data can be used in combination with social services agency and programmatic budgets to estimate quantity of resources consumed and the local prices for providing them. Importantly, within the social services domain, programmatic budgets alone are not sufficient for estimating prices. The infrastructure costs of the service providers also must be included in the price estimates, and often can be derived only from agency operating budgets. Lastly, evaluations of workforce participation in cost savings analyses generally focus on impacts on wealth, income, and tax revenue, requiring access to tax and asset records.

While a cost-savings analysis generally would consider only one of these domains at a time, a full BCA would leverage these records to assess impact across systems and arrive at a full net benefit of the intervention that accounted for savings in one system and increased costs in another. Outcome evaluation of interventions for children, youth, and families ideally requires longitudinal data on changes in disparate aspects of well-being: education, health, safety, housing, employment, happiness, and so on.

While administrative data sets contain much of the information needed for CA, CEA, cost-savings analysis, and BCA, these data may not be available. Administrative data often are not stored centrally. Local data systems tend to use varied formats, archive differing information, use incompatible file formats, and sometimes overwriting data instead of archiving them. Some systems are not even automated. Even if data are centralized, local cost recovery objectives may preclude retrieving them from the central source. Centralized data also tend to be a snapshot in time and place, while local data may be updated.

Even automated data often are not readily accessible. Privacy rules differ between health care and education data, but they often preclude access to identifiable records. Even signed consent will not enable access to identifiable tax records or Social Security earnings records.

The problem becomes especially acute when data cut across silos. The department funding a trial usually will try to contribute the data it owns to an evaluation, but may lack the leverage to convince other departments to spend resources on providing data or breaking barriers to support an evaluation.

The private sector now has data that dwarf the amount of public data. Every credit card swipe goes into a commercial database that documents buying habits and often also into a vendor database with details of who purchased what, where, and when. Sensors in crash-involved vehicles provide driving and impact data in millisecond intervals. And medical records increasingly are electronic. Thus, the data needed to answer many policy questions are housed in private data systems. Increasingly, the same is true of data needed to answer questions about the long-term outcomes of randomized controlled trials. The pressing question is how those data can be accessed affordably and ethically.

Access to data from randomized controlled trials also may be limited in ways that hamper maximizing the lessons learned from the trials. Trial managers are protective of their data. They fear confidentiality could be breached. They lack the resources to document and share deidentified data and answer questions about the data posed by prospective users. And they worry that their data could be misanalyzed. Yet meta-analyses are more powerful and accurate if unit record data can be pooled. It is unclear where the proper balance lies here.

CONCLUSION: *Federal agencies maintain large data sets, both government-collected and resulting from evaluations, that are not readily accessible. Privacy issues and silos compound the challenges of making these data available. Improving access to administrative data and evaluation results could provide opportunities to track people and outcomes over time and at low cost.*

CONCLUSION: *Without a commitment by government to the development of linkages across administrative data sets on education, health, crime, and other domains, both longitudinally and across systems, efforts to expand the evidence base on intervention impacts and evidence of economic returns will be limited.*

FACTORS THAT CAN FACILITATE THE
USE OF ECONOMIC EVIDENCE

Factors related both to organizational culture and management practices and to collaborative relationships can facilitate the use of economic evidence.

Organizational Culture and Management Practices

Organizational culture and management practices, including leadership, openness to learning, accountability, performance management, and learning forums, can promote more optimal use of economic evaluation. The focus in this section is on the dynamics within decision-making bodies. Some of the factors that provide an impetus for an organization to conduct economic evaluation are briefly reviewed in Box 4-3.

Leadership and Openness to Learning

Some organizations have a culture or characteristics that are supportive of the use of evidence, including the results of economic evaluation, such as leaders and managers who value economic evaluations and have sufficient

---

BOX 4-3
The Impetus for Economic Evaluation: Examples

Proposals internal to an organization, as well as legislation with a direct impact on the organization's budget, will frequently generate cost analysis (CA). The Congressional Budget Office (CBO), for example, requires CA for passage of federal legislation with a budget impact. Because CAs provide important information about the economic impacts of legislation, they may be accompanied by cost-effectiveness analysis (although CBO is likely to include such information in separate, program-related studies). As a routine matter, however, legislation often is not accompanied by information relating costs to the effectiveness of particular interventions (benefit-cost analysis) or assessing an intervention's cost-effectiveness relative to other options with the same goal.

As another example, the White House Office of Information and Regulatory Affairs administers Executive Order 12866 58 FR 51735, which requires federal agencies considering alternatives to rulemakings to provide an analysis of the costs and benefits of these alternatives. In theory this requirement has led to improved decision making, although there is not a strong evidence base indicating that it has in fact resulted in more cost-effective rules (Harrington and Morgenstern, 2004).

knowledge to understand and make use of them. Such characteristics have been known to influence the extent to which economic evaluation is used to make programmatic or budgetary decisions (Armstrong et al., 2014; Brownson et al., 2009; Jennings and Hall, 2011). Researchers, both internal and external, can promote the use of economic evaluation when they understand the organization, develop relationships with leaders and other potential users who become involved in joint decision making involving the evidence (Nutley et al., 2007; Palinkas et al., 2015; Williams and Bryan, 2007), and communicate results in ways that increase understanding and use of the evidence (National Research Council, 2012; Tseng, 2012).

Organizations open to discussion and learning are more receptive to the use of evidence, including rigorous economic evaluations, that may run counter to their experiences and beliefs (Cousins and Bourgeois, 2014). Changes in the organizational culture may therefore be required to make an organization receptive to the use of economic evidence. Such changes may entail not only leadership and support from the top of the organization, but also external support and access to the resources needed to achieve a shared vision for the acquisition and use of such evidence (Blau et al., 2015; Hoyle et al., 2008). Changes also may entail attention to future needs, including the data required for economic evaluation. (See the section above on budget considerations for discussion of budgeting for the development of data in advance of future economic evaluations.) Further discussion of the importance of a culture of learning is included in the section below on performance management.

Wholey and Newcomer (1997) argue that organizations and their cultures should be examined before a study is undertaken to determine whether the organization is, in fact, prepared to use the evidence produced by the study. Funders, both public and private, who want to promote the use of economic evidence might choose to place their resources in organizations that are more receptive to doing so—thereby also providing incentives for other organizations to perform more economic evaluation.

CONCLUSION: *Economic evidence is more likely to be used if it has leadership support and if the organizational culture promotes learning.*

Accountability

Accountability involves delegation of a task or responsibility to a person or organization, monitoring the delegate to observe performance, and delivering consequences based on that performance. It arises in such relationships as supervisors' evaluation of employees' performance, auditors' concerns with fiscal accountability, shareholders' interests in company performance, and funders' concerns with the success of the projects they fund.

Accountability is a central tenet of representative democracy (Greiling and Spraul, 2010), as citizens want to know how well the government to which they have delegated power has performed, and then deliver consequences through elections or other feedback channels.

Vesel**ý** (2013) notes that "accountability" is one of the most frequently used terms in public administration, but has many different meanings. He identifies four current usages, including "good governance" and a means to ensure the quality and effectiveness of government. Lindberg (2013) found more than 100 different subtypes and usages of accountability in the scholarly literature; he sees the major subtypes as political, financial, legal, and bureaucratic.

As the accountability movement has continued, its drawbacks, or unintended side effects, have become more obvious. These efforts can take time and resources away from an organization's primary goals; that is, accountability, too, involves a cost that must be related to benefits. Sometimes standards are unrealistic, or criteria for judging are contradictory. Agencies may focus on success of the tasks being measured or on one type of benefit, and neglect other goals or the broader picture. Accountability typically involves a top-down approach, whereas economic evaluation should be considered valuable in strengthening, not just threatening, decision makers. Those promoting the use of economic evidence would do well to understand why greater accountability can but not necessarily does promote the use of economic evidence or better performance (Halachmi, 2002; Vesel**ý**, 2013). The example in Box 4-4 illustrates the potential negative effects of an emphasis on accountability.

One bottom line is that economic evaluation first and foremost provides valuable information for constructive problem solving. If people think that results of evaluations and other data will be used against them (e.g., for budget cuts or other unfavorable consequences), they will react accordingly (Asen et al., 2013; Lorenc et al., 2014). They may aim to improve the specific outcomes being measured without actually improving anything— for instance, by serving only those who are most likely to achieve some outcome or by manipulating the data (Brooks and Wills, 2015).

Nevertheless, the interest in accountability will continue, and rightly so. The theory is somewhat incontrovertible: if people are accountable for their actions, they usually will respond to the incentives involved. It is in the application of accountability schemes that difficulties arise. There is a learning agenda implied by the above-described mixed experience with accountability frameworks. As Coule (2015) puts it, there is increasing recognition that the notion of accountability as "a somewhat benign and straightforward governance function" is, instead, "a challenging, complex choice" (p. 76).

BOX 4-4
Illustrative Example of Accountability: No Child Left Behind

An example of the ways in which strong accountability systems can overtake the gains available from a good information and economic evaluation system and even result in unintended consequences is the K-12 accountability provisions contained in the federal No Child Left Behind Act.* The act's goal of academic proficiency for all students as measured by state standardized tests of math and English language arts has resulted in a system highly focused on improving test scores. As a result, untested subjects, such as foreign languages or social studies, may be given short shrift. Students well below or well above proficiency have received less attention than others since they are less likely to contribute to a school's overall measures of progress. The National Research Council's (2011) report suggests that test-based incentive systems have had little effect on student achievement and that high school exit exams "as currently implemented in the United States, decrease the rate of high school graduation without increasing achievement" (pp. 4-5).

At the same time, by promoting the use of measures of progress, No Child Left Behind holds considerable promise for leading to many types of economic evaluation of different approaches to teaching, learning, and use of school resources. A more modest and attainable accountability system might first emphasize obtaining better measures of individual student progress that are useful to teachers and principals (e.g., as early warning signals of a student's no longer making progress), as well as for performing multiple levels of experimentation amenable to future economic evaluation.

---

*In December 2015, the No Child Left Behind Act was replaced by the Every Student Succeeds Act (Public Law No:114-95).

Performance Management

Closely related to accountability systems are performance management and monitoring. The theory or logic model entails monitoring performance to achieve greater accountability and then better performance. Government-wide reforms, such as the Government Performance and Results Act (GPRA) of 1993, the George H.W. Bush-era Program Assessment Rating Tool (PART), and the current GPRA Modernization Act of 2010 are prime examples of the creation of performance management systems aimed at making data more widely used in decision making. Policy-specific changes in such areas as safety-net programs (the Personal Responsibility and Work Opportunity Act of 1996) and education (the No Child Left Behind Act of 2002 and the Race to the Top initiative of 2009) provide further incentive for the use of performance measures within specific policy areas.

Economic evaluation can and has played an important role in performance management.

An area ripe for further research is the role of continuous improvement or continuous quality improvement both in supporting the implementation of evidence-based practices and in ensuring that the implementation of those practices is helping to improve outcomes. As part of the Maternal, Infant, and Early Childhood Home Visiting Program, for example, states are required to submit an implementation plan to the federal government. Among the items they must include is a plan for using data for continuous quality improvement. This requirement suggests that it is important not only to use data and evidence to identify which types of programs or practices can produce outcomes or savings that offset their costs, but also to have a system to continually monitor the implementation of these efforts and ensuring that implementation and outcomes are both moving in the expected direction. As noted earlier in this report, the implementation of interventions can strongly influence whether they produce the expected outcomes. Other factors—including community-level factors, historical context, and the choice of a counterfactual—also can affect outcomes. Thus, it is important in promoting evidence-based practice to identify ways in which governments and providers can monitor their programs continuously to ensure that they are producing the desired benefits.

Moynihan (2008) argues that performance data (of which economic evaluation is one type) is not comprehensive. For any complex program or task, there are multiple ways of capturing performance, and performance data could not reasonably be expected to replace politics or to erase information asymmetries in the policy process. This does not mean that these data are not useful if applied in a realistic system of improvement, rather than one focused on some final determination of merit. Moynihan also points out that performance data are more likely to be used purposefully in homogenous settings, where individuals can agree on the basic goal of a program.

Techniques such as BCA certainly have an appeal in being less susceptible to subjectivity than the selection of a simple performance target. But even as the importance and sophistication of BCA have risen, the political process should not be expected to cede decision making to even the best technical analysis. Organizational learning remains the central management benefit of performance data, including economic evidence, for complex tasks. Learning requires a willingness to observe and correct error, which depends in turn on frank discussions about what is working and what is not, as well as the limitations of even the highest-quality analysis.

Learning Forums

A classic error governments have made in efforts to link data to decisions is to pay inadequate attention to creating routines for the use of data. Learning forums are structured routines that encourage actors to closely examine information, consider its significance, and decide how it will affect future action. The meaning of data is not always straightforward; even the answer to such basic questions as whether performance is good or bad may be unclear. Learning forums provide a realm where performance data are interpreted and given shared meaning. More complex questions, such as "What is performance at this level?" or "What should we do next?" cannot be answered simply by looking at the data, but require deeper insight and other types of knowledge that can be incorporated into learning forums (Moynihan, 2015).

Such routines are more successful when they include ground rules to structure dialogue, employ a nonconfrontational approach to avoid defensive reactions, feature collegiality and equality among participants, and include a diverse set of organizational actors responsible for producing the outcomes under review (Moynihan, 2008). Moynihan and Kroll (2015) note that although no learning forum will be perfect, following principles and routines—for example, focusing on important goals and on some of the factors discussed in this and the previous chapter, such as committed leadership, timely information, a staff well trained in analyzing data, and high-quality data—can make a forum successful. A learning forum also will be more effective if it incorporates different types of relevant information. Quantitative data are more useful when they can be interpreted by individuals with experiential knowledge of process and work conditions that explain successes, failures, and the possibility of innovation (Moynihan, 2008). The latter type of information also might be derived from some type of evaluation, ideally with treatments and controls, a BCA, or a CEA.

A Potential Role for Funders

How might the broad conclusions on organizational culture and a continuous learning process presented in this section influence public and private funders? In sponsoring economic evaluation, funders often explicitly or implicitly seek or rely on a theory of causality: How do particular activities in this particular analysis result in specific outcomes? That question can beg how the evaluation and the theory itself should adapt in a process of newer learning and continuous improvement. Funders might consider granting funds to support the use of monitoring systems and feedback loops, thereby enabling nonprofits or government agencies to use economic and other data and evidence to learn, adapt, and incorporate new understandings into an ongoing cycle of improvement.

CONCLUSION: *Economic evidence is most useful when it is one component of a continuous learning and improvement process.*

Collaborative Relationships

"There is a process involved to get individuals who are not naturally researchers to think about how they should use this type of information. It is building relationships. It is building trust. It is not a one shot thing."
—Dan Rosenbaum, senior economist, Economic Policy Division, Office of Management and Budget, at the committee's open session on March 23, 2015.

Studies relating to the use of economic evidence in policy making suggest that the "disjuncture between researchers and decision-makers in terms of objective functions, institutional contexts, and professional value systems" (Williams and Bryan, 2007, p. 141) requires considering an interactive model of research utilization that would increase the acceptability of economic evidence (Nutley et al., 2007). Tseng (2012) argues that improving the quality of research itself is insufficient, noting that "relationships are emerging as key conduits for research, interpretation, and use. Policymakers and practitioners rely on trusted peers and intermediaries. Rather than pursuing broad-based dissemination efforts, there may be value in understanding the existing social system and capitalizing on it" (p. 13).

A systematic review of 145 articles on the use of evidence in policy making in 59 different countries found that the factor that most facilitated use was collaboration between researchers and policy makers, identified for two-thirds of the studies in which use was achieved (Oliver et al., 2014a). Other facilitating factors included frequent contact; relevant, reliable, and clear reports of findings; and access to high-quality, relevant research.

However, developing relationships takes time and effort. Studies of use conclude that research should be conducted with sustained personal contact, dialogue, and collaboration between researchers and decision makers to benefit both the policy-making and research development processes (Davies et al., 2008; Elliott and Popay, 2000; Mitton et al., 2007; National Research Council, 2012; Orton et al., 2011; Palinkas et al., 2015). The need for regular communication among researchers, practitioners, and policy makers is a lesson that has been learned among those involved in scaling up evidence-based programs (Supplee and Metz, 2015), as well as those advocating for evidence-based policy making (Innvaer et al., 2002; Kemm, 2006).

In addition to developing relationships with potential users, researchers can communicate with local decision makers. Mitton and colleagues (2007) recommend using a steering committee composed of local representatives from different sectors to help guide the research and recommend strategies for dissemination. The steering committee members then become important conduits to the community, informing others about the study, their trust in the research, the results, and their implications.

In some cases, researchers find potential users among community leaders or what those studying public policy term policy entrepreneurs (Oliver et al., 2014b; Orton et al., 2011; Tseng, 2012). Regular, open dialogues with consumers can alert researchers to how the evidence might be used—for example, instrumentally (directly, for a decision) or conceptually (to influence beliefs about the problem or the approach and to inform future planning).

It is also important to recognize that economic evaluations may be applied to questions and settings beyond the original purpose of the evaluation. Consumers of economic evidence may wish to generalize and translate results of a study when they consider implementing an intervention elsewhere. In such circumstances, translators or intermediaries can play a critical role in helping to bridge the divide that often exists between producers and consumers of economic evidence (Armstrong et al., 2013; Bogenschneider and Corbett, 2010; Tseng, 2012). These translators or intermediaries are often people who already have established relationships with leaders in the agency and the community and thus are familiar with the contexts in which the results of economic evaluation may be applied. Further, they are, or can become, a trusted source with the skills to identify and interpret relevant research results in an informed, unbiased manner. They can engage in ongoing dialogue with users and help them translate research results into action that is consistent with the results.

The function performed by these translators or intermediaries is often referred to as **knowledge brokering**, whose primary objective is to "link decision makers with researchers so they can understand each other's goals, cultures, and constraints, and can thus collaborate on how best to use evidence in decision making" (Conklin et al., 2013, p. 2). A knowledge broker may, therefore, be someone who operates independently at the intersection between producers and consumers, or may be someone affiliated more strongly with one group, such as an evaluator involved in evaluation and program planning who can help link empirical evidence with decisions made in practice settings (Donnelly et al., 2014; Urban and Trochim, 2009). Furthermore, Dobbins and colleagues assert that knowledge brokering is not limited to single intermediaries but "can be carried out by individuals, groups and/or organizations, as well as entire countries" (Dobbins et al., 2009, p. 2; Ward et al., 2009). The important point to remember is that it is the function of brokering to facilitate the diffusion and uptake of knowledge, regardless of the entity that provides it, that is essential to reducing the divide often experienced between research and practice. Fostering relationships between producers and consumers of economic evidence also can enhance the credibility and perceived relevance of research among potential users, since trust in the evidence appears to be closely tied to trust in its source (Fielding and Briss, 2006; Tseng, 2014).

Examples exist of such intermediary relationships or partnerships. Armstrong and colleagues (2013) describe success in Australia in implementing an Evidence-Informed Decision Making model, designed in accordance with research on knowledge transfer, to help decision makers better utilize scientific evidence. Such models are intended to integrate the best available research evidence with local contextual factors, such as community norms, political preferences, and available resources, leading to decisions better tailored to the local context (Tseng, 2014).

A promising development in efforts to connect research with policy and practice is the increasing focus on research-practice partnerships. Coburn and colleagues (2013) provide an overview of such partnerships in the field of education, defining them as "long-term mutualistic collaborations between practitioners and researchers that are intentionally organized to investigate problems of practice and solutions for improving district outcomes" (p. 2). Several such research-practice partnerships already exist, particularly in education.

According to Coburn and colleagues (2013), research-practice partnerships have five characteristics: (1) they are long-term, operating over several years and sometimes decades, which allows the partnership to focus on complex issues that may not be resolved with one study or simple or rapid analyses; (2) they focus on the problems of practice that districts find most pressing and important; (3) they are committed to mutualism, with research agendas being developed together by the researchers and practitioners and continually revisited to ensure that they are meeting the needs of each; (4) they use intentional strategies to foster partnerships, such as formal data sharing agreements and structured processes for developing research and sharing evidence; and (5) they produce original analyses, so the relationship is not just about translating or sharing findings but also about developing new studies to answer pressing questions.

These partnerships have the potential to address some of the ongoing challenges entailed in connecting research, practice, and policy (Innvaer et al., 2002; Oliver et al., 2014a). They build ongoing communication between researchers and practitioners to ensure that the research being produced answers the questions of interest to the practitioners or policy makers. This ongoing dialogue and relationship also allows for multiple conversations between researchers and practitioners to help translate findings into action in a way that is consistent with the evidence. Because researcher-practitioner partnerships center around the needs of and data from the community, including the framing of research questions of interest, they also address concerns among practitioners and decision makers about the generalizability and relevance of evidence from other contexts to their communities (Orton et al., 2011).

There are a number of examples of success in the use of economic evidence in decision making. Both the National Institute for Health and Care Excellence (NICE) in the United Kingdom and the Health Intervention and Technology Assessment Program (HITAP) in Thailand have statutory authority to use economic evidence to inform decisions about health care coverage. In Canada and Australia, knowledge transfer models are used to integrate research findings and contextual factors, such as community preferences, resources, and other local issues, to foster evidence-based decision making in local public health settings (Armstrong et al., 2013; Lavis et al., 2003); one of these efforts is described in Box 4-5. Finally, Blau and colleagues (2015) report on the success of training for medical professionals in four low- and middle-income countries (Albania, Azerbaijan, Croatia, and Georgia) in the use of economic evidence to inform decisions on immunization. The methods learned were then used in all four countries to improve estimates of the burden of disease, and led to policy changes in each country. These cases illustrate that effective use of economic evidence can occur, but they are the exceptions.

CONCLUSION: *Interactive, ongoing, collaborative relationships between decision makers and researchers and trusted knowledge brokers are a promising strategy for improving the use of economic evidence.*

EXAMPLES OF EFFORTS TO IMPROVE THE USE OF EVALUATION EVIDENCE

This chapter has reviewed factors that influence the use of economic evidence by decision makers. This section describes examples of ongoing efforts to address these factors. The examples in this section are intended to be illustrative of the points discussed throughout the chapter; they do not represent the total range of innovative ways in which state and local governments across the country are partnering with practitioners and intermediaries to improve the use and usefulness of research evidence in general and economic evidence in particular.

BOX 4-5
Knowledge Translation Strategies

Knowledge translation, defined as a range of strategies that help translate research evidence into practice, holds promise for guiding efforts to improve the use of economic evidence in decision making. Knowledge translation strategies are informed by theories underlying diffusion, dissemination, and implementation sciences and are designed to improve the capacity of both individual users and organizations to access and use evidence (Armstrong et al., 2013). The work of Armstrong and colleagues at the University of Melbourne in Australia is one of the few studies available to articulate and begin to test a theory of change around knowledge translation strategies. These researchers found that the knowledge base on the effectiveness of knowledge translation strategies in changing behaviors in the clinical medicine and allied health fields was more substantial than that on the effectiveness of these knowledge translation strategies in public health settings. Their formative research suggested that for their approach to be effective it would need to support change at the individual and organizational levels. As a result, they set out to develop the capacity of key personnel in local government agencies in Victoria to access research evidence, assess its trustworthiness, and apply it to the local context, as well as to implement strategies that could foster an organizational culture supporting evidence-informed decision making across these agencies. A statewide survey and a series of individual interviews with members of the target audience helped shape the development of a multi-pronged, resource-intensive intervention that included tailored organizational support, group trainings, targeted communications, and the development of evidence summaries of relevant content, all of which contributed to both individual and organizational improvements in the use of evidence. Strategies for improving the use of evidence among local government leaders included the implementation of training sessions to build the skills of project officers and senior management in basic research methods and ways of identifying high-quality empirical evidence, as well as the utilization of networks to promote evidence sharing, particularly if network activities also served to strengthen relationships between local agency staff and researchers.

Washington State Institute for Public Policy (WSIPP)

WSIPP is an example of efforts to use economic evidence to guide investment decisions by state government. WSIPP was created in 1983 by the Washington State legislature to conduct "practical, nonpartisan research at the direction of the legislature or the institute's board of directors" (Institute of Medicine and National Research Council, 2014, p. 9). The institute essentially functions as an advisor on spending decisions for the state. WSIPP has developed a three-step process for determining the economic impacts of decisions. First, it applies a meta-analytic approach to identify and summarize the results of all rigorous evaluations relevant to the policies being analyzed. Second, it uses a systematic analytical framework to calculate the benefits, costs, and risks to the state's population of a policy change. Finally, it analyzes the expected economic impact of investing in portfolios of programs that address a particular policy goal (Institute of Medicine and National Research Council, 2014).

WSIPP has become a valuable resource for state legislators by addressing several of the factors discussed in this chapter. First, it has strong relationships with lawmakers, which have helped both analysts and decision makers understand how to work effectively with each other. Second, WSIPP has managed to create and maintain the perception that its work is relevant to decision makers across various contexts by building a portfolio of work in many policy areas over many years. Third, it has developed a systematic process that it applies in all its BCAs, which includes the reporting of results in an easy-to-understand format, standardized across policy sectors. Finally, WSIPP has ensured that external conditions are conducive to the use of its work by remaining systematically nonpartisan, making recommendations that follow objectively from its work regardless of which political faction will identify most with them (Institute of Medicine and National Research Council, 2014; National Research Council and Institute of Medicine, 2009).

Pew-MacArthur Results First Initiative

A joint project of the Pew Charitable Trusts and the John D. and Catherine T. MacArthur Foundation, Results First works with states to implement WSIPP's approach to conducting BCA. This initiative helps states develop capacity to both produce and use economic evidence by offering government agencies WSIPP's analytical tools, training policy makers and their staff in how the model can help inform their decision making, and helping agencies and decision makers establish working groups to guide and implement the model (Institute of Medicine and National Research Council, 2014). Results First also ensures that analyses are relevant to the local context by replacing Washington State's data with data specific to each jurisdiction and by helping to implement analyses requested by states. Finally, Results First creates an effective incentive structure by requiring demonstrated commitment from both executive and legislative bodies to implementing WSIPP's model and considering the results in policy deliberations (Pew-MacArthur Results First Initiative, 2014).

At the committee's March open session, panelist Gary VanLandingham, director of Results First, stated that one of the major barriers facing the initiative is that "it is difficult to bring information into the policy process to come in as an outsider and bring information into the relationships . . . because of all of the gatekeepers that exist and the [need to gain] the policymaker's confidence." Thus part of Results First's strategy is to identify actors who already have those relationships—who are at "the nexus of influence nodes"—and work with them to build their capacity to do this type of analysis and bring it into the system.

University of Chicago Consortium on Chicago School Research (UChicago CCSR)

The example of the UChicago CCSR illustrates factors that facilitate the use of evidence and the perception that evidence is relevant to local decision making; lessons from this work apply to increasing the use of economic evidence. The UChicago CCSR was created in 1990 in a partnership among researchers from the University of Chicago, the Chicago public schools, and other organizations. The consortium's initial objective was to study the impact of the decentralization of Chicago's public school system. Since then, it has contributed to many of the city's reform efforts, a number of which have informed efforts in other jurisdictions.

Several features distinguish the UChicago CCSR from other research organizations, many of them related to factors that influence the use of evidence. First, by focusing on one place—Chicago—the consortium builds a perception among its main target group of users that its work is relevant to the local context. Second, it builds strong relationships and trust with users of its work by actively engaging a diverse group of stakeholders in the design of research, communicating the results of its work, and asking for input on the interpretation of its findings. In addition, its multipartisan steering committee includes representatives from state and local agencies, the teachers' union, civic leaders, education researchers, and community-based organizations. Finally, another unique feature of the UChicago CCSR is its commitment to reporting its work to a diverse range of audiences by translating research findings into publicly accessible reports that are widely disseminated.

Investing in Innovation Fund

The example of the Investing in Innovation Fund (i3) does not focus on economic evidence per se, but does highlight how evidence of impact is directly tied to decisions about investments in interventions benefiting children, youth, and families. Established in 2009 under the American Recovery and Reinvestment Act, i3 provides competitive grants to applicants that have established evidence of improving student achievement and attainment. By using evidence as an entrance requirement, i3 creates an incentive structure that encourages local educational agencies (LEAs) to generate solid evidence of the impact of their programs. In addition, because non-profit organizations are eligible for i3 funding only if they partner with one or more LEAs or a consortium of schools, i3 incentivizes the development of relationships and a political environment conducive to the effective use of the evidence generated by funded activities. At the committee's March open session, panelist Nadya Dabby, assistant deputy secretary for innovation and improvement at the U.S. Department of Education, stated that i3 gives "the support and incentive to create evidence coming out of the program . . . public investments should benefit [public education] beyond the direct beneficiaries."

EPISCenter

The example of EPISCenter illustrates efforts to shift investments toward proven practices through collaborative relationships and technical assistance aimed, in part, at building capacity to realize anticipated program and economic impacts. A partnership between the Pennsylvania Commission on Crime and Delinquency and Penn State University's Prevention Research Center, EPISCenter aims to advance high-quality implementation, impact assessment, and sustainability for interventions that have been proven effective through rigorous evaluations. In addition to outreach and advocacy to promote the adoption of evidence-based interventions, EPISCenter provides technical assistance, educational opportunities, and resources to communities. Examples of the programs promoted by the center include the following:

- **Communities that Care (CTC)**—a structured system designed at the University of Washington to help communities prevent adolescent problem behaviors and promote positive youth development. CTC communities collect local data on risk and protective factors associated with delinquency, violence, substance use, and educational attainment. Communities then identify specific risk and protective factors on which to focus, and seek out evidence-based programs and strategies for addressing those priorities. After a few years of implementing these strategies, communities reassess their risk and protective factors to measure impact and identify new and emerging priorities.
- **Standardized Program Evaluation Protocol (SPEP)**—a data-driven scoring system, developed at Vanderbilt University, for evaluating the effectiveness of juvenile justice programs in reducing recidivism. To determine an SPEP score, services being implemented are compared with characteristics that have been shown to predict

reduced youth recidivism. SPEP translates evidence into a technical assistance resource for analyzing current investments and their relationship to the evidence base.

Although EPISCenter's activities do not focus specifically on economic evidence, much of the center's approach to promoting the use of evidence in general can be adapted to promoting the effective use of economic evidence. In addition, the center disseminates estimates of the return on investment of some of the interventions it promotes.[6]

Pay for Success/Social Impact Bonds

"I would say that Pay for Success approaches have changed the conversation more rapidly and more dramatically than anything else I have been engaged in over my career. I have rarely seen key decision makers from counties, states, service providers, foundations, and other [stakeholders] come together in a shorter period of time and get so intensely interested in the outcomes of a program. What is the evidence? What would it take for us to get that evidence? People put their own money at risk on the proposition that some social program is actually going to achieve a set of outcomes. Having sufficient evidence that people are going to put their money down on it is very powerful."

> —Jerry Croan, senior fellow, Third Sector Capital, at the committee's open session discussion on March 23, 2015.

In March 2010, the United Kingdom's Ministry of Justice and Social Finance, a not-for-profit organization created in 2007, launched a pilot program aimed at reducing recidivism among prisoners released from the Peterborough prison. The key feature of this pilot was its financial arrangement: private parties, mainly charitable trusts and foundations, provided approximately £5 million to fund the program, while the ministry agreed to pay them up to £8 million after 7 years, according to observed recidivism among program participants. Furthermore, if the program failed to achieve a reduction in recidivism of 7.5 percent, investors would lose their money (Disley et al., 2011; Nicholls and Tomkinson, 2013).

The Peterborough pilot was the first financial arrangement of its kind. Such financing models—referred to here as pay for success (PFS) but also known by various other names, such as social impact bonds, outcome-

---

[6]See, for example, a brief discussion of the return on investment of Functional Family Therapy at http://www.episcenter.psu.edu/sites/default/files/ebp/MST-Three-Year-Report-ROI.pdf [November 2015].

based financing, and payment-by-results models[7]—have attracted a significant amount of interest in recent years. Since the original pilot was conducted, PFS programs have been explored in several countries on at least three continents (Azemati et al., 2013).

In particular, PFS financing has garnered growing interest within the United Kingdom and the United States (Callanan and Law, 2013; Corporation for National and Community Service, 2015). This financing tool leverages private investment to support preventive services that lead to public savings (Liebman, 2013). Typically, when a PFS contract is considered to be successful, the private investors receive back the initial capital outlay that supported service delivery as well as a percentage return, while the public sector benefits from the remaining cost aversion or savings (often in the form of reduced service utilization).[8] This financing structure makes PFS contracts of particular interest to programs designed to intervene in developmental processes that otherwise lead to downstream costs (Finn and Hayward, 2013).

The PFS model has a number of benefits highlighted by its proponents (Bridges Ventures, 2014; Costa and Shab, 2013; Crowley, 2014; Galloway, 2014; Greenblatt and Donovan, 2013). These benefits include the following:

- PFS reduces governments' financial risk from funding social programs. If the expected results are not achieved, the government's financial losses are reduced or completely eliminated, as in the Peterborough pilot.
- It allows private agents—individuals or organizations—to align their investments with their social values while creating an opportunity for positive return on their investment.
- It incentivizes service providers to innovate because the focus on outcomes allows them to adapt their programs to improve results without having to worry about the up-front expenditures often required in traditional pay-for-performance arrangements.
- It increases society's trust in how tax revenues are spent. Unsuccessful programs are not funded at the taxpayers' expense, and—because payments are determined by the economic value of positive outcomes, including government cost savings—successful programs provide societal value that exceeds their cost.

---

[7]In the present context, these terms are used to refer to financing instruments, but in other contexts, they are used differently. In international development, for example, outcome-based financing and pay for performance (P4P) more commonly refer to incentive-based payment mechanisms.

[8]Certain investors (e.g., private foundations) may be interested primarily in breaking even on their investment. Breaking even may allow the investors to reinvest the percentage return and sustain the program of interest.

- It increases the focus of public officials on economic evidence and the details of expected outcomes.

Conversely, others have been more cautious in embracing PFS (Stid, 2013), citing the following challenges:

- PFS contracts are complex and involve numerous parties—government agencies, service providers, investors, program evaluators, and intermediaries connecting all these parties. Governments may have difficulty adapting their procurement mechanisms to these arrangements.
- Complete transfer of financial risk from government agencies to investors may be difficult to achieve in all cases. In fact, recent contracts in the United States have required third parties to guarantee a maximum loss to investors if programs do not achieve their outcomes.
- To date, most PFS investors have been charities and foundations. To become a major model in social program financing, PFS will need to attract a wider—profit-seeking—range of investors.
- To foster innovation, PFS financing will require funding untested programs with inherently higher risk than is posed by models with rigorous evidence of effectiveness. It is still unclear whether investors will be willing to absorb higher degrees of risk, and governments will be willing to guarantee the corresponding larger payments.
- Although PFS arrangements theoretically remove government agencies from the management of program implementation, traditional principal-agent problems are not necessarily solved because the intermediaries who manage most aspects of PFS programs may face strong incentives to create situations in which positive outcomes are reported.

Since the 2010 Peterborough pilot, several U.S. municipalities and states have launched PFS arrangements to fund programs with an empirical record of preventing recidivism among juvenile offenders, reducing emergency care costs for children with asthma, and reducing utilization of special education among at-risk youth (Brush, 2013; Olson and Phillips, 2013). Interest in these arrangements is increasing at the federal and state levels—especially for early childhood programs, in which the return on investment may be the greatest (Heckman et al., 2010). In the United States, as of August 2015, PFS projects had been launched in 6 states and were being explored in 27 others.[9]

The Social Innovation Fund's (SIF) Pay for Success program is a U.S. federal initiative aimed at supporting PFS projects. SIF itself is an initiative of the Corporation for National and Community Service, with a stated goal of finding what works and making it work for more people. SIF seeks to accomplish this goal by creating a learning network of organizations working to implement innovative and effective evidence-based solutions to local and national challenges. As part of the 2014 and 2015 congressional appropriations, SIF was authorized to use up to 20 percent of its grant funds to support PFS implementation. In 2014, eight grantees were selected to receive funding for up to 3 years to provide technical assistance and promote capacity building for state and local governments and nonprofit organizations interested in implementing PFS strategies. SIF's grantees include university-based PFS initiatives, nonprofit organizations focused on specific policy areas (e.g., housing, crime and delinquency, children), and organizations that specialize in supporting PFS projects (Corporation for National and Community Service, 2015).[10]

Two key objectives of PFS financing are identifying programs that work and limiting government financing of those that do not work. Although success in public policy is usually identified with programs that achieved their objectives, a recent example highlights how implementation of the PFS framework can lead to finding success even when programs do not meet their targets. In 2012, New York City began implementing a 4-year PFS project designed to reduce recidivism among adolescents incarcerated at Rikers Island. Under the terms of the agreement, had the program reduced recidivism by 10 percent, the city would have paid private funders their $9.6 million investment, and would have paid more for a larger impact. In July 2015, however, an independent evaluator announced that the program had failed to show any decrease in recidivism (Vera Institute of Justice, 2015), and the program was canceled after only 3 years. Despite the evident disappointment in the program's failure, its implementation under a PFS approach meant that New York City did not pay for an ineffective intervention,[11] and it now can turn its attention to alternative approaches for reducing recidivism among this population. Moreover, these findings

---

[9] U.S. PFS activity tallied by the Nonprofit Finance Fund, see http://payforsuccess.org/pay-success-deals-united-states [June 2016].

[10] The full list of SIF's 2014 PFS grantees, subgrantees, and subrecipients can be found at http://www.nationalservice.gov/programs/social-innovation-fund/our-programs/pay-success#grantees [November 2015].

[11] Private funders did not lose the entirety of their investment. Bloomberg Philanthropies, a private foundation, provided a loss-guarantee that reduced private losses from $7.2 to $1.2 million.

may lead to further scrutiny of the limitations of the type of cognitive-behavioral therapy (CBT) implemented at Rikers, a significant development in itself because CBT had considerable evidence of prior success (MDRC, 2015).

Key to the future success of PFS agreements is government partners' willingness to work with intermediaries, program providers, and investors. Often contract development will reveal regulations or laws that prevent successful use of economic evidence to develop performance-based financing. For instance, efforts to structure PFS agreements around reducing the need for special education have been hindered by federal restrictions on Individuals with Disabilities Education Act (IDEA)-B funding. Specifically, states that invest in effective pre-K efforts will lose IDEA-B funding downstream. Related to "wrong pocket" issues discussed in Chapter 3, without greater flexibility and coordination between levels of government, using economic evidence can be more difficult.

> CONCLUSION: *Growing interest in performance-based financing efforts is likely to increase the importance of economic evidence in decisions on investments in children, youth, and families.*

RECOMMENDATIONS

RECOMMENDATION 3: If aiming to inform decisions on interventions for children, youth, and families, public and private funders of applied research[12] should assess the potential relevance of proposed research projects to end-users throughout the planning of research portfolios.

Strategies for implementing this recommendation might include the following:

- Engage groups of end-users in assessing high-priority research questions, key populations and contexts of interest, and capacity and resources for implementation in real-world conditions. Funders should then emphasize those areas in funding announcements.
- Review criteria in funding announcements to ensure that they encompass the extent to which the proposed research relates to the interests and needs of end-users.

---

[12] "Funders" here might include staff in public agencies (e.g., the National Institutes of Health, the Institute for Education Sciences, the Centers for Disease Control and Prevention), as well as staff in private philanthropic or other organizations.

- Engage end-users in review panels to assess aspects of relevance in proposal scoring and funding decisions.
- Fund long-term partnerships between researchers and practitioners and between researchers and policy makers that are centered around the needs of the practitioners or policy makers.
- Ensure that funding announcements require the publication of information of relevance to end-users, such as information on the context in which the study was implemented, the costs of both implementation and supports for implementation, and the population with which the study was conducted.
- Make ongoing learning and improvement a priority alongside demonstrating outcomes in assessment of grantees' performance.
- Require the publication of research findings in different formats targeted toward different audiences.
- Ensure that sufficient time and resources are provided to support a planning stage during which researchers can engage in such activities as developing relationships with organizations and key actors, refining research questions, building advisory groups, and learning the local context.

RECOMMENDATION 4: To achieve anticipated economic benefits and optimize the likelihood of deriving the anticipated outcomes from evidence-based interventions, public and private funders[13] should ensure that resources are available to support effective implementation of those interventions.

Strategies for implementing this recommendation might include the following:

- Support intermediary organizations that can provide training and technical assistance in the implementation of evidence-based interventions and work collaboratively with implementing organizations to ensure effective implementation.
- Ensure that resources and fidelity assurances are available for the implementation of evidence-based practices, including resources that support professional development, technical assistance, and monitoring of implementation.
- Facilitate linkages between decision makers and researchers through convening, information-sharing, or grant-making initiatives.

---

[13] "Funders" here might include elected officials at the local, state, or federal level; leadership of public grant-making agencies or regulatory bodies; and private funders of interventions for children, youth, and families.

RECOMMENDATION 5: Providers of postsecondary and graduate education, on-the-job training, and fellowship programs designed to develop the skills of those making or seeking to inform decisions related to children, youth, and families should incorporate training in the use of evidence, including economic evidence, in decision making.

RECOMMENDATION 6: Government agencies[14] should report the extent to which their allocation of funds—both within and across programs—is supported by evidence, including economic evidence.

REFERENCES

Aarons, G.A., Hurlburt, M., and Horwitz, S.M. (2011). Advancing a conceptual model of evidence-based practice implementation in public service sectors. *Administration and Policy in Mental Health and Mental Health Services Research, 38*(1), 4-23.

Anderson, L.M., Brownson, R.C., Fullilove, M.T., Teutsch, S.M., Novick, L.F., Fielding, J., and Land, G.H. (2005). Evidence-based public health policy and practice: Promises and limits. *American Journal of Preventive Medicine, 28*(5), 226-230.

Armstrong, R., Waters, E., Dobbins, M., Anderson, L., Moore, L., Petticrew, M., Clark, R., Pettman, T.L., Burns, C., Moodie, M., Conning, R., and Swinburn, B. (2013). Knowledge translation strategies to improve the use of evidence in public health decision making in local government: Intervention design and implementation plan. *Implementation Science, 8,* 121.

Armstrong, R., Waters, E., Moore, L., Dobbins, M., Pettman, T., Burns, C., Swinburn, B., Anderson, L., and Petticrew, M. (2014). Understanding evidence: A statewide survey to explore evidence-informed public health decision-making in a local government setting. *Implementation Science, 9*(1), 188.

Asen, R., Gurke, D., Solomon, R., Conners, P., and Gumm, E. (2011). "The research says:" Definitions and uses of a key policy term in federal law and local school board deliberations. *Argumentation and Advocacy, 47,* 195-213.

Asen, R., Gurke, D., Connors, P., Solomon, R., and Gumm, E. (2012). Research evidence and school-board deliberations: Lessons from three Wisconsin school districts. *Educational Policy, 26.* doi:10.1177/0895904811429291.

Asen, R., Gurke, D., Conners, P., Solomon, R., and Gumm, E. (2013). Research evidence and school board deliberations: Lessons from three Wisconsin school districts. *Educational Policy, 27*(1), 33-63.

Atkins, D., Slegel, J., and Slutsky, J. (2005). Making policy when the evidence is in dispute: Good health policy making involves consideration of much more than clinical evidence. *Evaluating Evidence, 24*(1), 102-113.

Azemati, H., Belinsky, M., Gillette, R., Liebman, J., Sellman, A., and Wyse, A. (2013). Social impact bonds: Lessons learned so far. *Community Development Investment Review, 9*(1), 23-33.

---

[14] The key actors in "government agencies" here would include agency leadership, budget offices, and others with management and budget functions in executive and legislative branches at the federal, state, and local levels.

Barnoski, R.P. (2002). *Washington State's Implementation of Functional Family Therapy for Juvenile Offenders: Preliminary Findings*. Olympia: Washington State Institute for Public Policy. Available: http://www.wsipp.wa.gov/ReportFile/803/Wsipp_Washington-States-Implementation-of-Functional-Family-Therapy-for-Juvenile-Offenders-Preliminary-Findings_Full-Report.pdf [October 2015].

Bergin, T. (2013). Markets for suspicion: Assessing cost-benefit analysis in criminal justice. *InterDisciplines*, 4(2), 59-84.

Blau, J., Hoestlandt, C., Clark, A., Baxter, L., Felix Garcia, A.G., Mounaud, B., and Mosina, L. (2015). Strengthening national decision-making on immunization by building capacity for economic evaluation: Implementing ProVac in Europe. *Vaccine*, 33(Suppl. 1), A34-A39.

Bogenschneider, K., and Corbett, T.J. (2010). *Evidence-Based Policymaking: Insights from Policy-Minded Researchers and Research-Minded Policymakers*. New York: Taylor & Frances Group.

Bogenschneider, K., Little, O.M., and Johnson, K. (2013). Policymakers' use of social science research: Looking within and across policy actors. *Journal of Marriage and Family*, 75(2), 263-275.

Bowen, S., and Zwi, A.B. (2005). Pathways to "evidence-informed" policy and practice: A framework for action. *PLoS Medicine*, 2(7), 0600-0605.

Bridges Ventures. (2014). *Choosing Social Impact Bonds: A Practitioner's Guide*. London, UK: Bridges Ventures, LLP.

Brooks, J., and Wills, M. (2015). *Core Principles*. Washington, DC: National Governors Association Center for Best Practices.

Brown, D.W., Kowalski, A.E., and Lurie, I.Z. (2015). *Medicaid as an Investment in Children: What Is the Long-Term Impact on Tax Receipts?* Cambridge, MA: National Bureau of Economic Research.

Brownson, R.C., Fielding, J.E., and Maylahn, C.M. (2009). Evidence-based public health: A fundamental concept for public health practice. *Annual Review of Public Health*, 30, 175-201.

Brush, R. (2013). Can pay for success reduce asthma emergencies and reset a broken health care system? *Community Development Investment Review*. Available: http://www.frbsf.org/community-development/files/pay-for-success-reduce-asthma-emergencies-reset-broken-health-care-system.pdf [March 2016].

Callanan, L., and Law, J. (2013). Pay for success: Opportunities and risks for nonprofits. *Community Development Investment Review*. Available: http://www.frbsf.org/community-development/publications/community-development-investment-review/2013/april/pay-for-success-opportunities-risks-nonprofits [November 2015].

Chaikledkaew, U., Lertpitakpong, C., Teerawattananon, Y., Thavorncharoensap, M., and Tangcharoensathien, V. (2009). The current capacity and future development of economic evaluation for policy decision making: A survey among researchers and decision makers in Thailand. *Value in Health*, 12(Suppl. 3), S31-S35.

Chambers, J.D., Cangelosi, M.J., and Neumann, P.J. (2015). Medicare's use of cost-effectiveness analysis for prevention (but not for treatment). *Journal of Health Policy*, 119(2), 156-163.

Chetty, R., Hendren, N., and Katz, L.F. (2015). *The Effects of Exposure to Better Neighborhoods on Children: New Evidence from the Moving to Opportunity Experiment*. Cambridge, MA: National Bureau of Economic Research.

Coburn, C.E., Penuel, W.R., and Geil, K.E. (2013). *Research-Practice Partnerships: A Strategy for Leveraging Research for Educational Improvement in School Districts*. New York: William T. Grant Foundation. Available: http://w.informalscience.org/images/research/Research-Practice-Partnerships-at-the-District-Level.pdf [October 2015].

Cohodes, S., Grossman, D., Kleiner, S., and Lovenheim, M.F. (2014). *The Effect of Child Health Insurance Access on Schooling: Evidence from Public Insurance Expansions.* Cambridge, MA: National Bureau of Economic Research.

Conklin, J., Lusk, E., Harris, M., and Stolee, P. (2013). Knowledge brokers in a knowledge network: The case of seniors health research transfer network knowledge brokers. *Implementation Science, 8*(7), 1-10.

Corbacho, B., and Pinto-Prades, J.L. (2012). Health economic decision-making: A comparison between UK and Spain. *British Medical Bulletin, 103*(1), 5-20.

Corporation for National and Community Service. (2015). *State of the Pay for Success Field: Opportunities, Trends, and Recommendations.* Available: http://www.nationalservice. gov/sites/default/files/documents/CNCS%20PFS%20State%20of%20the%20Field%20 Document%20Final%204-17-15%20sxf.pdf [March 2016].

Costa, K., and Shab, S. (2013). Government's role in pay for success. *Community Development Investment Review, 9*(1), 91-96.

Coule, T.M. (2015). Nonprofit governance and accountability: Broadening the theoretical perspective. *Nonprofit and Voluntary Sector Quarterly, 44*(1), 75-97.

Cousins, J.B., and Bourgeois, I. (Eds.). (2014). Organizational capacity to do and use evaluation. *New Directions for Evaluation, 2014(141).* doi:10.1002/ev.20075.

Crowley, M. (2014). The role of social impact bonds in pediatric health care. *Pediatrics, 134*(2), e331-e333.

Crowley, M. (2015). *Opportunities for Administrative Data to Support the Use of Economic Estimates in Decision-Making.* Presentation at Administration for Children & Families' Office of Planning Research and Evaluation meeting on The Promises and Challenges of Administrative Data in Social Policy Research, October 1-2, Washington, DC.

Damschroder, L.J., Aron, D.C., Keith, R.E., Kirsh, S.R., Alexander, J.A., and Lowery, J.C. (2009). Fostering implementation of health services research findings into practice: A consolidated framework for advancing implementation science. *Implementation Science, 4*(1), 50.

Davies, H., Nutley, S., and Walter, I. (2008). Why "knowledge transfer" is misconceived for applied social research. *Journal of Health Services Research & Policy, 13*(3), 188-190.

Disley, E., Rubin, J., Scraggs, E., Burrowes, N., and Culley, D.M. (2011). *Lessons Learned from the Planning and Early Implementation of the Social Impact Bond at HMP Peterborough.* Santa Monica, CA: RAND Corporation.

Dobbins, M., Robeson, P., Ciliska, D., Hanna, S., Cameron, R., and O'Mara, L. (2009). A description of a knowledge broker role implemented as part of a randomized controlled trial evaluating three knowledge translation strategies. *Implementation Science, 4*(23), 1-16.

Dobrow, M.J., Goel, V., and Upshur, R.E.G. (2004). Evidence-based health policy: Context and utilisation. *Social Science & Medicine, 58*(1), 207-217.

Dobrow, M.J., Goel, V., Lemieux-Charles, L., and Black, N.A. (2006). The impact of context on evidence utilization: A framework for expert groups developing health policy recommendations. *Social Science & Medicine, 63*(7), 1811-1824.

Donnelly, C., Letts, L., Klinger, D., and Shulha, L. (2014). Supporting knowledge translation through evaluation: Evaluator as knowledge broker. *Canadian Journal of Program Evaluation, 29*(1).

DuMont, K. (2015). *Leveraging Knowledge: Taking Stock of the William T. Grant Foundation's Use of Research Evidence Grants Portfolio.* New York: William T. Grant Foundation.

Eddama, O., and Coast, J. (2008). A systematic review of the use of economic evaluation in local decision-making. *Journal of Health Policy, 86*(2-3), 129-141.

Elliott, H., and Popay, J. (2000). How are policy makers using evidence? Models of research utilization and local NHS policy making. *Journal of Epidemiology & Community Health, 54*(6), 461-468.

Fielding, J.E., and Briss, P.A. (2006). Promoting evidence-based public health policy: Can we have better evidence and more action? *Health Affairs (Millwood), 25*(4), 969-978.

Finn, J., and Hayward, J. (2013). Bringing success to scale: Pay for success and housing homeless individuals in Massachusetts. *Community Development Investment Review, 9*(1). Available: http://www.frbsf.org/community-development/files/bringing-success-scale-pay-for-success-housing-homeless-individuals-massachusetts.pdf [December 2015].

Flitcroft, K., Gillespie, J., Salkeld, G., Carter, S., and Trevena, L. (2011). Getting evidence into policy: The need for deliberative strategies? *Social Science & Medicine, 72*(7), 1039-1046.

Galloway, I. (2014). Using pay-for-success to increase investment in the nonmedical determinants of health. *Health Affairs, 33*(11), 1897-1904.

Goldhaber-Fiebert, J.D., Snowden, L.R., Wulczyn, F., Landsverk, J., and Horwitz, S.M. (2011). Economic evaluation research in the context of child welfare policy: A structured literature review and recommendations. *Child Abuse & Neglect, 35*(9), 722-740.

Gordon, E.J. (2006). The political contexts of evidence-based medicine: Policymaking for daily hemodialysis. *Social Science & Medicine, 62*(11), 2707-2719.

Gottfredson, D.C., Cook, T.D., Gardner, F.E.M., Gorman-Smith, D., Howe, G.W., Sandler, I.N., and Zafft, K.M. (2015). Standards of evidence for efficacy, effectiveness, and scale-up research in prevention science: Next generation. *Prevention Science, 16*(7) 893-926.

Greenblatt, J., and Donovan, A. (2013). The promise of pay for success. *Community Development Investment Review, 9*(1), 19-22.

Greiling, D., and Spraul, K. (2010). Accountability and the challenges of information disclosure. *Public Administration Quarterly, 34*(3), 338-377.

Halachmi, A. (2002). Performance measurement, accountability, and improved performance. *Public Performance & Management Review, 25*(4), 370-374.

Hanney, S.R., Gonzalez-Block, M.A., Buxton, M.J., and Kogan, M. (2003). The utilisation of health research in policy-making: Concepts, examples and methods of assessment. *Health Research Policy and Systems, 1*(1), 2.

Harrington, W., Morgenstern, R.D., and Sterner, T. (2004). *Comparing Instruments and Outcomes in the United States and Europe.* Washington, DC: Resources for the Future.

Heckman, J.J., Moon, S.H., Pinto, R.R., Savelyev, P.A., and Yavitz, A. (2010). *A New Cost-Benefit and Rate of Return Analysis for the Perry Preschool Program: A Summary.* NBER Working Paper 16180. Available: http://www.nber.org/papers/w16180.pdf [December 2015].

Hoffmann, C., and Von Der Schulenburg, J.-M. (2000). The influence of economic evaluation studies on decision making: A European survey. *Health Policy (Amsterdam, Netherlands), 52*(3), 179-192.

Holmes, L., Landsverk, J., Ward, H., Rolls-Reutz, J., Saldana, L., Wulczyn, F., and Chamberlain, P. (2014). Cost calculator methods for estimating casework time in child welfare services: A promising approach for use in implementation of evidence-based practices and other service innovations. *Children and Youth Services Review, 39*, 169-176.

Hoyle, T.B., Samek, B.B., and Valois, R.F. (2008). Building capacity for the continuous improvement of health-promoting schools. *Journal of School Health, 78*(1), 1-8.

Institute of Medicine and National Research Council. (2014). *Considerations in Applying Benefit-Cost Analysis to Preventive Interventions for Children, Youth, and Families.* S. Olson and K. Bogard (Rapporteurs). Board on Children, Youth, and Families. Washington, DC: The National Academies Press.

Innvaer, S., Vist, G., Trommald, M., and Oxman, A. (2002). Health policy-makers' perceptions of their use of evidence: A systematic review. *Journal of Health Services Research & Policy*, 7(4), 239-244.

Jacob, R.R., Baker, E.A., Allen, P., Dodson, E.A., Duggan, K., Fields, R., Sequeira, S., and Brownson, R.C. (2014). Training needs and supports for evidence-based decision making among the public health workforce in the United States. *BMC Health Services Research*, 14(1), 564.

Jennings, E.T., Jr., and Hall, J.L. (2011). Evidence-based practice and the uses of information in state agency decision making. *The Journal of Public Administration Research and Theory*, 22, 245-255.

Kaufman, J.S., Crusto, C.A., Quan, M., Ross, E., Friedman, S.R., O'Rielly, K., and Call, S. (2006). Utilizing program evaluation as a strategy to promote community change: Evaluation of a comprehensive, community-based, family violence initiative. *American Journal of Community Psychology*, 38(3-4), 191-200.

Kemm, J. (2006). The limitations of "evidence-based" public health. *Journal of Evaluation in Clinical Practice*, 12(3), 319-324.

LaRocca, R., Yost, J., Dobbins, M., Ciliska, D., and Butt, M. (2012). The effectiveness of knowledge translation strategies used in public health: A systematic review. *BMC Public Health*, 12(751), 1-15.

Lavis, J.N., Robertson, D., Woodside, J.M., McLeod, C.B., and Abelson, J. (2003). How can research organizations more effectively transfer research knowledge to decision makers? *Milbank Quarterly*, 81(2), 221-248.

Lens, M.C. (2015). Measuring the geography of opportunity. *Progress in Human Geography*, 1-23. doi: 10.1177/0309132515618104. Available: http://phg.sagepub.com/content/early/2015/11/30/0309132515618104.full.pdf+html [June 2016].

Lessard, C., Contandriopoulos, A.P., and Beaulieu, M.D. (2010). The role (or not) of economic evaluation at the micro level: Can Bourdieu's theory provide a way forward for clinical decision-making? *Social Science & Medicine*, 70(12), 1948-1956.

Liebman, J.B. (2013). *Building on Recent Advances in Evidence-Based Policymaking*. Washington, DC: The Hamilton Project, The Brookings Institution.

Lindberg, S.I. (2013). Mapping accountability: Core concept and subtypes. *International Review of Administrative Sciences*, 79(2), 202-226.

Lorenc, T., Tyner, E.F., Petticrew, M., Duffy, S., Martineau, F.P., Phillips, G., and Lock, K. (2014). Cultures of evidence across policy sectors: Systematic review of qualitative evidence. *European Journal of Public Health*, 24(6), 1041-1047.

MDRC. (2015). *Statement on Rikers PFS Failure*. Available: http://www.mdrc.org/news/announcement/mdrc-statement-vera-institute-s-study-adolescent-behavioral-learning-experience [December 2015].

Merlo, G., Page, K., Ratcliffe, J., Halton, K., and Graves, N. (2015). Bridging the gap: Exploring the barriers to using economic evidence in healthcare decision-making and strategies for improving uptake. *Applied Health Economics and Health Policy*, 13(3), 303-309.

Miller, T.R., and Hendrie, D.V. (2012). Economic evaluation of public health laws and their enforcement. *Public Health Law Research*. Available: http://publichealthlawresearch.org/sites/default/files/downloads/resource/EconomicEvaluationPHL-Monograph-Miller Hendrie2012.pdf [March 2016].

Mitton, C., Adair, C.E., McKenzie, E., Patten, S.B., and Waye Perry, B. (2007). Knowledge transfer and exchange: Review and synthesis of the literature. *The Milbank Quarterly*, 85(4), 729-768.

Moynihan, D.P. (2008). *The Dynamics of Performance Management*. Washington, DC: Georgetown University Press.

Moynihan, D.P. (2015). *Using Evidence to Make Decisions: The Experience of U.S. Performance Management Initiatives.* Commissioned paper for the Committee on the Use of Economic Evidence to Inform Investments in Children, Youth, and Families. Available: http://sites.nationalacademies.org/cs/groups/dbassesite/documents/webpage/dbasse_171855.pdf [June 2016].

Moynihan, D.P., and Kroll, A. (2015). Performance management routines that work? An early assessment of the GPRA Modernization Act. *Public Administration Review.* doi: 10.1111/puar.12434.

National Research Council. (2011). *Incentives and Test-Based Accountability in Education.* Committee on Incentives and Test-Based Accountability in Public Education. M. Hout and S.W. Elliott (Eds.). Board on Testing and Assessment, Division of Behavioral and Social Sciences and Education. Washington, DC: The National Academies Press.

National Research Council. (2012). *Using Science as Evidence in Public Policy.* Committee on the Use of Social Science Knowledge in Public Policy. K. Prewitt, T.A. Schwandt, and M.L. Straf (Eds.). Division of Behavioral and Social Sciences and Education. Washington, DC: The National Academies Press.

National Research Council and Institute of Medicine. (2009). *Strengthening Benefit-Cost Analysis for Early Childhood Interventions.* A. Beatty (Rapporteur). Committee on Strengthening Benefit-Cost Methodology for the Evaluation of Early Childhood Interventions. Board on Children, Youth, and Families. Division of Behavioral and Social Sciences and Education. Washington, DC: The National Academies Press.

Nelson, S.R., Leffler, J.C., and Hansen, B.A. (2009). *Toward a Research Agenda for Understanding and Improving the Use of Research Evidence.* Portland, OR: Northwest Regional Educational Laboratory.

Neumann, P.J. (2004). Why don't Americans use cost-effectiveness analysis? *American Journal of Managed Care, 10*(5), 308-312.

Neumann, P.J., and Weinstein, M.C. (2010). Legislation against use of cost-effectiveness information. *New England Journal of Medicine, 363*(16), 1495-1497.

Nicholls, A., and Tomkinson, E. (2013). *The Peterborough Pilot Social Impact Bond.* Oxford, UK: Saïd Business School, University of Oxford.

Nutbeam, D., and Boxall, A.-M. (2008). What influences the transfer of research into health policy and practice? Observations from England and Australia. *Public Health, 122*(8), 747-753.

Nutley, S.M., Walter, I., and Davies, H.T.O. (2007). *Using Evidence: How Research Can Inform Public Services.* Bristol, UK: The Policy Press.

Oliver, K., Invar, S., Lorenc, T., Woodman, J., and Thomas, J. (2014a). A systematic review of barriers to and facilitators of the use of evidence by policymakers. *BMC Health Services Research, 14,* 2.

Oliver, K., Lorenc, T., and Innvaer, S. (2014b). New directions in evidence-based policy research: A critical analysis of the literature. *Health Research Policy and Systems, 12,* 34.

Olson, J., and Phillips, A. (2013). Rikers Island: The first social impact bond in the United States. *Community Development Investment Review.* Available: http://www.frbsf.org/community-development/files/rikers-island-first-social-impact-bond-united-states.pdf [December 2015].

O'Reilly, III, C.A. (1982). Variations in decision makers' use of information sources: The impact of quality and accessibility of information. *Academy of Management Journal, 25*(4), 756-771.

Orton, L., Lloyd-Williams, F., Taylor-Robinson, D., O'Flaherty, M., and Capwell, S. (2011). The use of research evidence in public health decision making processes: Systemic review. *PLoS One, 6*(7), 1-10.

Palinkas, L.A., Garcia, A.R., Aarons, G.A., Finno-Velasquez, M., Holloway, I.W., Mackie, T.I., Leslie, L.K., and Chamberlain, P. (2014). Measuring use of research evidence the structured interview for evidence use. *Research on Social Work Practice, 1-15.* Available: http://rsw.sagepub.com/content/early/2014/12/01/1049731514560413.full.pdf [June 2016].

Palinkas, L.A., Short, C., and Wong, M. (2015). *Research-Practice Policy Partnerships for Implementation of Evidence-Based Practices in Child Welfare and Child Mental Health.* New York: William T. Grant Foundation.

Pew-MacArthur Results First Initiative. (2014). *Results First in Your State.* Available: http://www.pewtrusts.org/~/media/assets/2013/results-first-in-your-state-brief.pdf [December 2015].

Pew-MacArthur Results First Initiative. (2015). *Legislating Evidence-Based Policymaking: A Look at State Laws that Support Data-Driven Decision-Making.* Available: http://www.pewtrusts.org/~/media/assets/2015/03/legislationresultsfirstbriefmarch2015.pdf?la=en [January 2016].

Ribisl, K.M., Leeman, J., and Glasser, A.M. (2014). Pricing health behavior interventions to promote adoption: Lessons from the marketing and business literature. *American Journal of Preventive Medicine, 46*(6), 653-659.

Saldana, L., Chamberlain, P., Bradford, W.D., Campbell, M., and Landsverk, J. (2014). The Cost of Implementing New Strategies (COINS): A method for mapping implementation resources using the stages of implementation completion. *Children and Youth Services Review, 39*(2), 177-182.

Simoens, S. (2010). Use of economic evaluation in decision making: Evidence and recommendations for improvement. *Drugs, 70*(15), 1917-1926.

Stid, D. (2013). Pay for success is not a panacea. *Community Development Investment Review, 9*(1), 13-18.

Supplee, L.H., and Metz, A. (2015). Opportunities and challenges in evidence-based social policy. *Social Policy Report, 28*(4). Available: http://www.srcd.org/sites/default/files/documents/spr_28_4.pdf [June 2016].

Tseng, V. (2012). *Social Policy Report: The Uses of Research in Policy and Practice.* New York: William T. Grant Foundation.

Tseng, V. (2014). Forging common ground: Fostering the conditions for evidence use. *Journal of Leisure Research, 46*(1), 6-12.

Urban, J.B., and Trochim, W. (2009). The role of evaluation in research—practice integration working toward the "golden spike." *American Journal of Evaluation, 30*(4), 538-553.

van Dongen, J.M., Tompa, E., Clune, L., Sarnocinska-Hart, A., Bongers, P.M., van Tulder, M.W., van der Beek, A.J., and van Wier, M.F. (2013). Bridging the gap between the economic evaluation literature and daily practice in occupational health: A qualitative study among decision-makers in the healthcare sector. *Implementation Science, 8*(57), 1-12.

Vera Institute of Justice. (2015). *Impact Evaluation of the Adolescent Behavioral Learning Experience (ABLE) Program at Rikers Island: Summary of Key Findings.* Available: http://www.vera.org/sites/default/files/resources/downloads/adolescent-behavioral-learning-experience-evaluation-rikers-island-summary-2.pdf [January 2016].

Veselý, A. (2013). Accountability in Central and Eastern Europe: Concept and reality. *International Review of Administrative Sciences, 79*(2), 310-330.

Ward, V., House, A., and Hamer, S. (2009). Knowledge brokering: The missing link in the evidence to action chain? *Evidence & Policy: A Journal of Research, Debate and Practice, 5*(3), 267.

Wholey, J.S., and Newcomer, K.E. (1997). Clarifying goals, reporting results. *New Directions for Program Evaluation, 76*, 95-105.

Williams, I., and Bryan, S. (2007). Understanding the limited impact of economic evaluation in health care resource allocation: A conceptual framework. *Health Policy, 80*(1), 135-143.

Zardo, P., and Collie, A. (2014). Predicting research use in a public health policy environment: Results of a logistic regression analysis. *Implementation Science, 9*, 142.

5

A Roadmap for Improving the Use of High-Quality Economic Evidence

The conclusions and recommendations in this report reflect the unrealized potential of economic evidence to increase the returns to society from investments in children, youth, and families. Suggestions are offered throughout the preceding chapters for improving current practices in the production and use of economic evidence. After providing a brief overview of those chapters, this chapter consolidates these suggestions into a roadmap for achieving this goal. This roadmap encompasses fostering multi-stakeholder partnerships to address cross-cutting issues related to the use of economic evidence, understanding what consumers and producers of economic evidence want each other to know, building a coordinated infrastructure to support the development and use of economic evidence, and providing stronger incentives for the production and use of better evidence—all with a foundational understanding that recognizing the needs of end-users is a critical prerequisite for success.

OVERVIEW OF THE PRECEDING CHAPTERS

The committee's charge was to study how to improve the use of economic evidence to inform policy and funding decisions concerning investments in children, youth, and families. Chapters 3 and 4 detail two vital ways in which this goal can be advanced: by developing higher-quality economic evidence (Chapter 3) and by devoting significant attention to the context in which investment decisions are made (Chapter 4), captured by the report's guiding principles: (1) *quality counts* and (2) *context matters*. If researchers, funders, and policy and administrative officials dealing with investments in children, youth, and families make concerted efforts to apply both of these principles, the committee believes it will have carried out its charge successfully. Even under significant resource constraints, too many studies lack sufficient quality, and too many efforts at integrating economic evidence into decision making neglect the context in which the evidence will be used.

To provide a foundation for the report's key messages, Chapter 2 offers an overview of the common methods used in economic evaluation; describes categories of stakeholders in the use of evidence resulting from such evaluation; provides selected examples of current uses of economic evidence related to children, youth, and families; highlights current challenges in the use of such evidence; and describes the role of this evidence within the broader evidence ecosystem. Chapter 2 also provides a list of many of the current issues related to the quality, use, and utility of economic evidence (Box 2-6). Many of these issues are addressed throughout this report, particularly within the conclusions and recommendations of Chapters 3 and 4.

Chapter 3 addresses issues related to the report's first principle, *quality counts*. The committee offers guidelines and best practices for the design, conduct, and reporting of high-quality economic evaluations so that the evidence produced is useful to its intended end-user(s). The committee recommends that, to the extent possible, stakeholders implement these guidelines and best practices to increase the overall use and utility of economic evidence. At the same time, the committee considers it vital that decision makers are aware of the limitations of the evidence as well (see Box 5-1).

In Chapter 4, the committee maintains that even if the highest-quality economic evidence is made available, the use and utility of this evidence depend largely on the context in which end-users consider it—that is, *context matters*. This chapter reviews an array of context-related issues that affect the use of evidence in decision-making processes, including the relevance of the evidence, the capacity to acquire and make use of the evidence, and such factors as politics and values. Many of the recommendations in this chapter are targeted to public and private funders (see Box 5-2).

A ROADMAP FOR SUCCESS

Fostering Multi-Stakeholder Partnerships to Address Cross-Cutting Issues Related to the Use of Economic Evidence

The conclusions offered in Chapters 3 and 4 make clear that many of the challenges to the quality, use, and utility of economic evidence affect multiple stakeholder groups. For example, poor methodological quality (as discussed in Chapter 3) affects all stakeholders in economic evidence, not just in any particular project at hand, but also weakens the demand for

---

BOX 5-1
Recommendations from Chapter 3

RECOMMENDATION 1: In support of high-quality economic evaluations, producers[1] of economic evidence should follow the best practices delineated in the checklist below for conducting cost analyses (CAs), cost-effectiveness analyses (CEAs), benefit-cost analyses (BCAs), and related methods. Producers should follow the core practices listed and, where feasible and applicable, the advancing practices as well. Consumers of economic evidence should use these recommended best practices to assess the quality of the economic evidence available to inform the investment decisions they are seeking to make.

RECOMMENDATION 2: In support of high-quality and useful economic evaluations of interventions for children, youth, and families, producers of economic evidence should follow the best practices delineated in the checklist below for reporting the results of cost analyses, cost-effectiveness analyses, and benefit-cost analyses and related methods.

---

[1]Chapter 2 identifies in detail the producers of economic evidence.

---

future economic evaluations. The best practices outlined in Chapter 3 are relevant to both the producers (e.g., researchers) who perform and report on economic evaluations and the consumers (e.g., funders, policy makers) who interpret and apply the resulting evidence in their investment decisions. Additional examples of cross-cutting issues are given throughout Chapters 2 through 4. Arguably, the issues that have the highest shared relevance among consumers and producers of economic evidence, as well as intermediaries, are those related to inadequate incentives to use high-quality and high-utility economic evidence; development of the necessary capacity and infrastructure for access to, analysis of, and dissemination of the evidence; and reporting of and access to evidence that is clear, credible, and generalizable. These failures often disconnect the production of economic evidence from its real-world application.

Such cross-cutting issues suggest a shared responsibility among stakeholders for improving the status quo. Based on its research and information gathered in its open sessions, the committee identified a significant need for the formation and support of multi-stakeholder collaborative efforts to help address these issues (August et al., 2006; Brown et al., 2010; Crowley et al., 2014). At a minimum, such efforts could encourage researchers and those engaged in decisions about policies and investments related to children, youth, and families to engage in open dialogue about their unique

BOX 5-2
Recommendations from Chapter 4

RECOMMENDATION 3: If aiming to inform decisions on interventions for children, youth, and families, public and private funders of applied research[a] should assess the potential relevance of proposed research projects to end-users throughout the planning of research portfolios.

RECOMMENDATION 4: To achieve anticipated economic benefits and optimize the likelihood of deriving the anticipated outcomes from evidence-based interventions, public and private funders[b] should ensure that resources are available to support effective implementation of those interventions.

RECOMMENDATION 5: Providers of postsecondary and graduate education, on-the-job training, and fellowship programs designed to develop the skills of those making or seeking to inform decisions related to children, youth, and families should incorporate training in the use of evidence, including economic evidence, in decision making.

RECOMMENDATION 6: Government agencies[c] should report the extent to which their allocation of funds—both within and across programs—is supported by evidence, including economic evidence.

---

[a]Funders" here might include staff in public agencies (e.g., the National Institutes of Health, the Institute for Education Sciences, the Centers for Disease Control and Prevention), as well as staff in private philanthropic or other organizations.

[b]Funders" here might include elected officials at the local, state, or federal level; leadership of public grant-making agencies or regulatory bodies; and private funders of interventions for children, youth, and families.

[c]The key actors in "government agencies" here would include agency leadership, budget offices, and others with management and budget functions in executive and legislative branches at the federal, state, and local levels.

perspectives, interests, and incentives. Such dialogue could serve as the first step in bridging the gaps among stakeholders. These efforts might build on existing effective multi-stakeholder organizations that seek to support the production of high-quality economic evidence and its use for policy-making and intervention decisions, including the Jameel Poverty Action Lab (supported by the Hewlett, MacArthur, and Nike Foundations), the Prevention Economics Planning and Research (PEPR) Network (supported by the National Institutes of Health), and Human Capital and Economic Opportunity (supported by the Institute for New Economic Thinking). (See Chapter 4 for additional discussions of partnerships.)

Lasting, effective change in the quality, use, and utility of economic evidence will require support for the efforts of such intermediaries in collaborative partnerships between the producers and consumers of economic evidence (Pew-MacArthur Results First Initiative, 2012, 2013; The Pew Charitable Trusts, 2012). As emphasized in observations made at the committee's open sessions, here lies some of the greatest potential for the improved use of economic evidence (Aos et al., 2004; Crowley, 2013; National Research Council and Institute of Medicine, 2009).

A number of ongoing efforts have achieved advances in bridging the gap between consumers and producers of evidence through the establishment of multi-stakeholder collaborations. For instance, work by the Pew-Macarthur Results First Initiative is working to build infrastructure that provides tailored estimates of the fiscal impact of investing in different interventions for children, youth, and families. The Arnold Foundation's Evidence-Based Policy and Innovation initiative seeks to advance efforts—including support for evidence-based decision making and deployment of rigorous evaluations—that both build the evidence base for social interventions and make use of that evidence. These efforts (as well as those discussed as examples in Chapter 4) can serve as a guide for future collaborative endeavors aimed at unifying the often siloed interests and efforts of producers and consumers of economic evidence.

CONCLUSION: *Long-term, multi-stakeholder collaborations that include producers, consumers, and intermediaries can provide vital support for the improved use of economic evidence to inform decisions on investments in interventions for children, youth, and families.*

Understanding What Consumers and Producers of Economic Evidence Want Each Other to Know

Recognizing the inherent difficulties faced by both consumers and producers of economic evidence and their often limited time for developing the types of relationships that a collaborative can help foster, the committee generated the listing in Box 5-3 of what consumers and producers of economic evidence want each other to know, regardless of the setting.

BOX 5-3
What Consumers and Producers of Economic Evidence
Want Each Other to Know

Five Things Consumers of Economic Evidence
Want Producers to Know

1. Many factors other than economic evidence (including political pressures and capacity) influence the decision-making process.
2. The time frames for research outcomes and investment decisions can be very different and affect the value of the evidence.
3. Seldom do all the benefits realized from investment decisions accrue to those who make the decisions or their community.
4. Existing evidence is not always aligned with the evidence needed by the decision maker.
5. Real-world constraints that affect the implementation fidelity and scale-up of an intervention need to be identified before further investments are made.

Five Things Producers of Economic Evidence
Want Consumers to Know

1. Better investment decisions can be made with a foundational understanding of precisely what economic evidence is, the ways it can be used, its limitations, and considerations of causality and external validity.
2. Either directly or through intermediaries, consumers need to be able to distinguish between higher- and lower-quality economic evaluations.
3. Clearinghouses reveal only which interventions have attained success, usually relative to some alternative and according to certain specified criteria; accordingly, they cannot and generally should not be considered adequate to indicate which programs are best suited to a particular organization, context, or goal.
4. To support sound investments in children and facilitate high-quality program implementation, investment is required in the infrastructure needed to collect, analyze, and disseminate high-quality economic evidence; crucial here are data tracking children's well-being over time so that future, often not-yet-specified, evaluations can be conducted.
5. Investing in education, training, technical assistance, and capacity building often leads to successful development, analysis, and implementation of interventions.

Building a Coordinated Infrastructure to Support the Development and Use of Economic Evidence

"Users of the data need to become more statistically literate. This is not easy data to use. It is not easy. You have to think differently. It is achievable."

—Fritz Scheuren, senior fellow and vice president,
NORC at the University of Chicago, at the
committee's open session on June 1, 2015.

The committee's review of the literature and inquiry with experts in the use of economic evidence revealed the importance of developing new infrastructure for the production and use of such evidence. The establishment of a coordinated infrastructure system, directed by the needs and interests of diverse stakeholder groups, could significantly increase the quality, utility, and use of economic evidence. A coordinated infrastructure to support the production and use of high-quality economic evidence would include (1) improved access to administrative data, (2) a database of estimates of outcome values, (3) improved efforts to track children and families over time, (4) a data archive to support the development of shadow prices, (5) training of future producers and consumers of economic evidence, and (6) tools for tracking nonbudgetary resource consumption.

As discussed in Chapter 4, administrative data often provide the most efficient and least costly way of developing high-quality estimates that are relevant to consumers. Integrated, longitudinal administrative data systems could be used to generate proxy estimates of the economic value of certain outcomes (i.e., shadow prices; see Chapter 3) and could be leveraged for assessment of the fiscal and economic impacts of interventions (English et al., 2000; Garnier and Poertner, 2000). Multi-stakeholder groups could support access to these data sets by developing trusting relationships with those who own and manage the data. Ideally, these groups would invest in core facilities available to researchers for linking research subjects and trial participants to administrative records (Drake and Jonson-Reid, 1999).

One current effort aimed at supporting access to administrative data is PEPR's Administrative Data for Accelerating Prevention Trials (ADAPT) initiative (Crowley and Jones, 2015). This effort is deploying a flexible data infrastructure and robust security architecture to increase researcher's access to key federal and state administrative data systems. The goal is to reduce the research and time costs of gaining access to these systems so as to increase their use in trials of preventive interventions. If educational, health, and other outcomes for children reflected in administrative data over time can be accessed, it will become much easier and more cost-effective to develop experiments to test interventions aimed at improving those outcomes. Such access includes the ability to link trial participants through direct or indirect matching with the administrative records. In this manner, the ADAPT initiative is an example of how estimation of interventions' fiscal and economic impacts can be greatly facilitated.

Key to supporting the production of high-quality economic evidence—particularly in cost savings or benefit-cost analyses—is the availability of monetary conversion factors or shadow prices for valuing different outcomes (see Chapter 3). Examples of such estimates include the public and private value of graduating from high school, the cost of an aggravated assault, and the average cost of an emergency department visit (Boardman et al., 1997; Cohen and Piquero, 2008; Karoly, 2008). Historically, these estimates have been dispersed throughout the literature, crossing disciplinary and methodological boundaries. The field needs a central resource for finding these estimates, developing reasonable ranges of estimates for such costs, and comparing estimates from different studies. One example of such a resource is the RAND Valuing Outcomes of Social Programs (VOSP) database, a centralized web-based repository for use by researchers and policy makers (Karoly, 2015). This database includes estimates of economic or fiscal value in the areas of child welfare, crime, education, health, labor market, means-tested benefits, cognitive and noncognitive skills, and substance abuse. Such efforts could be augmented with increased stakeholder participation.

Additional infrastructure efforts are also needed to develop new and more robust economic values for key outcomes of interventions for children, youth, and families (Cohen, 2005; Karoly, 2008; Levin et al., 2006). In particular, despite their growing importance in programming for children, youth, and families, estimates of the economic value of noncognitive or socioemotional skills are limited (Duckworth, 2011; Jones et al., 2015; Moffitt et al., 2011). Longitudinal data sets measuring these skills could be leveraged to develop estimates of their economic value whenever possible. More generally, these data sets could be archived and made available to other researchers—with appropriate data protections—to accelerate the creation of new shadow prices or monetary conversion factors. Such a data repository would be an international resource that could greatly accelerate the production of better estimates of the economic value of investing in children, youth, and families.

Multi-stakeholder groups also could augment the capacity of the field of economic evaluation by training more producers of economic evidence, as well as helping to develop more informed consumers. To this end, these groups could engage in strategic trainings focused on best practices and methodologies for generating high-quality economic evidence. Recommendations offered in Chapter 3 provide one starting point for such curricula. These trainings could occur within both formal academic and professional settings. The Centers for Disease Control and Prevention (CDC), for example, offers the Steven M. Teutsch Prevention Effectiveness Fellowship Program, which provides postdoctoral training in cost-effectiveness analysis. This program has trained a number of researchers who produce new economic estimates. Other government agencies could benefit from offering similar fellowships. The recent National Institutes of Health (NIH) notice clarifying priorities for health economic research (NOT-OD-16-025) explicitly identifies areas of highest priority for research funding, which will necessitate a workforce trained to carry out these priorities. Unfortunately, this notice does not include priority areas for training (National Institutes of Health, 2015a). Professional societies such as the Society for Prevention Research, the American Society of Health Economists, and the Society for Benefit-Cost Analysis periodically offer trainings in economic evaluation of prevention and health promotion programs within workshops and preconferences (Hay, 2010; Kuklinski and Crowley, 2014). Importantly, to ensure the production of high-utility estimates, future trainings will have to ensure that consumer needs discussed in Chapter 4 are well reflected. Further, trainings for consumers, such as legislative education, courses within master of public policy programs, or concise briefings to decision makers, would advance consumer literacy and the use of high-quality economic evidence.

Improvements in the estimates of the costs of interventions for children, youth, and families could be supported and accelerated through new and better tools for conducting cost analyses. One such tool, recently released by the Center for Benefit-Cost Studies in Education, is the Cost Toolkit,[1] which provides spreadsheets for collecting cost information. Innovative tools that increase the automation of cost estimates could affect an important change in the field.

CONCLUSION: *Multi-stakeholder groups can play a larger and more impactful role in building coordinated infrastructure to support the development and use of high-quality economic evidence.*

The committee identified an important role for foundations and government funders not simply in sponsoring or even requiring economic evaluation, but also in building up the infrastructure that supports its use at various levels. At the same time, the committee recognizes that such an infrastructure is still in its formative stages, and given both the strengths and limitations of economic evaluations, believes that a competition among ideas from multiple sources would be healthy for its development. Among the many possibilities are to (1) strengthen and support appropriate efforts of professional associations, such as the Association for Public Policy Analysis and Management, the American Evaluation Association, and the

---

[1]For more information, visit http://www.cbcsecosttoolkit.org [May 2016].

Society for Prevention Research (or an international affiliate), where a sufficient body of researchers and policy analysts in this field would be expected to convene and compare ideas; (2) examine opportunities within curricula (including those addressing medical, legal, and public policy) at various graduate schools where future users of such information are being taught; (3) attend to progressive data requirements, including structured processes for data sharing[2] and longitudinal tracking of individuals to enable costs and benefits to be tracked over time; and (4) provide resources, where appropriate, for better integrating evaluations into budget processes to accommodate the needs of decision makers at various levels of government.[3] While the committee recognizes the value of existing foundation and government efforts made to date, it believes that multiple approaches to developing such an infrastructure would further advance the quality and utility of economic evidence.

> CONCLUSION: *Investments are needed to help build an infrastructure that will support the most effective production and use of high-quality economic evidence.*

Providing Stronger Stakeholder Incentives for the Production and Use of Better Evidence

"There has to be an incentive within the way federal funds are dispersed and state funds are dispersed, incentives for the use of evidence, for the uptake of evidence, and for the building of evidence."
—Jon Baron, president, Coalition for Evidence-Based Policy, at the committee's open session on March 23, 2015.

Multiple stakeholder groups—including funders, policy makers, program developers, program evaluators, and publishers engaged in science communication—contribute to the production of economic evidence. Each of these groups can either facilitate or impede the production and use of high-quality, high-utility economic evidence.

Funders

Funding priorities impact the advance of science, cultivating new fields or weakening areas of inquiry. Funders—whether research- or policy-centered, public or private, academic or nonacademic, contract or grant—have

---

[2] Also relevant are the legal and ethical issues related to data-sharing efforts.
[3] Observations made at the committee's open sessions on March 23, 2015, and June 1, 2015; see Appendix A.

an opportunity to increase the pace of the production and use of high-quality economic evidence. For instance, the NIH Common Fund Health Economics Program recently showcased research on the economics of prevention supported by the Health Economics program. A key message in the final report is the current need to "increase support for methods development" (National Institutes of Health, 2015b, p. 15).

Both public and private funding agencies generally have expressed significant interest in understanding the economic impact of interventions for children, youth, and families. (Eddama and Coast, 2008; Finkelstein and Corso, 2003; Hoffmann et al., 2002; Pew-MacArthur Results First Initiative, 2013. In fact, NIH's recent notice (NOT-OD-16-025) affirms the importance of health economic work for all institutes' funding portfolios, and states that one of the highest-priority areas identified by NIH includes research that seeks to "understand behavioral, *financial*, and other factors that influence the implementation, adherence, dissemination, and adoption of medical discoveries into health care [emphasis added]" (National Institutes of Health, 2015a). This research would include cost analyses of program resource consumption (i.e., understanding financial factors influencing implementation and adherence), as well as benefit-cost work (i.e., understanding financial factors influencing dissemination and adoption). Thus, increasing large-scale funding incentives for the use of economic evidence is one important means of adding to the knowledge base in this area.

One way to incentivize the production and use of high-quality economic evidence would be to designate a portion of the budget for many or most interventions for such purposes. An example of this approach is the Nurse-Family Partnership Program (see Chapter 2). Federal tiered funding initiatives are another incentive structure that supports the use of evidence (McNeil, 2010; Thompson et al., 2011). Although not specifically focused on economic evidence, these initiatives are designed to support the use of evidence-based evaluations in funded interventions. An example from the education sector is the Investing in Innovation Fund (i3), which, as described in Chapter 4, provides competitive grants to applicants who have established evidence of improving student achievement and attainment. By using evidence as an entrance requirement, i3 creates an incentive structure that encourages local education agencies to generate solid evidence of the impact of their programs. Building on these examples, funders could craft analogous incentive structures around the goal of producing high-quality, high-utility economic evidence for many types of interventions for children, youth, and families.

Policy Makers

Policy makers could create incentive structures making economic evidence a priority and ensuring its use in decision making. Under federal budget rules, for example, legislation that would have a direct effect on the federal budget must be accompanied by a cost analysis developed by the nonpartisan Congressional Budget Office (CBO).[4] These cost analyses provide important information about the economic effects of legislative programs that are moving through the congressional process. Greater visibility of the impact of a given program at the time of decision making could improve the effective use of this information. As another example, from the executive branch, the White House Office of Information and Regulatory Affairs administers Executive Order 12866,[5] which requires federal agencies to consider alternatives to rulemakings through a specific requirement for an analysis of the costs and benefits of these alternatives. In theory, this requirement has led to improved decision making, although the evidence that these requirements have in fact led to more cost-effective rules is not strong (Harrington and Morgenstern, 2004). Within and across federal programs, a growing movement to focus on what works has placed a spotlight on the need to incentivize the production of stronger evidence before new programs are supported and scaled.

Program Developers

Programs developed within a local setting often face limited resources. As a consequence, only a few such programs are evaluated to determine their full actual impact (Crowley et al., 2014; Foster et al., 2003). Conversely, programs developed within a broader scientific setting may not reflect sufficient attention to the limited resources of implementing agencies (e.g., constrained capacity, time, and personnel; participant costs) or to the need to reach more participants with a given level of funding (Gruen et al., 2008; Israel et al., 1998). The result is the development of programs that are too costly for many practice or policy contexts. Program development could benefit from cost analyses conducted prospectively to assist decision makers in understanding how the structure, setting, or scope of an intervention will ultimately influence downstream costs, such as the costs of implementation (Gorksy and Teutsch, 1995; Haddix et al., 2003). This broader set of information would better support the development of cost-effective, impactful interventions. Once implemented, moreover, interven-

---

[4]For more information, visit https://www.cbo.gov/about/processes [March 2016].
[5]Executive Order 12866. Regulatory Planning and Review, 3 CFR, 1993 Comp., p. 638.

tions could continue to be optimized through the use of estimates from economic evaluation.

Program Evaluators

Requirements for program evaluation of interventions for children, youth, and families often lead to opportunities for increased economic evaluation. Of particular relevance here is evaluation of resource needs, program impacts, and economic value.

When preparing to undertake an economic evaluation of a program, evaluators can often go beyond a simple review of the literature on existing evaluations of the same or similar programs; they can identify end-users and consider opportunities to assess their needs for economic evidence (e.g., Yates, 1996). The particular form and structure of the evidence and perspectives extend beyond those of society at large to those of the participant, agency, level of government, and private sector, among others. Also crucial are the time horizon and scope of a program, the representativeness of the population served by the program, and the generalizability of estimates. Deeper needs assessments may reveal key assumptions that should be tested within the analysis (i.e., through sensitivity analyses).

Further, evaluators could play a key role in advocating for prospective economic evaluations. Specifically, as discussed in Chapter 3, evaluators could facilitate early planning for capturing those program costs and outcome data that foster higher-quality economic evaluations (Crowley et al., 2012; Drummond, 2005; Levin and Belfield, 2013). Otherwise, evaluators must use secondary records to glean limited cost information. Evaluators could incentivize support for such prospective work in a number of ways—even as simple as expressing a preference for high-quality economic evaluation during consultations, on professional websites, or when working with professional organizations to advertise and publish papers on program evaluation that promote prospective analyses.

Program evaluators also could support the production and use of higher-quality and more useful economic evidence by working to access administrative data systems that may house key information on program costs or outcomes (see Chapter 4). In particular, when evaluators gained access to a new administrative system, they could work to help owners of those data (government agencies, health care providers, school systems, nonprofits) develop a sustainable approach to making the data accessible to other evaluators (Drake and Jonson-Reid, 1999).

Publishers

Publishers could increase incentives for the production of high-quality economic evidence. Chapter 3 outlines the committee's conclusions and recommendations on reporting standards for economic evaluations that publishers could adopt and promote during the review process. Whenever possible, publishers could also engage reviewers with methodological expertise in economic evaluation. Additionally, publishers could consider opportunities to promote more extensive use of economic evidence for those substantive topics for which such evidence could prove most productive. Importantly, publishers could subject economic evidence to the same rigorous scrutiny as other types of evidence. Issues of replicability and rigor are of great importance to the integrity of economic evidence, as it lends itself directly to policy and budget making.

In raising the standard for the quality of economic evidence produced, it is also important to attend to the issue of publication biases. These biases, noted across diverse fields of study, often derive from the policies and practices of journal editors and peer reviewers who favor positive and statistically significant findings (Ioannidis, 2005; Ncayiyana, 2010). To support the use of high-quality economic evidence, publication biases are among the many incentives that need direct attention. For certain substantive topics, the stakeholders of evidence may find it useful to review results of well-designed research studies that have varying degrees of significance, are historical or new, or are pooled across multiple studies. By exploring these opportunities, publishers could help advance the production and use of high-quality economic evidence.

> CONCLUSION: *Funders, policy makers, program developers, program evaluators, and publishers engaged in science communication each have unique opportunities to advance the quality, utility, and use of economic evidence.*

RECOMMENDATIONS

RECOMMENDATION 7: **Program developers, public and private funders, and policy makers should design, support, and incorporate comprehensive stakeholder partnerships (involving producers, consumers, and intermediaries) into action plans related to the use of economic evidence.**

A strategy for implementing this recommendation might include the following:

- The formation of a strategic action plan by foundations and governments to develop, fund, and convene these partnerships with researchers and end-users of evidence.

RECOMMENDATION 8: Multi-stakeholder groups should seek to build infrastructure that (1) supports access to administrative data; (2) maintains a database of estimates of outcome values; (3) archives longitudinal data for multiple purposes, including improved tracking of children and families and the development of better estimates of long-term impacts and shadow prices; (4) educates future producers and consumers of economic evidence; and (5) develops tools for tracking nonbudgetary resource consumption.

RECOMMENDATION 9: To support sustainable action toward the production and use of high-quality economic evidence, public and private funders should invest in infrastructure that supports (1) the regular convening of producers, consumers, and intermediaries of economic evidence; (2) enhanced education and training in economic evaluation; (3) efforts to attend to progressive data requirements and data-sharing management needs; and (4) the integration of economic evaluations into budget processes.

RECOMMENDATION 10: Public and private funders, policy makers, program developers, program evaluators, and publishers engaged in science communication should strengthen the incentives they provide for the production and use of high-quality economic evidence likely to be of high utility to decision makers.

Strategies for implementing this recommendation might include the following:

- Funders in the public and private sectors (including the National Institutes of Health and Institute of Education Sciences):
  - For a reported percentage of all funded programs, set aside sufficient resources for economic evaluation, at a minimum for collection of the data needed for prospective cost analysis in support of cost-effectiveness or benefit-cost analysis.
  - Increase internal capacity to review economic evaluations by engaging experienced program evaluators.
  - Expand competitive grants and fellowship opportunities that support training for the next generation of evaluators.
- Policy makers (including the Congressional Budget Office, the U.S. Government Accountability Office, the Congressional Research

Service, and other agencies reporting on performance or policy options):

- In issued reports, provide documentation of the extent to which program outcomes are backed by economic evidence, including economic evaluation (this is not a requirement to produce the evidence, but to report on what has been produced or is being produced by the various programs).
- For agencies reporting on performance or policy options, require economic evidence in general, with economic evaluation data when possible.

- Program developers:
  - Consider program costs within program development and early feasibility analyses.
  - Develop detailed logic models linking program activities to proximal and distal outcomes.
  - Use current economic estimates to optimize program effectiveness and economic impact.
- Program evaluators:
  - Conduct needs assessment of end-users to determine the most useful estimates and the most useful ways of communicating them.
  - Advocate for prospective planning of economic evaluation as a way of improving program evaluation.
  - Work with government agencies to access administrative data systems and develop those longitudinal data sets most likely to be useful for economically evaluating future, not just current, interventions, as in the areas of children's education and health.
- Publishers:
  - Modify reporting standards for economic evaluation to require reporting on program costs both measured and not measured in each study.
  - Engage reviewers with proven experience and content expertise in economic evaluation.
  - Foster greater demand for high-quality economic evidence.

REFERENCES

Aos, S., Lieb, R., Mayfield, J., Miller, M., and Pennucci, A. (2004). *Benefits and Costs of Prevention and Early Intervention Programs for Youth.* Available: http://www.wsipp.wa.gov/pub.asp?docid=04-07-3901 [February 2016].

August, G.J., Bloomquist, M.L., Lee, S.S., Realmuto, G.M., and Hektner, J.M. (2006). Can evidence-based prevention programs be sustained in community practice settings? The early risers' advanced-stage effectiveness trial. *Prevention Science, 7*(2), 151-165.

Boardman, A.E., Greenberg, D.H., Vining, A.R., and Weimer, D.L. (1997). "Plug-in" shadow price estimates for policy analysis. *The Annals of Regional Science, 31*(3), 299-324.

Brown, L.D., Feinberg, M.E., and Greenberg, M.T. (2010). Determinants of community coalition ability to support evidence-based programs. *Prevention Science, 11*(3), 287-297.

Cohen, M.A. (2005). *The Costs of Crime and Justice.* London, UK and New York: Routledge. Available: http://search.ebscohost.com/login.aspx?direct=true&scope=site&db=nlebk&db=nlabk&AN=115423 [February 2016].

Cohen, M.A., and Piquero, A.R. (2008). New evidence on the monetary value of saving a high risk youth. *Journal of Quantitative Criminology, 25*(1), 25-49.

Crowley, D.M. (2013). Building efficient crime prevention strategies considering the economics of investing in human development. *Criminology & Public Policy, 12*(2), 353.

Crowley, D.M., and Jones, D. (2015). Financing prevention: Opportunities for economic analysis across the translational research cycle. *Translational Behavioral Medicine,* 1-8.

Crowley, D.M., Jones, D.E., Greenberg, M.T., Feinberg, M.E., and Spoth, R. (2012). Resource consumption of a diffusion model for prevention programs: The PROSPER Delivery System. *Journal of Adolescent Health, 50*(3), 256-263.

Crowley, D.M., Hill, L.G., Kuklinski, M.R., and Jones, D. (2014). Research priorities for economic analyses of prevention: Current issues and future directions. *Prevention Science, 15*(6), 789-798.

Drake, B., and Jonson-Reid, M. (1999). Some thoughts on the increasing use of administrative data in child maltreatment research. *Child Maltreatment, 4*(4), 308-315.

Drummond, M.F. (2005). *Methods for the Economic Evaluation of Health Care Programmes.* New York: Oxford University Press.

Duckworth, A.L. (2011). The significance of self-control. *Proceedings of the National Academy of Sciences, 108*(7), 2639-2640.

Eddama, O., and Coast, J. (2008). A systematic review of the use of economic evaluation in local decision making. *Health Policy, 86*(2-3), 129-141.

English, D.J., Brandford, C.C., and Coghlan, L. (2000). Data-based organizational change: The use of administrative data to improve child welfare programs and policy. *Child Welfare, 79*(5), 499-515.

Finkelstein, E., and Corso, P. (2003). Cost-of-illness analyses for policy making: A cautionary tale of use and misuse. *Expert Review of Pharmacoeconomics & Outcomes Research, 3*(4), 367-369.

Foster, E.M., Dodge, K.A., and Jones, D. (2003). Issues in the economic evaluation of prevention programs. *Applied Developmenal Science, 7*(2), 76-86.

Garnier, P.C., and Poertner, J. (2000). Using administrative data to assess child safety in out-of-home care. *Child Welfare, 79*(5), 597-613.

Gorsky, R.D., and Teutsch, S.M. (1995). Assessing the effectiveness of disease and injury prevention programs: Costs and consequences. *Morbidity and Mortality Weekly Report, 44*(RR-10), 1-10.

Gruen, R., Elliott, J., Nolan, M., Lawton, P., Parkhill, A., McLaren, C., and Lavis, J. (2008). Sustainability science: An integrated approach for health-programme planning. *The Lancet, 372*(9649), 1579-1589.

Haddix, A.C., Teutsch, S.M., and Corso, P.S. (Eds.). (2003). *Prevention Effectiveness: A Guide to Decision Analysis and Economic Evaluation.* New York: Oxford University Press.

Harrington, W., and Morgenstern, R.D. (2004). *Evaluating Regulatory Impact Analyses.* Washington, DC: Resources for the Future.

Hay, J. (2010). *Economic Evaluation of Drugs, Devices and other Medical Interventions.* Ithaca, NY: American Society of Health Economists. Available: http://ashecon.org/conference/2010/preconference/economic-evaluation-drugs-and-medical-technology.pdf [February 2016].

Hoffmann, C., Stoykova, B.A., Nixon, J., Glanville, J.M., Misso, K., and Drummond, M.F. (2002). Do health-care decision makers find economic evaluations useful? The findings of focus group research in UK health authorities. *Value in Health*, 5(2), 71-78.

Ioannidis, J.P. (2005). Why most published research findings are false. *PLoS Med*, 2(8), e124.

Israel, B., Schulz, A., Parker, E., and Becker, A. (1998). Review of community-based research: Assessing partnership approaches to improve public health. *Annual Review of Public Health*, 19, 173-202.

Jones, D.E., Greenberg, M., and Crowley, M. (2015). Early social-emotional functioning and public health: The relationship between kindergarten social competence and future wellness. *American Journal of Public Health*, 105(11), 2283-2290.

Karoly, L.A. (2008). *Valuing Benefits in Benefit-Cost Studies of Social Programs*. Santa Monica, CA: RAND. Available: http://www.rand.org/content/dam/rand/pubs/technical_reports/2008/RAND_TR643.pdf [February 2016].

Karoly, L.A. (2015). *Valuing Outcomes of Social Programs: The RAND Database of Shadow Prices for Benefit-Cost Analysis of Social Programs*. Presented at the Society for Prevention Research, May, Washington, DC. Available: https://spr.confex.com/spr/spr2015/webprogram/Paper22878.html [February 2016].

Kuklinski, M.R., and Crowley, M. (2014). *Building the Economic Case for Prevention: Methods and Tools for Assessing the Resource Needs and Economic Costs for Preventive Intervention*. Presented at the Society for Prevention Research, May, Washington, DC. Available: http://www.preventionresearch.org/2014-annual-meeting/pre-conference-workshops-and-international-networking-forum [February 2016].

Levin, H., and Belfield, C. (2013). *Guiding the Development and Use of Cost-Effectiveness Analysis in Education*. New York: Center for Benefit-Cost Studies of Education, Columbia University. Available: http://cbcse.org/wordpress/wp-content/uploads/2013/08/Guiding-the-Development-And-Use-of-Cost-effectiveness-Analysis-in-Education.pdf [February 2016].

Levin, H., Belfield, C., Muennig, P.A., and Rouse, C. (2006). *The Costs and Benefits of an Excellent Education for All of America's Children*. New York: Columbia University. Available: http://www3.nd.edu/~jwarlick/documents/Levin_Belfield_Muennig_Rouse.pdf [February 2016].

McNeil, M. (2010). Duncan carving deep mark on policy. *Education Week*, 1-18.

Moffitt, T.E., Arseneault, L., Belsky, D., Dickson, N., Hancox, R.J., Harrington, H., Houts, R., Poulton, R., Roberts, B.W., Ross, S., Sears, M.R., Thomson, W.M., and Caspi, A. (2011). A gradient of childhood self-control predicts health, wealth, and public safety. *Proceedings of the National Academy of Sciences of the United States of America*, 108(7), 2693-2698.

National Institutes of Health. (2015a). *Clarifying NIH Priorities for Health Economics Research*. Available: https://grants.nih.gov/grants/guide/notice-files/NOT-OD-16-025.html [February 2016].

National Institutes of Health. (2015b). *Economics of Prevention Workshop Summary*. Available: https://commonfund.nih.gov/sites/default/files/Final_August_2015_Economics_of_Prevention_Workshop_Summary_REV_11-06-15_ld_508_0.pdf [February 2016].

National Research Council and Institute of Medicine. (2009). *Strengthening Benefit-Cost Analysis for Early Childhood Interventions*. A. Beatty (Rapporteur). Committee on Strengthening Benefit-Cost Methodology for the Evaluation of Early Childhood Interventions. Board on Children, Youth, and Families. Division of Behavioral and Social Sciences and Education. Washington, DC: The National Academies Press.

Ncayiyana, D.J. (2010). "Truth" in medical journal publishing. *SAMJ: South African Medical Journal*, 100(2), 71-72.

Pew-MacArthur Results First Initiative. (2012). *Better Results, Lower Costs: Washington State's Cutting-Edge Policy Analysis Model.* Washington, DC. Available: http://www. pewtrusts.org/~/media/legacy/uploadedfiles/pcs_assets/2012/resultsfirstwashington casestudypdf.pdf [February 2016].

Pew-MacArthur Results First Initiative. (2013). *States' Use of Cost-Benefit Analysis Improving Results for Taxpayers.* Available: http://www.pewtrusts.org/~/media/legacy/uploadedfiles/ pcs_assets/2013/pewresultsfirst50statereportpdf.pdf [February 2016].

The Pew Charitable Trusts. (2012). *Results First.* Available: http://www.pewstates.org/projects/ results-first-328069 [February 2016].

Thompson, D.K., Clark, M.J., Howland, L.C., and Mueller, M.-R. (2011). The Patient Protection and Affordable Care Act of 2010 (PL 111-148): An Analysis of maternal-child health home visitation. *Policy, Politics, & Nursing Practice, 12*(3), 175-185.

Yates, B.T. (1996). *Analyzing Costs, Procedures, Processes, and Outcomes in Human Services.* Thousand Oaks, CA: Sage.

Appendix A

Public Session Agendas

**PUBLIC INFORMATION-GATHERING SESSION AGENDA
MEETING 1**

January 26, 2015

The National Academies Keck Center
500 Fifth Street, NW
Washington, DC 20001

1:10 pm   **Welcome, Introductions, and Opening Remarks**
Eugene Steuerle, Committee Chair

1:30 pm   **Remarks on Study Statement of Task from Sponsors**
Valerie Chang, MacArthur Foundation
Kerry Anne McGeary, Robert Wood Johnson Foundation
Simon Sommer, Jacobs Foundation (via phone)

1:45 pm   **Committee Discussion with Sponsors**

2:35 pm   **Public Comments (as needed)**

2:45 pm   **Adjourn Open Session**

PUBLIC INFORMATION-GATHERING SESSION AGENDA
MEETING 2

March 23, 2015

National Academy of Sciences Building
2101 Constitution Ave, NW
Washington, DC 20418

1:00 pm   **Welcome, Introductions, and Opening Remarks**
Eugene Steuerle, Committee Chair

1:15 pm   **Panel 1: The Use of Economic Evidence Decisions**
Moderator: *Jennifer Brooks, Committee Member*

Speakers:
- *Uma Ahluwalia, Montgomery County Maryland, Department of Health and Human Services*
- *Barry Anderson, Office of the Executive Director, National Governors Association*
- *Nadya Dabby, U.S. Department of Education*
- *Dan Rosenbaum, Economic Policy Division, Office of Management and Budget*
- *Henry Sobanet and Erick Scheminske (via phone), Colorado Governor's Office of State Planning and Budgeting*

2:45 pm   **Break**

3:00 pm   **Panel 2: Facilitating and Overcoming Barriers to the Use of Economic Evidence in Investments**
Moderator: *Daniel Max Crowley, Committee Member*

Speakers:
- *Jon Baron, Coalition for Evidence-Based Policy*
- *Sandra Bishop-Josef, ReadyNation*
- *Jerry Croan, Third Sector Capital Partners*
- *Stephanie Lee, Washington State Institute for Public Policy*
- *Gary VanLandingham, Pew-MacArthur Results First Initiative*

4:30 pm   **Public Comments (as needed)**

4:45 pm   **Adjourn Open Session**

PUBLIC INFORMATION-GATHERING SESSION AGENDA
MEETING 3

June 1, 2015

The National Academies Keck Center
500 Fifth Street, NW
Washington, DC 20001

9:45 am   **Welcome, Introductions, and Opening Remarks**
                Eugene Steuerle, Committee Chair

10:00 am   **Panel 1: Bridging the Gap between Producers and**
                Consumers of Economic Evidence
                Moderator: *Ted Miller, Committee Member*

                Speakers:
- *Will Aldridge, FPG Child Development Institute, University of North Carolina at Chapel Hill*
- *Danielle Berfond, The Bridgespan Group*
- *John Q. Easton, Spencer Foundation (via WebEx)*
- *Mark W. Lipsey, Peabody Research Institute, Vanderbilt University (via WebEx)*

11:15 am   **Break**

11:30 am   **Panel 2: Barriers to and Advances in the Use of**
                Administrative Data/Integrated Data Systems
                Moderator: *Rachel Nugent, Committee Member*

                Speakers:
- *Robert M. Goerge, Chapin Hall at University of Chicago*
- *Carlise King, Early Childhood Data Collaborative, Child Trends*
- *Fritz Scheuren, NORC at the University of Chicago*
- *Beth A. Virnig, Research Data Assistance Center, University of Minnesota*

1:00 pm   **Adjourn Open Session**

Appendix B

Biographical Sketches of Committee Members and Staff

EUGENE STEUERLE (*Chair*) is Richard B. Fisher chair and institute fellow at the Urban Institute and a syndicated columnist. Previously, he served in a variety of government positions, including deputy assistant secretary for tax analysis in the U.S. Department of the Treasury and as organizer of the department's study that led to the Tax Reform Act of 1986. He has also been federal executive fellow at the Brookings Institution and a columnist for the *Financial Times*. His work as an economist has focused broadly on the federal budget, fiscal policy, and the economy He currently serves on advisory panels or boards for the Congressional Budget Office, the Government Accountability Office, the Joint Committee on Taxation, the Committee for a Responsible Federal Budget, the Independent Sector, the Aspen Institute Initiative on Financial Security, the National Committee on Vital and Health Statistics, and the Partnership for America's Economic Success. He received a Ph.D. in economics from the University of Wisconsin–Madison.

RICARDO BASURTO-DAVILA is a health economist with the Los Angeles County Department of Public Health. In his current position in the department's Policy Analysis Unit, he focuses on increasing the use of quantitative analysis in decision making by leading economic evaluations and policy analysis studies of policies and programs that affect population health. Previously, he held positions as a prevention effectiveness fellow at the U.S. Centers for Disease Control and Prevention, where he conducted economic evaluations of the efforts implemented by the United States and other countries to respond to the 2009 H1N1 influenza pandemic. He also previously was with the RAND Corporation, where his work focused on migration, social, and environmental determinants of health, and inequalities in health and health care. He has a B.A. in economics from Instituto Tecnológico de Monterrey in Mexico, an M.Sc. in economics from the University of Texas at Austin, and a Ph.D. in policy analysis from the Pardee RAND Graduate School.

JENNIFER BROOKS is a senior program officer at the Bill & Melinda Gates Foundation, where her work focuses on the development and implementation of a new national early learning portfolio at the foundation. Previously, she served as the director of Economic, Human Services and Workforce at the National Governors Association Center for Best Practices and as the team leader for Head Start research at the Administration for Children and Families at the U.S. Department of Health and Human Services. Her work focuses on using data and evidence to enhance policies and programs for low-income children in a variety of fields, including early learning, child welfare, cash assistance programs, and youth development. She has an M.A. in public policy from the University of Chicago and an M.Sc and a Ph.D. in human development and family studies from Pennsylvania State University.

JEANNE BROOKS-GUNN is the Virginia and Leonard Marx professor of child development at Teachers College and the College of Physicians and Surgeons and director of the National Center for Children and Families, all at Columbia University. Her research focuses on how lives unfold over time and factors that contribute to well-being across childhood, adolescence, and adulthood. She also designs and evaluates intervention programs for children and parents (home visiting programs for pregnant women or new parents, early childhood education programs for toddlers and preschoolers, two generation programs for young children and their parents, and after school programs for older children). She is a member of the National Academy of Medicine and the National Academy of Education, and she has received life-time achievement awards from the Society for Research in Child Development, the American Academy of Political and Social Science, the American Psychological Society, American Psychological Association, and the Society for Research on Adolescence. She has a M.Ed. from Harvard University and a Ph.D. in human learning and development from the University of Pennsylvania.

BARBARA CHOW is program director of education with the William and Flora Hewlett Foundation. Previously, she served as policy director for the Budget Committee of the U.S. House of Representatives, executive director of the National Geographic Education Foundation, and vice president for education and children's programs at National Geographic. She also previously served as special assistant to President Clinton for legislative affairs and as the White House liaison to Congress on economic, budget, and appropriation matters. She also previously worked in the U.S. Office of Management and Budget, where she was the program associate director for education, income maintenance, and labor; as the deputy director of the White House Domestic Policy Council; on the staff of the U.S. Senate Budget Committee; and as a manager of federal budget policy at Price Waterhouse. She has a master's degree in public policy from the University of California, Berkeley.

PHAEDRA CORSO is the University of Georgia Foundation professor of human health, founding head of the Department of Health Policy and Management, director of the Economic Evaluation Research Group in the College of Public Health, associate director of the Owens Institute for Behavioral Research, and adjunct faculty at the School of Public and International Affairs, all at the University of Georgia. Her research interests include economic evaluation of public health interventions; quality-of-life assessment for vulnerable populations; evaluation of preferences for health risks; and the prevention of violence, injury, and substance use. Previously, she held several positions at the U.S. Centers for Disease Control and Prevention, including as an economic analyst in the area of violence prevention. She has a Ph.D. in health policy from Harvard University.

DANIEL MAX CROWLEY is an assistant professor at Pennsylvania State University and a research fellow with the National Bureau of Economic Research studying the economics of investing in healthy development. He is particularly interested in preventing illness and criminal behavior through evidence-based interventions in early life. His work sits at the intersection of human development economics, and public policy. This research focuses primarily on (1) strengthening economic evaluations of preventive interventions, (2) facilitating evidence-based policy making through strategic investments in preventive services, and (3) evaluating the utility of performance-based financing to access new resources for improving health. He has a Ph.D. in human development and family studies from Pennsylvania State University.

JODY L. FITZPATRICK recently retired from the School of Public Affairs and director of the Master in Public Administration Program at the University of Colorado Denver. Her work has focused on conducting evaluations in education, social services, and employment, with a particular focus on women and families. Her interests include context and its influence on evaluation, evaluation use, and measurement. She has served on the board and as president of the American Evaluation Association She has a Ph.D. in program evaluation from the University of Texas at Austin.

LEIGH MILES JACKSON (*Study Director*) is a program officer with the Board on Children, Youth, and Families. Previously, she was a developmental psychopathology and neurogenomics research fellow at Vanderbilt University, where she investigated the role of chronic sleep disturbance on the health and epigenetic outcomes of adolescents. She has a bachelor's degree in chemistry from Wake Forest University and a Ph.D. in molecular and systems pharmacology from Emory University.

LYNN A. KAROLY is a senior economist at the RAND Corporation and a professor at the Pardee RAND Graduate School. Her recent research has focused on human capital investments, social welfare policy, child and family well-being, and U.S. labor markets. In the area of child policy, much of her research has focused on early childhood programs, particularly early care and education programs. For those programs, she has studied their use and quality, the system of publicly subsidizing them, professional development for their workforce, and quality rating and improvement systems. In related work, she has examined the costs, benefits, and economic returns of early childhood interventions and youth development programs, and she has assessed the use of benefit-cost analysis to evaluate social programs. She has a Ph.D. in economics from Yale University.

BRIDGET KELLY (*Senior Program Officer*) was on the staff of the Board on Children, Youth, and Families. Previously, she served as the study director for the Committee on the Science of Children Birth to Age 8: Deepening and Broadening the Foundation for Success. She also worked for projects on global chronic diseases; country-level decision making; benefit-cost analysis for early childhood interventions; prevention of mental, emotional, and behavioral disorders; and depression, parenting practices, and child development. She has a B.A. in biology and neuroscience from Williams College and an M.D. and a Ph.D. in neurobiology from Duke University.

NOAM KEREN (*Research Associate*) is on the staff of the Board on Children, Youth, and Families. In addition to his work on this study, he is working on the Forum on Promoting Children's Cognitive, Affective, and Behavioral Health. Previously, he conducted research in psychology and neuroscience, investigating the neurobiology underlying cognitive functions using behavioral measures and advanced neuroimaging methods. He also served as a science writer and foreign news editor for the *Israeli Air Force Magazine*. He has a B.Sc. in psychology from the University of Florida and an M.A. in psychology from Washington University in St. Louis.

MARGARET KUKLINSKI is a research scientist at the Social Development Research Group in the School of Social Work at the University of Washington. Her multidisciplinary work covers economics, clinical and community psychology, and child development. She is broadly interested in the design and analysis of prevention interventions that promote positive youth development and are economically viable. Her current projects include the Community Youth Development Study, a multisite randomized controlled trial of the Communities That Care prevention system, for which she is working on economic and benefit-cost analysis of long-term effects. She is also the principal investigator on an evaluation of the Seattle Public Schools High School Graduation Initiative, which aims to prevent students from dropping out and improve high school graduation rates, academic performance, and disciplinary problems among high-risk students. She has a Ph.D. in psychology from the University of California, Berkeley.

TARA MAINERO (*Associate Program Officer*) is on the staff of the Board on Children, Youth, and Families. In addition to her work on this project, she has served as staff lead for a consensus study dissemination strategy, a forum collaborative, and a workshop youth advisory group. Previously, she was on the staff of the Children's Defense Fund and with the D.C. Department of Youth Rehabilitation Services. She has a master's degree in social work with a concentration in social change.

TED R. MILLER is principal research scientist and director of the Public Services Research Institute at the Pacific Institute for Research and Evaluation. He is also an adjunct professor at West Virginia University School of Public Health and Curtin University Centre for Population Health Research. He is currently taking part in the Global Burden of Disease measurement effort. His work in the field of economics has concentrated on the costs of societal ills, savings from prevention, and methods for analyzing the return on investment in prevention. He has applied his cost estimates to estimate the return on investment and cost per quality-adjusted life year for more than 160 injuries, violence, and substance abuse interventions, most of them focused on youth. He has master's degrees in operations research and city planning and a Ph.D. in regional science (spatial economics) from the University of Pennsylvania.

RACHEL NUGENT is vice president of the Chronic Noncommunicable Diseases Global Initiative at RTI International. Prior to this position, she was a clinical associate professor in the Department of Global Health at the University of Washington. She is also the principal investigator of the Disease Control Priorities. Previously, she served as deputy director of Global Health at the Center for Global Development, director of health and economics at the Population Reference Bureau, program director of Health and Economics Programs at the Fogarty International Center of the National Institutes of Health, and senior economist at the Food and Agriculture Organization of the United Nations. She served as an adviser to the World Health Organization, various U.S. agencies, and nonprofit organizations on the economics and policy environment of noncommunicable diseases. She has a Ph.D. in economics from George Washington University.

OLGA ACOSTA PRICE is an associate professor in the Department of Prevention and Community Health at the Milken Institute School of Public Health at George Washington University. She is also director of the Center for Health and Health Care in Schools, a national resource and technical assistance center committed to building effective school health programs. Previously, she was director of the School Mental Health Program at the Department of Mental Health in Washington, D.C.; assistant professor at the University of Maryland's School of Medicine; and associate director of the Center for School Mental Health Assistance, a national technical assistance center, where she helped to promote the development of school-based mental health services across the country. She has a Ph.D. in clinical psychology from the State University of New York at Buffalo.

ANNE SHERIDAN is an independent consultant at Sheridan & Associates where she provides independent project management, outreach, research, and government relations services to political and issue organizations, and coalitions. Formerly, she served as the executive director of Office for Children for the governor of Maryland, where she chaired the Children's Cabinet, which is comprised of the secretaries of the Departments of Budget and Management, Disabilities, Health and Mental Hygiene, Human Resources, and Juvenile Services, as well as the state superintendent of schools. In that capacity, she worked on allocating funds for distribution to state agencies, local governments, and public and private organizations, and partnered with the local management boards to plan, coordinate, and monitor the delivery of priority services in local jurisdictions. Prior to this work, she managed the Maryland No Kid Hungry Campaign for Share Our Strength, a national nonprofit organization working to end childhood hunger. She has a B.A. in economics from Simmons College and an M.Sc. in foreign service from Georgetown University.

Glossary

Attrition: In the context of research studies, refers to the gradual loss of study participants, which can occur for a variety of reasons, including adverse effects of the treatment.

Average cost: Total cost divided by the quantity of output or the cost per unit of output. Also, in the context of this report, the total intervention cost divided by the number of participants. Average cost accounts for both fixed (or sunk) and variable costs. See also *marginal cost*.

Benefit-cost analysis (BCA): A method of economic evaluation in which both costs and outcomes of an intervention are valued in monetary terms, permitting a direct comparison of the benefits produced by the intervention with its costs (also referred to as cost-benefit analysis).

Benefit-cost ratio: A common way to express the results from a benefit-cost analysis. The ratio is calculated by dividing total intervention benefits by total intervention costs, after relevant discounting and inflationary adjustments have been made.

Break-even analysis: A method of economic evaluation that can be used when the outcomes of an intervention are unknown. Can be used to complement a cost analysis as a way of anticipating potential economic returns.

Budgetary impact analysis: A special case of cost-savings analysis that examines the impact, year-by-year, of an intervention on the government budget for aggregate or specific agencies.

Constant dollar: An adjusted value of currency used for comparison of dollar values from one time period to another, free of the effects of inflation. Because of inflation, the purchasing power of a dollar changes over time; current dollars, or actual dollars paid, include inflationary effects. Current, also referred to as "nominal," dollars can be converted to constant, or "real," dollars through the use of a price index (e.g., consumer price index [CPI]) that measures inflation in a given time period, often annually, through this formula: Constant dollars$_{year\ x}$ = Current dollars$_{year\ y}$ × $(CPI_{year\ x}/CPI_{year\ y})$.

Contingent valuation analysis: A method of obtaining estimates of the worth of a social good or benefit in which people are asked how much they would pay for a particular outcome given a particular hypothetical scenario.

Cost: In economic evaluation, the full economic value of the resources required to implement a given social intervention.

Cost analysis (CA): A type of cost and outcome evaluation that provides a complete accounting of the economic costs of implementing a given intervention. Cost analysis is one component of all other cost and outcome evaluation methods (see also *benefit-cost analysis*, *cost-effectiveness analysis*, and *cost-savings analysis*), although it may be of interest in its own right.

Cost-effectiveness (CE) ratio: A common way to express the results from a cost-effectiveness analysis. The ratio is calculated by dividing the intervention *costs net of monetized outcomes* (defined below) by the change in a focal outcome measured in its natural unit.

Cost-effectiveness analysis (CEA): A method of economic evaluation in which outcomes of an intervention are expressed in nonmonetary terms, typically their natural units. The outcomes and costs are compared with both the outcomes (using the same outcome measures) and the costs for competing interventions, or with an established standard, to determine whether the outcomes are achieved at reasonable monetary cost.

Cost-effectiveness acceptability curve: Displays the probability that an intervention yielded a positive return at different monetary values of a quality-adjusted life year (QALY).

Cost-savings analysis: A type of cost and outcome evaluation that entails performing a benefit-cost analysis but only from the perspective of the government sector. The present value of the intervention's costs is compared with the present value of the stream of future benefits to the government sector. See also *benefit-cost analysis*, *cost analysis*, and *cost-effectiveness analysis*.

Cost-utility analysis: A cost-effectiveness analysis that uses a quality-of-life measure (e.g., a disability-adjusted life year [DALY] or quality-adjusted life year [QALY]) as the unmonetized outcome.

Costs net of monetized outcomes: The cost of an intervention less the economic benefits resulting from the intervention's impacts that have been expressed in dollar terms.

Counterfactual: The base condition used as the basis of comparison when evaluating an intervention. No treatment, the current situation, and the best proven treatment are common counterfactuals.

DALY (disability-adjusted life year): A general measure of disease burden on quantity of life lived. One DALY can be thought of as one lost year of "healthy" life.

Dependent variable(s): The factor(s) that change as a result of an experimental treatment or intervention, such as the academic skills of children who have participated in an early childhood education program.

Direct costs: May refer to those resources required to provide services directly to participants of the intervention (e.g., classroom time, home visits).

Discount rate: A factor used to estimate the value of future cash flows (i.e., future benefits of avoided costs) at the current equivalent value, used with the goal of attempting to take into account likely changes in valuation, *opportunity costs* (defined below), and other factors.

Discrete choice: A method for estimating *shadow prices* (defined below), referring to experiments in which respondents' preferences are assessed from a sequence of hypothetical scenarios that vary on several attributes, which can include the price of the nonmarket commodity of interest.

Economic evidence (in the context of this report): The information produced from cost and cost-outcome evaluations, including cost analysis, cost-effectiveness analysis, and benefit-cost analysis.

Economies of scale: Advantages that accrue when an intervention is conducted on a larger scale than initially, and that result from opportunities to use resources more efficiently and reduce average costs.

Effect size: The magnitude of results, or effects on participants, of a particular intervention.

Fixed costs: Costs that do not change, over a certain range, with variation in the amount of goods produced or services provided. In social interventions, often refers to costs that do not vary with the number of participants served.

Government sector: Represents individuals collectively as taxpayers who may bear the costs of an intervention or experience benefits as a result of its impacts.

Government perspective: Narrowly focused on a specific government agency or level of government (e.g., federal, state, local).

Impact: A change in outcome(s) that can be attributed to an intervention.

Independent variable: One of the characteristics of an experiment's subjects that are considered in the study design, such as the age and gender of the participants in an early childhood intervention.

Indirect costs: May refer to the *overhead costs* (defined below) related to administrative functions of an intervention or to services not provided directly to but on behalf of the participants.

Intangible cost (or benefit): A cost (or benefit) that cannot be measured directly in dollar terms. In the case of the costs of crime, for example, intangible crime victim costs include pain and suffering and loss of the feeling of personal safety. See also *tangible cost (or benefit)*.

Intent to treat: An approach to analyzing the results of a trial in which all participants are treated as if they received the intervention as intended, even if some did not.

Internal rate of return: For a given intervention, the discount rate that equalizes the present value of the future stream of benefits with the present value of the future stream of costs (i.e., the discount rate that sets net present-value benefits to zero). Discount rates below the internal rate of return will result in positive net present-value benefits, while the reverse is true for discount rates above the internal rate of return. See also *benefit-cost ratio* and *net present-value benefits.*

Intervention: In the context of this report, a broad term used to denote programs, practices, and policies relevant to children, youth, and families.

Intervention specificity: When an intervention's specific purpose, intended recipients, approach to implementation, causal mechanisms, and intended impact can be described in sufficient detail.

Hidden costs: Additional resource costs needed to implement an intervention (e.g., resources for adoption, development, training, technical assistance, and sustainability). These costs may include resources required beyond the intervention to ensure full implementation

Knowledge brokering: A function often performed by translators or intermediaries who work at the intersection between producers and consumers of evidence to facilitate the diffusion and uptake of information.

Linked economic impacts: Impacts attributable to an intervention that are not directly caused by the intervention. For example, a delinquency intervention may have direct economic impacts on criminal justice system and victimization costs, as well as linked effects on lifetime earnings because of the relationship between reducing delinquency and increasing high school graduation.

Logic model: A pictorial representation of an intervention's theory of change. Logic models typically show the relationship among resources, or inputs, needed to carry out an intervention; major activities involved in the intervention; and the results of the intervention, expressed as outputs, outcomes, and/or impacts.

Marginal cost: The cost to produce one more unit of output given current levels of production (i.e., the marginal change in cost for one more unit at the current level of operation). Marginal cost typically excludes *fixed costs* (defined above).

Market price: The price that reflects an individual's or society's willingness to pay for an outcome of interest.

Monetize: In benefit-cost analysis, monetize refers to the conversion of intervention impacts from nonmonetary to monetary terms.

Monte Carlo simulation: The repeated drawing of uncertain parameters from assumed distributions to produce a distribution of possible outcomes. In benefit-cost analysis, used to translate uncertainty in predicted resource use, impacts, and their monetized values into a distribution of predicted net present-value benefits.

Multivariate regression model: A statistical procedure for examining the relationship among several variables. This statistical technique makes it possible to isolate the effect of an experiment on an outcome after the influence of other possible factors has been taken into account.

Net present-value (NPV) benefits: A summary measure from benefit-cost analysis, defined as the present value of the stream of benefits (or costs) that results from the impacts of an intervention less the present value of the stream of costs to implement the intervention. See also *benefit-cost ratio* and *internal rate of return.*

Net (present-value) savings: A summary measure from cost-savings analysis, defined as the present value of the stream of benefits (or costs) to the government sector that results from the impacts of an intervention less the present value of the stream of costs for the public sector to implement the intervention. See also *internal rate of return.*

Opportunity cost: The value of alternatives not chosen and calculated as part of an analysis of the costs of the alternative that was chosen.

Outcome: An attitude, action, skill, behavior, etc. that an intervention is intended to causally influence.

Overhead: Ongoing costs of carrying out an intervention or running an organization, such as space and administrative staff costs, that have not been tied specifically to a particular activity.

P-value: In the context of this study, the probability that an outcome was produced by chance rather than as a result of an intervention.

QALY (quality-adjusted life year): A general measure of disease burden on the quality and quantity of life lived. The QALY for a year in perfect health is valued at 1, less optimal health is valued at less than 1, and death is assigned a value of 0.

Quasi-experimental design: An experiment designed to produce evidence of causality when randomized controlled trials are not possible, using alternative statistical procedures to compensate for nonrandom factors.

Randomized controlled trial: A study in which participants are assigned by chance to receive (or not receive) the intervention or treatment being studied. When the number of participants in the trial is sufficiently large, any differences among them that might influence their response to the treatment will be distributed evenly, and as a result, differences in response can be attributed to the treatment.

Return on investment (ROI): A method of economic evaluation used in special cases in which benefit-cost analysis is conducted for a specific stakeholder group.

Regression discontinuity design: A quasi-experimental analysis that can be used in program evaluation when randomized assignment is not feasible. It is based on the assumption that individuals who fall just above or below a cut-off point on a particular scale are likely to be similar, so that this group can be treated as varying randomly.

Revealed preference: An approach for estimating *shadow prices* (defined below). Estimates what people pay for products with the attributes that need to be valued but are not priced directly.

Selection bias: An unrecognized systematic difference between participants and controls that may explain differences in outcomes and therefore confounds assessment of intervention impact.

Sensitivity analysis: An analysis performed to address uncertainty in an economic evaluation.

Shadow price/shadow value: In the context of this study, the estimated true value of a resource or impact or cost of the results of a particular decision, as calculated when no market price is available or when market prices do not reflect the true value; a dollar value attached to an opportunity cost.

Societal perspective: Captures the public sector and the private sector and includes all stakeholders who have some relationship to an intervention as bearers of costs or as beneficiaries, as well as those who may be affected only indirectly.

Stakeholders: A person, group, or organization that has an interest in or use for cost and outcome evaluation. The broadest stakeholder is society as a whole. Society as a whole may be subdivided into specific stakeholders, typically defined as the government sector (or individuals as taxpayers), intervention participants (as private individuals), and the rest of society (intervention nonparticipants as private individuals).

Standard error: A sample's standard deviation divided by the square root of the sample size. The smaller the standard error, the more representative the sample will be of the overall population.

Stated preference: A method for estimating *shadow prices* (defined above) that uses survey data to estimate prices where markets do not exist or are distorted.

Tangible cost (or benefit): A cost (or benefit) that can be measured directly in dollar terms. In the case of the costs of crime, for example, tangible crime victim costs include medical expenses, property damage and loss, and lost wages. See also *intangible cost (or benefit)*.

Time horizon: The period of time applied to the economic evaluation. At minimum, this includes the period over which the intervention is implemented. It is of note that for discrete interventions, outcomes may be observed only during the intervention period, may extend further into the future after the intervention ends, or may be projected beyond the period when outcomes were last measured.

(Interrupted) Time series design: A type of quasi-experiment in which measures on a sample or a series of samples from the same population are obtained several times before and after a manipulated (e.g., an intervention) or naturally occurring event.

Total costs: An intervention's aggregate costs, calculated by multiplying all resources used by their unit costs and then summing these totals.

Variable costs: In contrast to fixed costs, those costs that vary as the amount of goods produced or participants served by an intervention varies.